Urban Futures

Urban Management Series

Series Editor: Nick Hall

Titles in the Urban Management Series:

Urban Futures
Economic Growth and Poverty Reduction

Edited by

Nabeel Hamdi with Jane Handal

ITDG
PUBLISHING

Published by ITDG Publishing
The Schumacher Centre for Technology and Development,
Bourton Hall, Bourton-on-Dunsmore, Rugby, CV23 9QZ, UK,
www.itdgpublishing.org.uk

This collection © ITDG Publishing 2005
© The individual contributors 2005

First published in 2005

ISBN 1 85339 599 4

ITDG Publishing is the publishing arm of the Intermediate
Technology Development Group.
Our mission is to build the skills and capacity of people in developing
countries through the dissemination of information in all forms,
enabling them to improve the quality of their lives and
that of future generations.

Cover photograph by Rachel Hamdi

Typeset by J&L Composition, Filey, North Yorkshire
Printed in Great Britain

Contents

The Urban Management Series

Nick Hall

The Urban Management Series focuses on the impacts of demographic and economic change in developing countries. The series offers a platform for practical, in-depth analysis of the complex institutional, economic and social issues that have to be addressed in an increasingly urban and globalized world. One of the UN's Millennium Development Targets calls for significant improvement in the lives of at least 100 million slum dwellers by 2020. This is a depressingly modest target because there could well be two billion new urban dwellers over the next 30 years. Well over 600 million people currently live in life- and health-threatening homes and neighbourhoods.

By 2025 it is estimated that two-thirds of the poor in Latin America and a third to almost half the poor in Africa and Asia will live in cities or towns. The urban poor face different issues and livelihood choices in comparison to the rural poor. The reduction of urban poverty requires appropriate policies and approaches. The livelihoods and rights of the poor must be at the centre of any strategy to reduce poverty and develop an inclusive society. This is equally true in urban areas.

Cities and towns, and the industrial and commercial activities located in them, are a positive force for national economic growth. This is why cities are popular: where you find the mass of bees is where to look for honey. Urban areas provide consumer markets and services for agricultural producers. They are also gateways to larger national, regional and international markets. But the opportunities from urban development have not been maximized by poor people. Their rights are curtailed and they are often excluded from accessing secure land, shelter, services, employment and social welfare due to the discriminatory practices of government, the private sector and civil society.

This series of books addresses the many challenges facing urban management professionals. First and foremost, they aim to improve understanding of the impact of urbanization on the livelihoods and living conditions of poor people. With better understanding the institutional and political conditions for poor people to participate and benefit from the urban development process may be improved. The lessons from research and dialogue should show how best to involve the private sector and civil society in mobilizing the necessary resources for inclusive and sustainable development; how to mitigate the impact that poor environments and natural hazards have on the poor; how to enhance the economic synergy between rural and urban economies; and how to strengthen efforts by the international community to coordinate support for a positive urbanization process.

Urban Futures presents some of the latest research on the most significant issues, by first rate writers. It poses difficult questions and offers some answers. For a start, it stresses that conventional approaches to planning must adapt to the economic and political realities of fast-changing cities. This book emphasizes that technical responses to the appalling conditions facing people in slums and informal settlements begin with a better understanding of power relationships. An overarching theme acknowledges that the poor in cities are part of the solution, not the problem.

We are left with the impression that for too many years urban investments have been undertaken and urban policies implemented on the basis of an impressionistic understanding of the problems at hand, of the complex conditions underlying them, and of the limited human and institutional resources available to manage them properly. The provocative concluding chapter of this book looks ahead optimistically. Whilst it asks a great many disturbing questions, their tone confirms that the rates of urbanization we have witnessed in the past few decades should be cause for celebration. Archeologists have shown us what life was like in the first cities built over 5000 years ago in Mesopotamia (Iraq and Syria). Now, architects, engineers, planners, sociologists and economists have a leading role to improve the quality of life for over half of the world's population. Urban research is a never ending quest.

Nick Hall
Series Editor

Foreword

Urban Futures offers a rich and diverse array of analysis that underscores the daunting challenges facing the developing world in the coming urban era. It spans cutting-edge questions of research methodology and illuminates emerging priorities, such as violence, and the urgent need to better understand the dynamics of urban poverty.

This book has its origins in the Second Urban Research Symposium that took place in Washington, DC in December 2003. The symposium, the second in what is hoped to become an ongoing series of such events held by the World Bank and partner agencies, was sponsored by the World Bank together with the German Federal Ministry for Economic Cooperation and Development and Deutsche Gesellschaft fur Technische Zusammenarbeit (GTZ), the Lincoln Land Institute, the Norwegian Ministry of Foreign Affairs, the Swedish International Development Agency (SIDA), and the U.K. Department for International Development (DFID). The objectives of the 2003 symposium were: to explore recent and ongoing research with policy and operational relevance to economic growth and poverty reduction in developing and transition economies; to foster networking and partnerships among international researchers working on problems of urban poverty; and to contribute to the formulation of a well-focused urban research agenda to guide their future collaboration.

The chapters in Part II are edited versions of a selection of the symposium papers. They present a rich body of work that is highly relevant to policy and operations; that reflects networking and partnerships as good practice, both as inherent features of the topics studied and in the manner of the research undertaken; and that is clearly situated among widely recognized current research priorities.

All of the papers in this volume support the case that the ongoing processes of rural-urban transition and the growth of urban settlements are phenomena that can favour increased productivity and opportunities for human development – thus contributing to increased incomes and enhanced welfare both at the national level and within the urban areas themselves. Poverty is multidimensional, encompassing both income and non-income factors. Raising welfare in all these dimensions requires developing a wide portfolio of assets – human, physical, natural, intellectual, financial and social capital. Sustainable economic growth and poverty reduction are phenomena deeply affected by institutions – the formal and informal norms, values and rules determining relations in society – which determine how assets are shared and used.

Just as the benefits from urbanization can be realized through well-functioning institutions – markets, government and social networks – that promote wide access to assets, to voice and to information, many of the visible problems accompanying urbanization reflect institutional failures. In particular, urban development fails to live up to its promise for economic growth or poverty reduction when basic institutions are weak or lacking, to promote property rights (e.g., secure tenure), to balance the interests of the many against the few, or to anticipate and commit to preparing for the future needs of a growing city.

More research, of the kind illustrated in this book, is needed that examines institutional factors of urban development that drive change (for better or worse) in the quality of life of cities, especially as it affects the urban poor – research that asks, for example:

- how the interests and demands of the poor and deprived residents are expressed and represented
- how coalitions and constituencies are formed to counter vested interests and advocate or negotiate change that is beneficial to the poor
- how critical information is made available and used in public discourse
- how knowledge is translated into effective policies and actions to reduce poverty at a significant scale and to make cities both more livable and more productive.

Christine Kessides
Senior Urban Advisor and Chair, Urban Research Symposium Committee
Transport and Urban Development Department
World Bank, Washington, DC

Figures

Tables

Acronyms and abbreviations

ACEG	African Centre for Economic Growth
ADB	Asian Development Bank
BHN	*Banco Hipotecario Nacional* (National Mortgage Bank)
CBD	Central Business District
CBO	community-based organization
CBS	Central Bureau of Statistics
CDF	Comprehensive Development Framework
CFH	Civic Forum on Housing
CMP	Community Mortgage Programme
COPE	Community Organization of the Philippines Enterprise
CTHC	Cone Textiles Housing Co-operative
DFID	Department for International Development
DHS	Demographic and Health Survey
ECLAC	Economic Commission for Latin America and the Caribbean
FGD	focus group discussion
FOMIN	Multilateral Investment Fund at the Inter-American Development Bank
FONAVI	*Fondo Nacional de Vivienda* (National Housing Fund)
FONHAPO	*Fondo Nacional de Habitaciones Populares* (Government Popular Housing Fund)
GDP	gross domestic product
GIDC	Gujarat Industrial Development Corporation
GIS	geographical information system
GJMC	Greater Johannesburg Metropolitan Council
GNP	gross national product
GUO	Global Urban Observatory
HBE	home-based enterprise
HIPC	Highly Indebted Poor Country
HUDCC	Housing and Urban Development Coordinating Committee
IADB	Inter-American Development Bank
IDP	Integrated Development Plan
IDRC	International Development Research Centre
IDS	Institute for Development Studies

IGA	income-generating activity
ILO	International Labour Organization
IMF	International Monetary Fund
INDEC	*Instituto Nacional de Estadísticas y Censos* (National Census and Statistics Institute)
INFONAVIT	*Instituto del Fondo Nacional de la Vivienda para los Trabajadores* (Institute of the National Housing Fund for Private Sector Workers)
IUDP	Integrated Urban Development Project
IUHP	Integrated Urban Housing Development in Kenya and India project
KASVIT	Kisumu Alliance of Street and Informal Traders
KLGRP	Kenya Local Government Reform Programme
K-REP	Kenya Rural Enterprises Programme
LA	local authorities
LAC	Latin American countries
LATF	Local Authority Transfer Fund
LSMS	Living Standards Measurement Survey
LUO	Local Urban Observatory
MCN	Municipal Council of Nakuru
MDG	millennium development goal
MENA	Middle East North Africa
MSE	micro and small-scale enterprise
NACHU	National Co-operative Housing Union
NAFTA	North American Free Trade Agreement
NAHECO	Nakuru Affordable Housing and Environmental Co-operative
NARC	National Rainbow Coalition
NCPC	Naga City People's Council
NCUPF	Naga City Urban Poor Federation
NGC	National Government Center (Philippines)
NGO	non-governmental organization
PECCO	Philippine Ecumenical Council on Community Organization
PHC	Pew Hispanic Centre
PIP	policy, institutions and processes
PO	people's organization
PRI	*Partido Revolucionario Institucional* (Institutional Revolutionary Party)
PRRC	Pasig River Rehabilitation Commission
PRSP	Poverty Reduction Strategy Process
ROK	Republic of Kenya
ROSCA	Revolving and Savings Credit Association
SACCO	savings and credit organization
SACTWU	Southern African Clothing and Textile Workers' Union

SAP	Structural Adjustment Programme
SBP	Single Business Permit
SDS	Society for Development Studies
SEWU	Self Employed Women's Union
SLF	Sustainable Livelihoods Framework
SPB	Single Business Permit
SPEED	Socialized Programme for Empowerment and Economic Development
ULAP	Powerful Alliance of Affected Families along the Pasig River
UMP	Urban Management Programme
UN	United Nations
WIEGO	Women in Informal Employment Globalising and Organising
ZOTO	Zone One Tondo Organization

Introduction

Nabeel Hamdi

Dozens of research reports, journals and published papers sit on bookshelves in our small office. Thousands are available in the libraries of universities and research institutes to which we have access. A simple search on any Internet search engine yields hundreds of thousands of documents, scores of which, if not more, are very informative and useful. When the subject of interest is something as current as community-based development, more is made available each day than we can download, let alone absorb. Yet there are so many improvements possible in our work, which we are somewhat aware of but not knowledgeable enough about to execute, so we continuously seek research that can guide us and address our concerns.

The greatest concern for us is always the sustainability of a community initiative after we, as an external agency, leave the scene on completion of a pilot project or campaign. We need to know what it is that can help programmes sustain and scale up on their own. We need to know how to turn pilot projects into ways of life. For this learning to take place, research needs to address the dynamics of communities – their wisdom, needs, operational strengths and ways in which they can work for their own good in a sustainable way which can be scaled up. We have so far not been able to derive this learning to a satisfactory level.

The primary reasons for our inability to fulfil our learning needs from the research already available to us are that in most cases it does not address self-sustenance issues and it is not packaged in a way which we can directly relate to our work context. It is rather difficult for our field operators to interpret the often intricate representation of findings and resultant models and theories, and to apply them at community level.

To address our content needs, it would be of great use to us if research efforts could address community dynamics and focus on issues of participation and governance through interventions at the level of knowledge and perceptions of civil society and duty bearers.

To address our methodological needs, it would help if some new research could look at how best to apply existing knowledge in practice, and how to interpret theories, models and manuals in simple, flexible and easy-to-adapt ways of working in the field. The dynamics of our urban systems are too complex to be made very simple; yet people who operate in field situations are too practical to be able to absorb complex research output. It really helps when the research community comes down to their level – the level of community practice.

Anshu Sharma
Sustainable Environment and Ecological Development Society (SEEDS) India

This book brings together a collection of essays from around the world on urban development and poverty. Its content is based largely on the Urban Research Symposium 'Urban Development for Economic Growth and Poverty Reduction', convened at the World Bank, 15–17 December 2003. The purpose of this book is threefold:

- to review selected examples of current international research with respect to some of the major themes that contribute to improving the equity and efficiency of urban systems
- to bridge the need for a strong theoretical understanding of the issues with the demand for an equal understanding of practical application
- to explore and set out methodologies for understanding qualitatively the dynamics of poverty and urban development.

BACKGROUND

In their introduction to the World Bank symposium, the organizers captioned a simple, yet still challenging premise in the field of development. Poverty reduction and economic growth are intrinsically related but are not always synonymous. Human well-being, they recognized, is as important to economic growth as growth is to well-being. Poverty is multidimensional, encompassing both income and non-income-related factors. Mobility, aspiration, dignity, respect, knowledge and information all feature importantly in our understanding of the dynamics of poverty.

Raising standards of well-being and reducing poverty demand a wide-ranging portfolio of initiatives designed to strengthen the assets of the poor and to improve access to essential goods, services and resources. The organizers recognized that sustainable economic growth, if it is to contribute to reducing poverty, demands significant institutional reforms – to increase efficiency in managing resources, to determine how assets can be shared and used equitability and, importantly, to restructure the balance of power in favour of a civil society and good governance.

The interdependency between rural and urban in relation to both economic and human development is by now well recognized. Many of the visible problems that accompany rapid urbanization reflect policy and institutional failures and a failure of governance. In particular, urban development has failed to live up to its promise of economic growth and poverty reduction when basic institutions at local levels are weak, corrupt or non-existent. When it comes to promoting rights and building livelihoods, there is an urgent need to balance the collective interests of the market with those of individuals, community-based organizations and small enterprise. There is a need to anticipate and commit to preparing for the future needs of fast-changing cities.

All this in the context of the widening gap between those who have and those who do not. It is estimated that 1.2 billion people worldwide are without safe drinking water and 2.9 billion lack adequate sanitation. Fifty-four countries saw the average income decline in the 1990s; 30 000 children die daily from preventable disease; 500 000 women a year die in pregnancy or childbirth; 13 million children were killed by diarrhoea in the 1990s. Human development, measured by the human development index, fell in 21 countries during the 1990s. One in five adults cannot read and 98% of these are in countries of the developing south – two-thirds of these are women. The statistics are even more sobering in the context of the projected doubling of cities (two billion new urban dwellers) over the next 30 years. This context underscores the need to face the institutional – governance – issues and start effective planning to ensure that urban demographic growth leads to poverty reduction and economic growth.

Various issues emerged during the World Bank Seminar, which are reflected in the title and content of chapters in this book:

- poverty research
- partnerships
- housing policy and tenure
- livelihoods
- economic reforms
- land
- enterprise.

In addition, a number of cross-cutting themes emerged, and are again reflected in different ways throughout this volume.

First, there continue to be questions about the effectiveness of planning in responding to the economic and political realities of fast-changing cities. The planning process inhibits more often than enables the creativity and flexibility that entrepreneurship demands, both formally and informally.

Second, there is the demand for good governance – for transparency and accountability when it comes to decision-making and for a good understanding of power relationships as a prelude to partnership formation and participatory work.

Inclusive governance demands an informed citizenship, a change in power relations, a commitment to basic rights, an emphasis on decentralized government. All these are worthy themes but difficult in practice, given the dynamic and often volatile politics and economic circumstances of countries and cities in the South.

Third, there is the need for more learning, more research and more effective data management. All this with a view to understanding better the dynamics of poverty, land markets, housing finance and tenure, jobs and livelihoods. Equally, there is the demand to improve the means of dissemination of ideas, experience and findings on a progressive basis, and for them to be accessible not only to other researchers, but also to

those who must use these results for formulating policy, improving practice methods, and designing projects and programmes. These include
government authority, practitioners, NGOs and donors.

Fourth, when it comes to poverty research there is the need again for a
universal definition of poverty, for agreed criteria with which to measure
the impacts of programmes on poverty reduction progressively and with
respect to discrete groups who are most at risk – women, children, the
elderly and disabled.

Finally, there is the imperative to bridge the gaps between research and
practice, project planning and policy design, informal processes and formal ones, the role of small organizations and larges ones, micro-level
action plans and macro-level strategic plans. There is the need, in other
words, to search for new partnerships between often competing interest
groups in the interests of moving forward.

STRUCTURE

This book adopts as its principal theme, poverty and the eradication of
extreme poverty, in the context of projected urban demographic growth.

Part I, The dynamics of poverty and urban poverty research, offers a
framework for understanding poverty and a methodology for research. It
identifies a range of broadly based, non-country-specific themes in respect
to the processes of urbanization, urban poverty and child poverty.

Part II, The dynamics of urban systems, includes a selection of country-
specific essays, each focused on an aspect of urban development and in
relation to poverty. Each essay offers first a theoretical overview in respect
to its theme topic (shelter, land, partnership, migration), then explores this
in practice through case examples. Each essay raises issues and defines
principles in its own right. The whole identifies selectively a range of key
topics for urban research.

Finally, in his epilogue, Shlomo Angel articulates a series of questions
designed to point the way forward for urban research. The questions are
grouped under ten themes, including processes of urbanization, land use,
poverty, housing finance, urban subsidies and urban research, among
others.

PART I

THE DYNAMICS OF POVERTY
AND URBAN POVERTY RESEARCH

CHAPTER ONE

Understanding urban and the management of change[1]

David Satterthwaite

INTRODUCTION

Urbanization is often mentioned as one of the most significant global changes of the last century; close to half the world's population now lives in urban areas compared to 15 per cent a century ago and the percentage continues to increase. But the most recent round of censuses (held since 1998) has shown that many nations are less urbanized and less dominated by large cities than had been predicted. The latest UN estimate for the world's urban population in 2000 had 270 million people fewer than the UN had predicted 20 years previously (United Nations, 1982, 2002). There were also fewer very large cities than anticipated, and there are doubts whether much of sub-Saharan Africa is continuing to urbanize.

However, the long-term trend towards an increasingly urbanized world has not changed. This chapter discusses the reasons for this and also why, when new census data become available, it is likely to show greater diversity in the scale and pace of urbanization (the rate of increase in the proportion of people living in urban centres) between nations.

AN URBANIZING WORLD

The world's urban population is now around 3 billion people – the same size as the world's total population in 1960. Many aspects of urban change in the past 50 years are unprecedented, including not only the world's level of urbanization and the size of its urban population, but also the number of countries becoming more urbanized and the size and number of very large cities. Many urban changes are dramatic, including dozens of cities whose populations grew tenfold in 30 years and others that sprawl for thousands of square kilometres and concentrate more than 15 million people. Around half the world's largest cities are now in Asia.

But the scale of these changes is often overstated. Most nations may be urbanizing but a large proportion of the world's urban centres are not growing rapidly. Discussions of urban growth focus on the rapidly growing centres and forget those that are not growing rapidly. Many urban centres have more people moving out than in – including many of the world's largest cities such as Mexico City, São Paulo, Buenos Aires, Calcutta and

Seoul. These are also among the many large cities that had several million fewer inhabitants in 2000 than had been predicted 25 years ago. The increasing number of 'mega-cities' with more than 10 million inhabitants may appear a cause for concern, but by 2000, there were only 16 such cities and they concentrated less than 4 per cent of the world's population.

Such statistics also tell us nothing about the very large economic, social, political and demographic changes that have underpinned the trend towards increasingly urbanized societies. It is important to understand these underpinnings. Urbanization is not happening in all locations. There is also an economic logic to the distribution of the world's largest cities since they are heavily concentrated within the world's largest economies. It is not surprising that Asia has so many of the world's largest cities, since throughout most of history this has been the case – and the growing number of large Asian cities reflects the region's growing importance within the world economy.

In addition, although rapid urban growth is often seen as a problem, it is generally the nations with the best economic performance that have urbanized most in the past 50 years. Perhaps surprisingly, given the problems evident in most large cities in Africa, Asia and Latin America, there is an association between rapid urban change and better living standards. The mega-cities may appear chaotic and out of control but most have life expectancies and provision for piped water, sanitation, schools and health-care that are well above the national average – even if the aggregate statistics for most mega-cities hide significant proportions of their population who are living in very poor conditions. Some of world's fastest-growing cities over the past 50 years have among the best standards of living within their nation – including Porto Alegre and Curitiba (Hardoy et al., 2001; Menegat, 2002). If our concern is to improve urban conditions, especially for the 700 million or so urban dwellers living in very over-crowded dwellings in tenements or shacks lacking basic infrastructure and services, a considerable part of our effort should focus on relatively small urban centres, including thousands that are not growing rapidly.

WHAT DRIVES URBAN CHANGE?

The population in each of the 50 000 or so urban centres in the world[2] and its rate of change are influenced by external factors and by factors related to each very particular local context. These include the quality of the site and natural resource availability (especially fresh water), location in rela-tion to consumers and markets, demographic structure, existing economy and infrastructure (the legacy of past decisions and investments), and the quality and capacity of public institutions. External influences range from the natural resources available close by, to trends within the regional and national economy (and the quality of each urban centre's connection to these through transport and communications), to decisions made by regional and national governments, local and national investors and the 30 000 or so global corporations who control such a significant share of the world's economy. Much urban change is driven by where profit-seeking enterprises choose to concentrate (or choose to bypass).

Understanding urban change within any nation is complicated. Consideration has to be given to changes in the scale and nature of its economy and the connections with neighbouring nations and with the world economy. Also to the structure of government (especially the division of power and resources between different levels of government) and the extent and spatial distribution of transport and communications investments. Virtually all nations that have urbanized quickly during the past 50 years have had long periods of rapid economic expansion and large shifts in employment patterns from agricultural and pastoral activities (dispersed among rural areas) to industrial, service and information activities (highly concentrated in urban areas). The internationalization of world production and trade (including the rapid expansion in the value of international trade) has influenced urban trends in most nations. Many cities owe their prosperity (or at least part of their employment base) to their roles within this increasingly internationalized production and distribution system. Although agriculture is often considered as separate from urban development, prosperous high-value agriculture combined with prosperous rural populations have underpinned rapid development in many cities (Hardoy and Satterthwaite, 1989). So too has tourism – but in different locations the stimulus may come from local, national or international tourists and with large differences in the extent to which tourism spending benefits the local economy.

Detailed analyses of urban change within any nation over time provide a reminder of the diversity of this change:

- the rising and falling importance of different urban centres; the largest cities are simply those that have managed to retain their economic and/or political importance
- the spatial influence of changes in government policies (for instance from supporting import substitution to supporting export promotion, the extent and nature of decentralization)
- the growing complexity of multinuclear urban systems in and around most major cities; and the changing patterns of in-migration and out-migration from rural to urban areas, from urban to urban areas and from urban to rural areas.

International migration has strong impacts on the population size of particular cities in most nations, but it is not only changing patterns of prosperity that explain these vast flows of people. Many cities have felt the impact of war or disaster, or of people fleeing such events. Major demographic change has also been apparent in all nations during the past 50 years which, in turn, has influenced urban change. This includes the rapid population growth rates in much of Latin America, Asia and Africa after

World War II (although in virtually all nations these have now declined significantly) and changes in the size and composition of households and in age structures.

THE REGIONAL DISTRIBUTION IN THE WORLD'S URBAN POPULATION

Most of the world's urban population is now outside Europe and North America (see Table 1.1). Asia alone contains almost half the world's urban population, even if more than three-fifths of its people still live in rural areas. Africa, which is generally perceived as overwhelmingly rural, now

Table 1.1   The distribution of the world's urban population by region, 1950–2010

Region	1950	1970	1990	2000	Projection for 2010
Urban population (millions of inhabitants)					
World	751	1357	2286	2862	3514
Africa	32	82	197	295	426
Asia	244	501	1023	1376	1784
Europe	287	424	521	534	536
Latin America and the Caribbean	70	164	313	391	470
Northern America	110	171	213	243	273
Oceania	8	14	19	23	26
Percentage of population living in urban areas					
World	29.8	36.8	43.5	47.2	51.5
Africa	14.7	23.1	31.8	37.2	42.7
Asia	17.4	23.4	32.2	37.5	43.0
Europe	52.4	64.6	72.1	73.4	75.1
Latin America and the Caribbean	41.9	57.6	71.1	75.4	79.0
Northern America	63.9	73.8	75.4	77.4	79.8
Oceania	61.6	71.2	70.8	74.1	75.7
Percentage of the world's urban population living in					
World	100	100	100	100	100
Africa	4.3	6.1	8.6	10.3	12.1
Asia	32.5	37.0	44.8	48.1	50.8
Europe	38.3	31.3	22.8	18.7	15.3
Latin America and the Caribbean	9.3	12.1	13.7	13.7	13.4
Northern America	14.6	12.6	9.3	8.5	7.8
Oceania	1.0	1.0	0.8	0.8	0.8

has a larger urban population than North America. UN projections suggest that most of the growth in the world's population between 2000 and 2010 will be in urban areas in Africa, Asia and Latin America.

As Table 1.1 shows, levels of urbanization in certain regions increased dramatically between 1950 and 2000 – for instance in Africa and Asia. Particular subregions had even larger changes – for instance Western Asia going from 27 per cent to 65 per cent urban in the same 50 years or Eastern Europe from 39 per cent to 68 per cent urban. However, the growth rates of urban populations and the rates of increase in levels of urbanization are not unprecedented; many countries in West Europe – and also the US and Japan – had periods when their level of urbanization increased as rapidly (Preston, 1979).

Some qualifications are needed in regard to the accuracy and precision of urbanization statistics. In terms of accuracy, the statistics for 2000 in Table 1.1 draw mainly on estimates, since for most nations, no census data were available after 1993. The lack of census data is particularly problematic for sub-Saharan Africa, where, for many nations, there were no census data available since the 1970s or early 1980s when the source of these statistics (UN, 2002) was written, so all figures for their urban (and rural) populations for 1990 and 2000 are based on estimates and projections. We do not know whether sub-Saharan Africa continued to urbanize during the 1990s; this calls into question the claim that sub-Saharan Africa was unusual because it continued to urbanize during the 1990s despite economic stagnation (Fay and Opal, 2000). Sub-Saharan Africa appears to urbanize during the 1990s in UN statistics because an assumption was made that it would do so in the methods used to estimate urban populations when no census data were available. Other sources suggest that most of sub-Saharan Africa urbanized much less than that suggested by the UN statistics (Potts, 1995, 2001; Bocquier, 2004).

In terms of precision, the level of urbanization in any nation is strongly influenced by how its government defines an urban centre, especially what proportion of 'small urban centres and large villages' end up classified as urban or rural. In virtually all nations, a significant proportion of the population lives in settlements with between 1000 and 20 000 inhabitants, most of which have both urban and rural characteristics. For instance, most have a significant proportion of their labour force working in agriculture and forestry, and many services and facilities that serve agriculture. Most also have urban characteristics – a significant proportion of their labour force earning a living from secondary and tertiary activities, and often a concentration of government employees and services (healthcare, education, police, etc.). The level of urbanization in a nation is much influenced by what proportion of these 'small towns or large villages' are classified as urban. India would be predominantly urban if all settlements with more than 1000 inhabitants were classified as urban, as much of its rural population lives in villages with more than 1000 inhabitants. Classify all these 'small urban centres and large villages' as rural and the nation is much less urbanized. By its 1996 census, 17.5 per cent of Egypt's population lived in settlements with between 10 000 and 20 000 inhabitants that had many urban characteristics, including significant non-agricultural economies and occupational structures. These were not classified as urban, although they would have been considered urban in most other nations (Bayat and Denis, 2000). If the Indian or Chinese government chose to change the criteria used in their censuses to define urban centres, this could increase or decrease the world's level of urbanization by several percentage points. Thus, the level of urbanization in the world, in each region and in each nation is best understood not as a precise figure. The world was not 47.7 per cent urban in 2001 but somewhere between 40 and 55 per cent, depending on what criteria are used to define urban centres.

THE WORLD'S LARGEST CITIES

Two aspects of the rapid growth in the world's urban population are the increase in the number of large cities and their historically unprecedented size (see Table 1.2). Just two centuries ago, there were only two cities with more than a million inhabitants – London and Beijing (then called Peking); by 2000 there were 388. Of these million-cities, a large (and increasing) proportion are in Africa, Asia and Latin America. However, many or the world's fastest-growing cities have been in the US – for instance Las Vegas and Fort Lauderdale are among the world's million-cities that had populations growing more than 20-fold in the past 50 years with Orlando, West Palm Beach and Phoenix growing more than tenfold.

The average size of the world's largest cities also increased dramatically. In 2000, the average size of the world's 100 largest cities was around 6.2 million inhabitants compared to 725 000 in 1900 and 187 000 in 1800. While there are various examples of cities with more than a million inhabitants over the past two millennia, the city with several million inhabitants is a relatively new phenomenon. London was the first to reach this size in the second half of the nineteenth century; by 2000, there were 39 such cities.

Table 1.2 also shows the changes in the regional distribution of the world's largest cities. The growing proportion in Africa, Asia and Latin America is often highlighted as a particular concern. However, this is not so much a dramatic shift as a return to what was apparent prior to the industrial revolution (Bairoch, 1988). Throughout most of recorded history, Asia has had a high proportion of the world's largest cities. South and Central America and North Africa have long had large cities too. The most dramatic change during the past two centuries is the appearance in the list of cities from Northern America and Oceania – related to the appropriation of the US, Canada and Australia by immigrants and the urban/industrial economies they developed. In 1800, neither of the US's two largest cities (Philadelphia and New York) was large enough to be within the world's 100 largest cities.

Table 1.2 The distribution of the world's largest cities by region over time

Region	1800	1900	1950	2000
Number of 'million-cities'				
World	2	17	85	388
Africa	0	0	2	35
Asia	1	4	31	195
Europe	1	9	29	61
Latin America and the Caribbean	0	0	7	50
Northern America	0	4	14	41
Oceania	0	0	2	6
Regional distribution of the world's largest 100 cities				
World	100	100	100	100
Africa	4	2	3	8
Asia	65	22	36	45
Europe	28	53	35	15
Latin America and the Caribbean	3	5	8	17
Northern America	0	16	16	13
Oceania	0	2	2	2
Average size of the world's 100 largest cities	187 000	725 000	2.1 million	6.2 million

Despite the speed of change in urban populations, there is continuity in the location of most important cities. Most of the largest cities in Europe, Latin America, Asia and North Africa today have been important cities for centuries. North America and sub-Saharan Africa stand out as having most 'new cities' among the world's largest cities today (cities that now have more than a million inhabitants but had not been founded or did not exist as urban centres by 1800). Table 1.2 also highlights how Europe had few of the world's largest cities by 2000, in contrast to 1900. In part, this reflects the growing economic importance of other regions. It also reflects the way that urban form has changed in high-income nations with more dispersed urban systems and with large sections of cities' working populations commuting from outside city boundaries. If the population of European cities is measured in ways that include the settlements that are primarily the homes of those who commute daily to these cities, the number of European million-cities increases considerably.

The population of any large city is influenced by how boundaries are defined. The current population of most of the world's largest cities can change by many million inhabitants, depending on which boundaries are used. City boundaries are not set according to universally agreed criteria but to local and national criteria. Most large cities have at least three different figures for their populations, depending on whether it is the city, the metropolitan area or a wider planning or administrative region that is being considered. The largest Chinese cities provide examples of this. The population figures that are usually given for cities such as Shanghai, Beijing and Tianjin are for the populations in large local government areas which include significant proportions of people living in rural areas and working in forestry and agriculture. Statistics for city populations also vary depending on how people are registered – for instance in Shanghai the population can vary by several million, depending on whether the 'floating' population is included. This confusion between local government area and city area explains why the city of Chongqing sometimes appears as the world's largest city with a population of 30 million. This is the population in the municipality, which covers 82 400 square kilometres (about the size of the Netherlands and Denmark combined); the city population is around 6 million. London could easily re-establish itself among the world's largest cities if the Greater London Authority was able to convince the national government that a new London municipality be created, incorporating neighbouring counties.

Some cities have boundaries that greatly understate their real populations because they have not been adjusted to include large, dense settlements that developed around them. For instance, the population of Colombo in Sri Lanka is often given as around 642 000, but this was the population in 2000 in 'Colombo municipal council'; the urban agglomeration of which this municipal council is the centre has a much larger population. Finally, different boundaries also mean different population growth rates – so London, Los Angeles, Tokyo, Buenos Aires or Mexico City can be correctly stated as having populations that are declining or expanding in recent decades, depending on which boundaries are used. In addition, large increases in a city's population between two censuses are often partly due to an expansion of boundaries which incorporate many settlements that had not been part of the city in the earlier census.

WHAT UNDERLIES URBAN CHANGE?

Cities and the global economy

There is an economic logic underlying the distribution of the world's urban population, including its largest cities. Table 1.3 shows the concentration of the world's 'million-cities' and 'mega-cities' in its largest economies. In 2000, the world's five largest economies (US, China, Japan, India and Germany) had nine of the world's 16 mega-cities and 46 per cent of its million-cities. Similarly, within each of the world's regions, most of the largest cities are concentrated in the largest economies – for instance Brazil and Mexico in Latin America, and China, India, Indonesia and the Republic of Korea in Asia.

Table 1.3   The distribution of the world's largest cities among its largest economies in 2000

Nations	No. of 'million' cities	No. of cities with 5–9.99 million inhabitants	No. of mega-cities (cities with 10 million-plus inhabitants)
The world's five largest economies			
US	37	1	2
China	91	3	2
Japan	6	0	2
India	32	3	3
Germany	13	1	0
The next five largest economies (France, UK, Italy, Brazil, Russian Federation)	37	3	2
The next five largest economies (Mexico, Canada, Republic of Korea, Indonesia, Australia)	32	1	2
The next five largest economies (Turkey, Argentina, Netherlands, South Africa, Thailand)	17	2	1
The world's other 187 nations and territories	123	9	2
TOTAL (for the world)	388	23	16

In general, the higher the per capita income of a nation or region within a nation, the higher the level of urbanization. Most of the nations with the most rapid increase in their level of urbanization between 1960 and 1990 were also the nations with the most rapid economic growth (UNCHS, 1996) and this is unlikely to have changed (but this will only become known when there are sufficient census data on urban populations for 2000).

There is an obvious association between the world's largest cities and globalization. Growing cross-border flows of raw materials, goods, information, income and capital, much of it managed by transnational corporations, underpin a network of what can be termed 'global cities' that are the key sites for the management and servicing of the global economy (Sassen, 2002). Most international investment is concentrated in a relatively small proportion of the world's cities. It is no coincidence that Tokyo, New York and London, the three most important global financial centres (Sassen, 1994), are also among the world's largest cities. This also helps explain reports of renewed population growth in London during the 1990s. Many of the world's fastest-growing cities are also the cities that have had most success in attracting international investment. The remittance flows created by large-scale international migration associated with globalization have also had a profound impact in many cities.

However, the association between globalization and large cities is moderated by two factors. The first is that advanced telecommunications systems allow a separation of the production from those who manage and finance it. For example, the economies of London and New York may depend heavily on growing markets for industrial goods but they have very little such industrial production themselves. The second, linked to this, is the more decentralized urban patterns that are possible within regions with well-developed transport and communications infrastructure. Many of the most successful regions have urban forms that are not dominated by a large central city, with new enterprises developing in a network of smaller cities and greenfield sites – for instance Silicon Valley and Orange County in California, and Bavaria in Germany (Castells and Hall, 1994), and the network of cities in south-east Brazil that have attracted much new investment away from São Paulo. In all high-income nations and many middle and low-income nations, there has been a growing capacity of cities outside the large metropolitan areas to attract a significant proportion of new investment. In the many nations that have had effective decentralizations, urban authorities in smaller cities have more resources and capacity to compete for new investment. Trade liberalization and a greater emphasis on exports have also increased the comparative advantage of many smaller cities.

Most of the large cities whose population growth rates remained high during the 1980s and 1990s were cities with strong economic performance and usually ones based on an increased role internationally – for instance Dhaka in Bangladesh and Bangalore in India. China has many examples of cities with rapid population growth rates, which is hardly surprising given the very rapid growth in China's economy sustained over the past two decades. For instance, the city of Shenzhen close to Hong Kong has grown from a small border town to a major metropolis in the past 20 years. But China also has many cities that grew slowly in recent decades.

The list of the world's largest cities includes many that articulate large national economies into the global system (such as Paris, Madrid and São Paulo) or subnational (regional) economies (Friedmann, 1993). However, some cities with key roles within the global economy are not so large – for instance Zurich and Singapore. Several of the world's largest cities do not owe their size and economic base to their role within global production or management but to being national capitals that concentrate political power – for instance Delhi, Cairo and, before the Nigerian capital was shifted to Abuja, Lagos.

One reason why the world is less urbanized in 2000 than expected is the slow economic growth (or economic decline) that many low and middle-income nations have experienced since 1980. This helps explain slower population growth rates for many cities in Africa and Latin America. Part of this is also related to structural adjustment policies that brought declines in employment, falling real incomes and declining urban welfare, and proved less successful than anticipated in stimulating economic growth.

Cities and political structures

It is tempting to compare urbanization trends between nations, not least because the data sets are available for each nation's level of urbanization and each major city's population from 1950 to 2000 (with projections to 2015). But doing so is fraught with danger. First, there are the limitations in the data noted above. Second, the factors underlying urban change often differ greatly between nations – or within each nation over time. It is rare to find careful analyses of urban change within any nation over time that recognizes the limitations in the data (for instance how changes in some urban boundaries between censuses affected urban trends) and that is able to link urban changes with underlying economic, political, social and demographic changes. Where these are produced, they discourage international comparisons because they show the diversity evident across any national territory and between censuses. For many nations, it is impossible to produce such a national review, because there are too few censuses available to do so.

To illustrate the complexity, consider the example of Pakistan. An analysis of Pakistan's 1998 census by the Pakistani urban scholar Arif Hasan (Hasan, 2004) highlighted the impossibility of understanding urban change without understanding the influence: of Partition in the late 1940s (which caused large migration flows to particular locations, especially to Karachi), of Pakistan's division (as Bangladesh became independent); of the civil war in Afghanistan (bringing many refugees to Pakistan and many Western agencies supporting the Afghans fighting the Soviet-backed government based in Pakistan); of the green revolution; of Pakistan's political structure and of a host of other factors. Inevitably, the very large population movements brought by these also brought many political conflicts – including those between long-term city-dwellers and immigrants from India, between Pakistanis and Afghans, and between urban interests and rural interests. Now the whole nation's urban system is being influenced by the erosion of the nation's light industry, because of cheap imports.

Perhaps the most important political influence on urban change in most nations in Africa and Asia over the past 50 years was the dissolving of the European powers' colonial empires. One reason why urban change has been so rapid in many nations is because it began from such a small base, as the colonial powers kept down urban populations by imposing restrictions on the rights of their national populations to live and work in urban centres. One reason why urban populations grew so rapidly just before or after the ending of colonial rule was the removal or weakening of the colonial *apartheid*-like controls on population movements (Potts, 1995). For instance, urban growth dynamics over the past 40 years in South Africa,

Namibia and Zimbabwe (formerly Rhodesia) cannot be understood without taking account of the profound impact of controls on people's movement imposed by white minority regimes on the composition and growth of cities (Potts, 1995).

Another reason for rapid urban population growth was the need for newly independent governments to build the institutions of governance that nation-states need and also expand the education and healthcare systems that had been so undeveloped under colonial rule. This obviously boosted growth in the urban centres that were the main political and administrative centres. Many commentators view the rapid growth of sub-Saharan African cities over the past 50 years as a serious problem. But if a large part of the rapid change in urban populations is related to the achievement of political independence and the removal of highly discriminatory controls on population, it suggests that this rapid change also has positive aspects. Political changes since independence also influence urban trends. For instance, in Uganda, urban growth was slower than expected during the early post-independence period when violence and political instability made economic development impossible, but then became more rapid when political stability was restored in most of the country and the economy expanded (Potts, 2001).

Political changes have also had a strong impact on urban change in many other regions, notably in the countries of the former Soviet Union and its economic bloc, and in China. In much of Latin America too, urban systems and trends have been reshaped during the 1980s and 1990s by the introduction of or a return to democratic rule, the shift in economic policies from import substitution to export promotion, serious economic problems and, in many nations, decentralization and stronger democracy within city and municipal governments.

Wars and civil conflicts in parts of Europe and Africa have also brought major shifts in populations. For instance, millions of people fled to urban areas in Angola, Mozambique and the Sudan during civil wars there during the 1980s and 1990s, just as they had done in Zimbabwe during the liberation struggle of the 1970s (Potts, 1995). It is difficult to know the exact dimensions of these movements – for instance Angola has had no full census since 1970. Yet during the 1980s, there were huge population displacements in Angola as many rural areas were insecure and people fled to small towns and inland cities as well as to cities near the Atlantic coast. The post-election war from 1992 to 2002 affected the inland cities more, so displaced populations headed more to the cities on the Atlantic coast (Cain et al., 2002). Changes are also brought about when conflicts cease. For instance, in both Mozambique and Zimbabwe, there was significant out-migration from some cities when conflict ended (Potts, 2001). The number of international refugees in Africa and Europe rose to unprecedented levels during the 1990s and a considerable proportion came to live in cities, seeking refuge or looking for new bases for their livelihoods (International Federation of Red Cross and Red Crescent Societies, 2001). Famines have also influenced urban trends in many African nations during the past 50 years, especially where urban centres provide rural populations with more chance of survival.

So, while reviews of tables showing urban population statistics for different nations may show some broad trends towards increasingly urbanized societies, the scale and nature of such trends and their underlying causes differ greatly from country to country. There are also differences between regions of the same country and over time. A focus on large cities forgets how most of the urban population in most nations live in urban centres with under half a million inhabitants, including many in urban centres with fewer than 50 000 inhabitants.[4] Even if globalization and the legal and institutional changes it brings are an increasing influence in most urban centres, it is important not to forget the unique mix of social, economic, political and demographic factors within each location that are influencing urban change. Or how different the impact of globalization is on each city.

CONCLUSIONS

The world is likely to be more urbanized in 10 to 15 years and to have more large cities – but perhaps less so than current projections suggest. There are good grounds for questioning whether most of the urban population will live in large cities. In high-income and many middle-income nations, more dispersed patterns of urban development are evident. Also, in high-income nations, much of the rural population receive the infrastructure and services that used to be associated with urban centres. They no longer work in agriculture and many work in urban centres (or telecommute with urban-based enterprises) so a growing proportion of rural-dwellers are urbanized in their lifestyles and occupations but still classified as rural. The need for more useful settlement classification systems than 'rural' and 'urban' are obviously needed (Champion and Hugo, 2003).

There are also grounds for questioning whether urbanization levels will continue to rise in virtually all nations. For instance, Africa will only become increasingly urban if most of its more populous nations have greater economic success than they had during the 1990s. There is no reliable basis for predicting future levels of urbanization globally, although statistics will be greatly influenced by the economic performance of those populous nations which currently have low levels of urbanization.

The problems that arise from rapid urban growth are not inherent to cities or to fast urban expansion. The knowledge of how to install and maintain the infrastructure and services that underpin good-quality city environments has developed over the past 150 years and cities have many economies of scale and proximity to support this. During the past 30 years has been added the knowledge of how to integrate this provision with a broader regional concern for sustainable resource use, good land-use management and minimizing wastes and pollution (Hardoy et al., 2001).

It is not rapid urban change but the lack of attention given to developing urban governance structures that underpins most urban problems (Hardoy et al., 2001). Many factors constrain the development of appropriate governance structures, especially where these raise costs and limit choices for politically powerful enterprises and populations. Good governance will set limits on where industries can locate and developers can build; also on what local water sources they can tap and what wastes they can dispose of. The latest information on global warming suggests that good governance will need to set limits on how frequently individuals can drive or fly, or on the amount of fossil fuel they can use (IPCC, 2001). Good governance recognizes the rights of all citizens, not just the wealthy ones. It has to include actions to ensure that infrastructure and services are available to all within its boundaries, and that revenues are raised from those who benefit from this. It will ensure 'the rule of law' through which the rights and entitlements of everyone and 'the public good' are protected and effective democratic processes are in place, including the values this implies such as accountability to citizens and transparency in the generation and use of public resources. This is a very different 'urban agenda' to the one that focuses on 'urban growth' as the problem.

CHAPTER TWO

Understanding poverty: urban longitudinal research methodology[1]

Caroline Moser

INTRODUCTION

Renewed concern with issues of urban poverty relate not only to the higher profile of poverty reduction generally – as illustrated by the World Development Report 2000/1 and the Millennium Development Goals – but also to the fact that by the year 2020, 80 per cent of the world's population will be living in urban areas. Linked to this is recognition that while economic growth is good for poverty reduction, the poor do not necessarily automatically benefit from such growth. This calls for more sustainable urban focused poverty-reduction strategies. To address this requires far better understanding of the long-term intergenerational transmission of poverty, of poverty dynamics and of social and economic mobility.

While chronic poverty studies focus on those who become poor and remain poor, it is also important to identify the characteristics (causes and consequences) of families and households that get out and stay out of poverty, rather than slipping back into poverty. Understanding the dynamics of poverty, particularly the intergenerational transmission of success or failure to move out, can provide important policy information relevant for future poverty reduction strategies.

In the past decade, a new generation of poverty research has broadened the definition and measurement of poverty from income/consumption measures to include those that encompass the complexity of vulnerability, exclusion and insecurity. In addition, important insights gained from qualitative anthropological and sociological studies as against quantitative research are more widely recognized. The continuum of methodologies now includes:

- quantitative household panel data sets that focus on the individual and household, conducted primarily by economists with repeat household surveys
- poverty mapping studies that use a combination of household and census data over time
- community panel data sets focusing on social change, whether at intra-household, household or community level. These are repeat longitudinal studies conducted by anthropologists and sociologists in the same urban 'community' over the past 10 to 30 years

- participatory methodologies focusing on perceptions of well-being/ill-being.

The fact that studies increasingly use different forms of 'mixed methodologies' poses important questions of robustness and representativeness as researchers seek to better understand what keeps some families and households in poverty, while others move out.

KEY ISSUES

Substantive issues: the contributions and limitations of longitudinal research to understanding poverty

The following key issues are important to consider when undertaking poverty research.

Poverty dynamics or economic and social mobility?

Is it meaningful to talk about movement in or out of poverty over a 25-year interval? A number of concerns were raised about the viable timescale for longitudinal poverty research. There was a general consensus that comparative data sets, particularly panel data with gaps of longer than a 10-year period, were less appropriate for tracking poverty dynamics (individuals or households moving in or out of poverty) and more useful for exploring issues relating to economic and social mobility over time.

Mobility studies requires consideration not only of large-scale contextual changes at the political, economic and social level, including phenomena such as natural disasters, but also, and possibly of even greater importance, recognition of the impact of various stages of the *life cycle*. For example, are people poorer because they are at a point when they are investing in their children's education? Here Jeanine Anderson (2003) used the concept of 'punctuated development' to describe the risks that parents experience launching the second generation and endowing them with the necessary resources. She described 'lines of upward movement' as 'punctuated' by particular events that require the reorganization/reallocation of resources. Following up on this Deepa Narayan[2] referred to launching the second generation (in terms of endowments provided) as the 'acid test' of moving out of poverty.

The non-poor as well as the poor?

Do studies of poverty focus too narrowly on the poor? Some research has identified the need for a broader field of study, bringing in comparative data from the non-poor. Phakama Mhlongo[2], for instance, identified how the longitudinal study in Kwa-Zulu Natal has identified four categories:

- those who stayed poor
- those who were never poor
- those who went into poverty
- those who moved out of poverty.

Others, such as Barbara Harriss-White (2003), described the importance of longitudinal research that focused entirely on the creation of productive wealth ('the merchant road to capitalist wealth') – in her case longitudinal research on enterprises in a South Indian town. These data are crucial to identify who falls in to poverty, as well as who climbs out. Researching the 'nearby rich', those with whom the poor interact, also brings into focus new issues such as trade, power and prestige, and is particularly important when respondents routinely leave their residential areas and commute to middle-income neighbourhoods for employment and other activities. A focus on the poor themselves in poor areas misses the relationships between the rich and the poor.

Poverty, inequality or subjective perceptions of well-being?

More widely recognized than before is the importance of measuring changes not only in poverty levels but also in inequality and opportunities. For instance, Susan Rigdon's (2003) construction of five generational 'genograms' from Oscar Lewis' Puerto Rico anthropological fieldwork notes illustrated the appalling inter-generational transference of inequality as measured in terms if illiteracy and ill health. Yet another variable concerns changes in perceptions of well-being and 'happiness'. Carol Graham's (2003) comparative research using data from Peru, Russia and the US highlighted non-economic reasons for upward mobility as well as introducing the concept of 'frustrated achievers' – better educated, particularly urban populations (with greater comparative reference groups) who in terms of subjective well-being saw themselves as worse off than before even though their income levels had increased – with an associated fear of becoming vulnerable to falling into poverty.

In this sense, moving out of 'poverty' may relate less to objective economic measures and more to subjective hopes and aspirations. In her longitudinal analysis of Guayaquil, Caroline Moser (2003) referred to 'rising aspirations and growing despair', while in Rio, Janice Perlman (2003) highlighted the growing exclusion that accompanied the increasing gap between rich and poor as people struggled over 30 years to be '*gente*' (people). Here, poverty was identified as a social construct – with globalization adding a dramatic spatial extension to the universe of reference groups studied longitudinally.

Getting out of poverty or acquiring 'urban savvy'?

Based on her intergenerational longitudinal research in Lima, Peru, Anderson (2003) identified the importance of acquisition of 'urban savvy' – knowledge of how urban institutions function as a critical intergenerational measure of 'making it' in cities. This slow accumulation of knowledge and information of the impacts of essential services on well-being is critical for upward mobility, and to avoid falling into destitution.

Breadth or depth in longitudinal research

To incorporate the growing agenda of new poverty-related issues means that choices often have to be made relating to the range of issues to be addressed longitudinally. The Young Lives project described by Trudy Harpham (see Chapter 3), for instance, has chosen 'breadth over depth' in including a range of questions relating to livelihood assets, social relations (social capital) and uptake of social services (and their associated institutional performance). In contrast to this, Narayan identified a balance between 'hard data' from a robust sampling frame and 'soft data' that adds value in providing subjective perceptions of well-being.

Differential gender-based intra-household impacts of economic crises

Longitudinal research has clearly acknowledged the differential impacts of poverty within the household. In Lima, Anderson (2003) identified the development of 'female domestic fronts' as an outcome of the Peruvian economic crisis. When men lost their jobs their wives were often forced to take on additional income-generating activities. To balance this with reproductive responsibilities, other female relatives were introduced into the household and the outcome was one of increased hostility between women and men. Male 'dethronement' often resulted in their being pushed out of the household. (Debby Bryson referred to a similar phenomenon in the Welsh context as 'men with cookers'.) This loss of prestige of adult men has important intergenerational implications in terms of the links between male identity and increased risks of substance abuse, now associated with urban youth.

Tracking poverty or mapping policy?

Research has recently prioritized longitudinal tracking of poverty trends rather than changes in urban policy *per se*. Although there are numerous contextual references to poverty reduction and infrastructure interventions, the interlinkages between the two are not generally explored in great detail. Indeed, as discussed in the sections below on causality and micro-macro linkages, assessments of the impact of policy on poverty are particularly difficult to analyse, as identified by Moser (2003) – and in all probability require researchers specifically mapping policy changes to make inferences in terms of impacts on poverty levels. The Young Lives project described by Harpham (2003) (see Chapter 3) hopes to develop the methodology to better understand the relationships between 'life-cyclical effects and policy effects'. Equally, Carol Rakodi[2] identified the importance of unpacking people's experiences of service delivery in terms of its impact on their well-being.

Changes in household (or individual) poverty or institutions that deliver for the poor?

Closely linked to the above is the issue as to whether tracking changes in household income or consumption levels sufficiently addresses institutional changes in the delivery of infrastructure and social services. David Satterthwaite (in Chapter 1) identifies the failure of institutions that are meant to deliver services for the poor as an important poverty-related issue and therefore a necessary focus for longitudinal research. Recent global experience of local-level organizations increasing their capacity to negotiate with the state for the delivery of such services, or to hold state institutions more accountable, has resulted in benefits for the poor even in non-growth economic contexts. As Moser (2003) concludes, the introduction into longitudinal research of concepts such as 'collective well-being' requires a shift in focus from individualistic 'getters-out of poverty' to a focus on 'collective activists' challenging structural power to achieve institutional change for local-level communities – heterogeneous in terms of poverty levels.

Longitudinal research design issues

The unit of analysis

Although the majority of longitudinal research projects use the household as the unit of analysis, there is considerable diversity over and above this. Thus while Narayan argued for a focus on the individual in tracking who gets out of poverty, others such as Chris Scott (2003) show how his longitudinal panel data research in Chile simultaneously used a number of units of analysis, including farms, household heads, households (the core panel) and communities. In this case, the movement of assets, rather than income, was used to measure change. Anderson (2003) used the term 'house' (as in the house of Windsor) to identify intergenerational structures that included founding parents and descendants. In Rio, Brazil, Perlman (2003) used the individual and the community as two units of analysis. Finally, Mike Thies and Samuel Adenekan[2] both mentioned tracking house buildings in Kaduna, Nigeria, as a particular asset the changing structure of which reflected shifting levels of well-being.

Representativeness

One of the key challenges specific to longitudinal research relates to bridging the time-gap between research periods. Of particular importance is the issue of 'representativeness', highlighted by contrasting discipline perspectives. While some have questioned the relevance of results from small-scale studies, others (mostly anthropologists) argue that small samples, and even case studies, can be effective in testing broader propositions. Others point out that cohorts that are not nationally representative, but representative of a particular group or community, could be equally useful. In addition it may be possible to retrofit non-random samples to other, random, data. Sample sizes ultimately relate to cost; a nationally representative sample can simply be too expensive, and therefore it may be necessary to 'maximize randomness' while minimizing cost. The identification of so-called 'sentinel site' sampling – purposely selecting sites with a poverty focus – provides an example that addresses both representativeness and costing simultaneously. In this respect, Narayan, for instance, identified the potential of selecting high growth/low growth areas to provide the comparative basis for longitudinal research.

Attrition

The issue of attrition is important both generally and as an issue affecting both ends of the spectrum (individuals moving out of the community either because they moved out of poverty or because they fell further into it). Even where no attrition occurs ageing is always a problem, with the need to 'top up' panel data sets. However, as Bob Baulch (2003) commented, panel data attrition rates in less developed countries can vary from 6 per cent to 50 per cent between rounds, and is more of a problem in an urban context given greater levels of mobility. Reducing the number of households over time alters the sample size, and therefore affects statistical precision, as well as losing a potentially crucial part of the overall picture. If attrition is non-random – and there have not been sufficient studies to establish whether it is random or not – the analysis will be non-representative.

The *costs* of tracking, and the associated need to identify who to track, and where, were of particular concern. Perlman's (2003) challenging efforts to track her original sample in Rio took a year and a half. She created student teams to find the 262 individuals eventually located in this process and relied heavily on the 'solidarity of the *favelas*' to reach them.

Suggested solutions to reduce the problem of attrition include:

■ using ID codes for households
■ recording a household's exact position through GPS (global positioning systems)

- collecting details of household networks of family and friends who can help in tracking (the close ties of people within certain marginal communities were often helpful)
- developing clear tracking protocols, including deciding who to invest in tracking when they move
- providing incentives for both participating households and interviewers.

Examples of incentives can include an annual birthday party, a free phone-in line to announce moves, and appointing individuals as site monitors and community gatekeepers to record significant events, as well as where people moved to.

Recall bias and associated measurement error

What can be done about this problem of bias in retrospective research? Even data on births and deaths look different when based on recall rather than on present recording. Various techniques are available, such as calendars of events, as well as asking the same question in several different ways. For example, 'How many days of work did you miss due to illness?', 'How much did you spend on healthcare?'. The use of life histories is also identified as a means of reducing recall bias, as well as group interviews with other household members present to help 'jog' each others' memories and provide some 'triangulation' and corroboration of events.

Retrofitting

Is it possible to retrofit research methodologies to incorporate new language, terms, issues and methodologies (usually qualitative or participatory) into longitudinal data sets? On the one hand the same language can be used in new rounds of surveys and interviews, on the other hand updating language may be considered more appropriate, even though there is a loss of continuity. Along with this, relevant concepts have also changed and new issues emerged, such as democracy and social capital, as well as experiences of violence and HIV/AIDS. Changes in the political context within which longitudinal research is undertaken can also influence the research context, as variously described by Scott (2003) and Perlman (2003).

Opinions vary on the issue of retrofitting. Some argue that it is not possible, because without a time sequence (more than one point in time) it is impossible to establish any idea of cause and effect; from this perspective, the opportunities for changing and adding to the methodology are limited. Others, however, argue that since the objective of longitudinal research is to monitor change, it is essential to address new phenomena if they arise. Consequently, research should reflect reality, and the way reality changes.

One strategy for this is to design a methodology with specific core modules of research, and to insert other 'flexible' modules at later visits to incorporate and reflect new issues as they emerge. Another strategy for retrofitting is the use of a subsample to address different issues at different stages of research, thus allowing for change.

Of particular interest, given the increased popularity of participatory methodologies, is the issue of unit of research for analysis. As Jeremy Holland (2003) describes, participatory urban appraisal focus group discussions provide the opportunity for an important process of refining of perceptions to reach a consensus about reality; yet there are tensions between research results based on the focus group as against the household. In this respect there is the issue of representativeness of participatory methodologies. Does the fact that the World Bank 'Voices of the poor' study included 40 000 men and women make it more representative than a participatory study with a small universe?

Longitudinal research data analysis issues

Causality

What do you have to show to *prove* causality? Moreover, will qualitative data ever be convincing? Correlation does not imply causality; while it is difficult to prove causality, it may be possible to identify strong pointers. Harpham (2003) has produced the following check list to help decide whether something is cause or effect:

- eliminate change through sampling
- prove the strength of association between two things
- postulate a mechanism (otherwise known as 'theory')
- consistency with other studies
- prove the time sequence.

Causality models were perceived as bearing little relation to daily-lived reality; for example, the poor themselves may list 60 causes of one issue. For this reason there was considerable concern to identify the linkage *mechanisms* between policy and the lives of respondents.

The macro-micro linkages

A key element of the causality debate relates to the need for analysis of both macro and micro levels as a means of effectively linking the two. It is also necessary to take into account the time-lags, or 'slow accumulations', between policy implementation, and the ensuing repercussions for communities or individuals. This is one of the advantages of longitudinal research – since research over shorter time periods cannot capture such long-term processes.

A number of strategies for benchmarking the linkages between macro and micro change to individual lives (context versus detail) are proposed. These include plotting time-lines of major social, political and economic changes, as well as mapping policy changes, and comparing these with what people reported in their life histories to see the 'effects of externalities'. This provides an example of the need to 'make sense of life histories' identified by Perlman (2003). For example, health problems associated with dirty water might decline some time after the installation of sewerage systems. Comparisons with other communities that experienced different policy interventions also provide a useful technique. Mixing data on large-scale events (such as timing the occurrence of natural disasters or political changes) with lived experience also allows for crosschecking to reduce recall bias. As with smaller-scale issues, relying on respondents' perceptions and recall of large-scale policy events without crosschecking can be problematic; people may remember vividly the day they got electricity, but may have confused knowledge about the timing or management of particular programmes.

Mixing qualitative and quantitative methods and data

Closely related to the issue of macro and micro linkages is the question of how to incorporate both quantitative and qualitative methods and data. The limitations of qualitative methods were identified as time-consuming and intensive, with their small sample unrepresentative. On the other hand, the potential advantages of qualitative methods relate to their capacity to document the complexity of daily life, which eludes quantitative surveys, and brings out the richness of intra-household dimensions.

There was a general consensus that the two kinds of methodology provide complementary sources of information, and should be used in tandem to link 'smaller stories to larger-scale ones'. Qualitative data can be used to help explain quantitative findings, and vice versa. Consequently there were many recommendations that qualitative and/or participatory elements should be embedded within larger surveys, or integrated in other ways. An effective example comes from Vietnam, where the poverty assessment included both quantitative household surveys and qualitative information from the participatory poverty assessment. This requires government support from the outset, with ownership built through the process, and considerable time (three years) plus associated donor support.

Practical issues emerge when combining qualitative methods with more traditional quantitative ones. For instance, in a study mixing survey data with respondents' *perceptions*, it is crucial to ask about perceptions prior to administering the survey. Using different methods also means that there may be triangulation, with different interpretations of data sometimes emerging. One study found that there was a significant difference between the researchers' interpretation of the survey data as to whether people moved in and out of poverty, and what the people themselves perceived had happened (Lanjouw and Stern, 1998).

Methodologies relating to longitudinal perceptions of change have identified the importance of including different reference points. For example, people's perceptions may alter in relation to those of their children. In addition they may differ in terms of different benchmarks, i.e. against others in their community, their country or against other global reference points.

BROADER POVERTY RESEARCH ISSUES WITH SPECIFIC RELEVANCE TO LONGITUDINAL RESEARCH

Ethical issues

While ethics are always important in social science research, they are even more acute in longitudinal studies. Participation over such a long time frame can be a burden for respondents. The issue of informed consent is very important here, as people may not understand what they are letting themselves in for. (In contrast to this, Perlman (2003) found that people were honoured that someone 'wanted to learn about their lives', and were hurt if not selected in the random sample – to the point where a 'pseudo-questionnaire' was created to appease them.) In studies considering using GPS tracking technology, there are obvious concerns with surveillance, as Jo Beall (2002) identified. In most research, there are no associated interventions to help reduce poverty: researchers simply 'watch' the poverty of respondents over time. While the issues raised by respondents are often immediate concerns, the research is long term; 'people die while researchers are still at the stage of deciding how to distribute their findings to policy-makers'.

In certain instances, researchers were met with mistrust and suspicion. Thus one telling comment from a respondent was the following:

> 'We're overresearched and underdeveloped; when researchers come they are thin, and when they return later, they are nice and fat, while we remain the same as always.'

In other contexts, as Harriss-White (2003) has commented, longitudinal researchers 'become better known to less and less people'.

Despite identifying ethics as being of major concern, researchers have revealed few practical suggestions as to how to address the issue. One innovative approach used three components to attempt to address the high costs to respondents, including explaining how the research should be useful in the long term, giving back the results of previous research and, as Harpham (2003) described, the preparation of a 'Very Useful Information

Package'. In Rio, Perlman (2003) identified respondents by their first names only so as to protect their anonymity, but this led to disaster when trying to track people years or even decades later.

Finally, the issue of stress experienced by the researchers themselves has been raised. Mholongo[2] describes the exhausting experience of trying to track households, particularly in contexts with high levels of violence, where people who had previously been within the study had been killed in the interval between the implementation of the panel studies.

SOME FINAL COMMENTS: PATHS FORWARD

- There have been calls to stop grappling with the issues of representation and causality within qualitative methodologies, to acknowledge that these are valid and to move forward. The use of 'smaller samples to get bigger pictures'.
- Many researchers have emphasized that the key is to develop new frameworks which integrate both traditional quantitative methodologies and qualitative and participatory ones, as together they contribute much to the study of poverty dynamics.
- Longitudinal research highlights the contradictions between policy-makers who require 'quick-fix' answers and the long-term natures of many poverty-related change issues.
- Another plea is to resist the temptation for enormous 'ask everything' studies that result in a large amount of unused data.
- Increasingly, adopted mixed methodologies use triangulation as an important way of crosschecking the validity of different types of data.
- In conclusion, 'evidence-based policy' makes longitudinal data more critical than ever before.

CHAPTER THREE

Young Lives: panel studies and child poverty[1]

Trudy Harpham, Ian Wilson and Sharon Huttly

INTRODUCTION: THE ATTRACTION OF PANEL STUDIES

The essence of the longitudinal survey is that it offers repeated observations of individuals over time. Such time-series design is often
encountered under the generic term *panel study*. The unit of analysis is
normally the individual and not (as in some cross-sectional surveys) the
family or household. This is because the nature of families or households can change across time. 'Panel studies should use the individual
rather than the household as the unit of analysis and map the relationship existing between the two at different points in time. One can use
the household as the unit of *measurement* but ought to use the individual as unit of *analysis*, attributing to each individual the characteristics of the household in which he or she lives' (Laurie and Sullivan,
1991: 122).

Rose (2000: 34) sums up the strengths of panel studies as follows:

> *'Essentially panel data allow us to distinguish between transitory and persistent
> aspects of phenomena such as poverty and unemployment. They allow us to
> examine gross change – flows as well as the stocks. As they mature, panels provide
> vital information on intergenerational issues, for example social mobility. . . .
> However, these advantages only emerge if panel surveys are well designed and are
> maintained so that the disadvantages inherent to panels – panel conditioning
> [respondents becoming atypical of the population because of their panel
> membership, wave non-response, attrition – are minimised'.*

'Transitory aspects' can only be captured if the frequency of observation is
high relative to the duration of the 'transitory' phenomenon.

Panel studies are analytically strong, provide an opportunity to link
macro-micro issues and are increasingly called for in the research recommendations of numerous projects. However, the disadvantages of
panel studies need to be borne in mind: they are costly and complex; it
takes a long time for results to become available; and determination of
aims at the outset may restrict the ability to respond to emerging policy
questions.

THE YOUNG LIVES PROJECT

The Young Lives project investigates the trajectories of poor children in Ethiopia, India (Andhra Pradesh only), Peru and Vietnam. It arose from the UK Department for International Development's (DFID) desire to monitor international millennium development goals (MDGs). The participating countries were selected, from over 20 who expressed interest, in order to illustrate a range of policy, social and economic issues on child poverty and well-being. Research capacity and contrasting contexts were sought.

The data collected are based on a broad understanding of child welfare, and include information on child development in addition to the more conventional nutritional and education measures. The project is taking a broad approach to poverty, including assessments of access to key services, work patterns and social relationships as well as core economic indicators such as assets.

The design of the long-term survey is based on studies of existing data relating to child poverty, and on the views of parents and children themselves collected using participatory methods during the preparatory phase of the project (see for example, Harpham et al., 2004).

The main components are as follows.

1. *Index children.* The study will follow a group of approximately 2000 children per country born in the year 2000/1. They were one year old at the first sweep. The children and their households will be surveyed again when the children are aged four, eight, 11 and 14.
2. *Eight-year-olds.* The study also collected information about approximately 1000 children in each country who were eight years old in 2002. This information can then be compared with the index children, when they reach age eight. The eight-year-olds will also be followed up in future sweeps of the survey.
3. *Community-level data collection.* Information about the social, economic and environmental context of each community was collected at the same time as the surveys.
4. *Thematic projects.* These will be in-depth investigations into key issues raised by the surveys, or issues which are felt to be best examined through qualitative approaches.

Preliminary reports from round one are available at www.younglives.org.uk. A key characteristic of the project has been early engagement with national policy-makers and planners. In the first three years of the project nearly as much money was spent on raising the profile of the project, advocacy and dissemination as on empirical research. This investment has reaped rewards. For example, although only preliminary, descriptive data were available from the first sweep of data at the end of 2003, the project achieved good acknowledgement in high-profile development documents like the Vietnam National Development Report. In addition, contracts with national media have been formed to ensure the use of popular channels.

ADDRESSING PROBLEMS OF PANEL STUDIES IN DEVELOPING COUNTRIES

Conceptual frameworks that link macro and micro contexts

'In the search for effective policies to combat poverty, bridging the gap between macro-level policy analysis and micro-level livelihoods analysis is an essential task, but not an easy one' (Shankland, 2001). Because panel studies are well suited to linking macro policy changes with micro individual or household changes, it is imperative to have a conceptual framework that links the two. A conceptual framework requires hypothetical linkages between risk factors (or determinants, depending on what discipline one is from) and outcomes. The Young Lives project has numerous outcomes such as a child's physical and mental health, her nutritional status and developmental stage for age, numeracy, literacy and the child's own, subjective perception of well-being. In addition, there are risk factors for such outcomes. These include aspects of child care (including use of services), work, play, education and household structure, including parental characteristics such as care givers' education status and physical and mental health. Careful consideration needs to be given to the measurement of wealth, socio-economic status and livelihoods. Young Lives uses a livelihoods framework and tries to capture shocks and various assets (such as social capital) which may buffer the effect of shocks. As Dercon (2001: 7) states: 'panel data . . . are crucial for increasing our quantitative understanding of shocks and their impact'. But all this is at the micro level; what about the macro? In between the two levels are community structures and institutions. It is useful to capture contextual information by implementing a community (ecologic) questionnaire. The sampling procedure can facilitate or hamper the collection of the most useful community-level data. We need enough communities to see variation in the effect of policy implementation (or to confirm its uniformity across the state). 'Within' communities we want all of a set of households to be part of the same 'community'.

Measuring change at the macro level requires monitoring policy over time and then, in analyses, linking such change to micro-level change at the household or community level. Studies may be concerned with specific sectors, such as health, or may be interested in broader issues such as poverty, in which case cross-sectoral policies have to be monitored (e.g. privatization). Evidence of policy implementation, not mere declarations or enactment, needs to be monitored. Thus, information is required on any differential implementation (between places (region, rural/urban), times or population groups). If inter-sweep tracking visits are made to cohort members, field workers can undertake checks of policy implementation at the local level during these visits. In addition, complementary longitudinal qualitative data may illuminate quantitative relationships observed (Laurie and Sullivan, 1991).

Another point to note about macro-micro linkages in panel studies is that a single cohort study is not able to inform us about trends. For life-course processes recorded for a single cohort, there is no scope to examine variation from cohort to cohort. Only a comparison *between* cohorts allows one to establish whether there has been change across time, for example whether children born 10 years later have better nutritional status (Dale and Davies, 1994). However, this substantially adds to costs and a single additional cross-sectional survey of children at a particular age (as was done in Young Lives) is a compromise that will at least provide some comparative data, provided it uses the same sampling basis as the original cohort. In addition, the panel data can be compared to secondary data sources (e.g. previous national surveys) if population groups are sufficiently similar. In the case of Young Lives, comparisons to Demographic and Health Surveys (DHS) and Living Standards Measurement Surveys (LSMS) are often useful.

Sampling the cohort in a cost-effective way

Sample selection for a panel study needs very careful consideration. In many cases it may be impractical to take a sample, representative of the relevant age group, from the general population. It would need to be very large and expensive to contain enough of any given target group.

If it has the aim of illuminating macro-micro issues, a study needs to focus on geographical areas 'sites') where it is meaningful to assess the local implementation of relevant policies and to collect a meaningful sample of micro-level information on individuals. The sampling strategy requires work at two levels: site selection and sampling of individual households within sites. Those individuals selected within sites studied will of course be personally unknown and anonymous to analysts concerned with the whole study, so the usual requirements of objectivity demand that sampling has the benefits associated with randomness, rather than being casual or opportunistic. Also, repeated follow-up makes it imperative that the selections made can be documented and traced, so the site sample can be reproduced without difficulty. In practice, this is likely to mean that a systematic form of sampling is used, carefully adapted to local conditions.

At the level of site selection, it can be anticipated that plausible entities that might become sampled sites will have numerous characteristics that are well known, at least regionally. For example, one site may be a centre of a particular form of child labour in an ill-regulated industry, a market for some specific products, the centre of intercommunal religious violence, and so on. Sampling sites at random disregards this plethora of information, and will only work well if there are a huge number of selected sites so that most important features are adequately represented. To keep down the workload and the corresponding costs, developing country studies are likely to have a relatively small number of sites, so these must be sampled purposively, ensuring they serve to illuminate macro-micro policy linkages known to be important at the outset, e.g. individual or combined impacts of legislation on child labour, and an improved commitment to industrial regulation. A claim to have avoided subjective selection biases depends on a very clear qualitative description of the site selection, e.g. how it draws on published data and was, for example, agreed by consensus of named experts.

Tracking individuals

Minimizing loss of individuals over time is perhaps one of the greatest challenges facing any panel study. Refusal to continue participation is the main reason for loss in developed country cohort studies, whereas in developing countries the principal problem is failure to trace participants (Hill, 2002). Tracking or tracing rates, naturally, vary according to factors such as the intersweep interval and local conditions. The selection of strategies to maximize tracing is determined by resources and local circumstances. These strategies range from the gathering of pertinent information to the use of technology. Information on key friends, neighbours and family of a participant can lead to useful sources of help when a cohort member has moved. Another possibility is to employ a local community member to conduct occasional tracing checks on cohort members. Improvements in communications technology bring new possibilities. Geographical Information Systems (GIS) provide exciting new opportunities for tracking in remote areas. Decisions must be taken on, for example, whether to follow individuals who move outside the study catchment areas. Large-scale studies have used a central tracking operation for cases that move beyond a local area. In the Young Lives study, information has been gathered in the first sweep of the study to establish tracking strategies for the different sentinel sites, according to factors such as within-site mobility and migration rates. Early data from Vietnam suggest a combined migration/death rate of one per cent of index children per year. It is expected that many of the migrated children will be maintained within the study, particularly in Vietnam, where official registration of migration is the norm.

Ethical issues

Ethical issues are particularly important in panel studies because of the increased burden on respondents. In some developing countries, appropriate ethical committees do not yet exist – they may have to be established before the implementation of a panel study (as was the case in Vietnam). An important aspect of successful tracking of cohort individuals is that on entry to the study they are aware of its longitudinal nature and that they consent to being traced over time. This is one ethical issue that differs from single cross-sectional studies. Panel studies, naturally, share many ethical concerns with other study designs and these are important to address. These include issues such as informed consent, how to deal with cases of illness or abuse encountered, and how to interview vulnerable groups such as children. An issue which perhaps bears greater significance in panel studies is that of incentives for participants. The question of whether to use incentives, in the form of cash or kind, particularly where there is no immediate benefit of participating in a study, is not straightforward. In the South African Birth to Twenty Project, for example, study participants receive simple, tangible reminders of the project such as stickers, key rings, annual calendars, fridge magnets, pens and rulers, all with a prominent study logo. Participants are refunded for any transport costs incurred and a limited social and health service has been incorporated into the study. A toll-free number has been installed in the project office to enable families to contact the study for advice and information. Referral notes to local services are given to families when serious health or social problems are detected. Incentives in the form of communication to make participants feel involved have also proved helpful to keep participants interested and to remind them to inform organizers about change of address. Examples include birthday cards, regular newsletters, reports on the study in the local media and a website (www.wits.ac.za/birthto20).

Data management and analytical challenges

Improvements in both computing software and hardware have helped put panel studies within easier reach of researchers. Nevertheless, their complexities for data management and analysis should not be underestimated and require considerable care in design and ongoing maintenance. Planning for data management and analysis at an early stage can also inform the design of data collection instruments such as questionnaires – for example, by clarifying the coding of variables or by evaluating the utility of a question, in an analysis plan with dummy tables. These points hold for other types of study, but for panel studies they are perhaps of even greater importance, since the early planning stages need to consider the data management and analysis requirements of later sweeps. A good foundation will reap many benefits at later stages.

To capitalize on the primary strength of panel studies means looking at data longitudinally, that is linking data measured at one point in time with measurements at later points. This requires consideration of how stable or transient variables are in assessing their use as determinants or correlates of later outcomes. A key problem is that of missing data, either when an individual is lost to follow-up entirely or misses a sweep but returns later. This is a methodological field of enquiry which is currently attracting considerable attention and likely to generate more sophisticated and accessible methods for dealing with missing data, such as imputation.

Finally, a crucial issue for long-term successful use of panel data is comprehensive documentation of procedures and structures. Few researchers will be involved with a long-term study for its entire duration and as the complexity of data sets increases, the need grows for clear metadata – explanatory information associated with the actual data, e.g. as to what was measured or recorded by whom and about whom, when and where; and any changes to datasets during 'cleaning'. These metadata should be securely locked on to the data themselves and all documentation and definitions should be of sufficient standard that the provenance of early data can still be fully understood 15 or 30 years hence. This requires rigorous attention to archiving of metadata, in turn requiring a high degree of selectivity about the data and metadata items preserved, to avoid too large a bureaucratic burden.

CONCLUSIONS

Panel studies are important in developed countries due to their ability to inform policy (Office for National Statistics, 1999; Institute for Social and Economic Research, 2000). As the call for evidence-based policy increases in developing countries the attraction of panel studies will grow. However, they are expensive and complex. As experience of implementing panel studies in developing countries increases, more guidelines can be formed regarding the challenges considered in this chapter: selecting a sample in the absence of a sampling frame; linking macro and micro contexts; tracking mobile populations; the need for ethics committee approval; and sophisticated data management and analysis. Panel studies should not be entered into lightly in any context, but in resource-constrained environments their added value needs careful consideration. They certainly require quite long-term robustness of funding and a stable institutional setting, and they require their backers to have sufficient vision and patience to accept limited value for money in terms of results from the early stages, the greater benefits accumulating in the study's mature years.

CHAPTER FOUR

Poverty and urban violence

Leo Thomas

INTRODUCTION

Poverty and urban violence have increasingly become dominant concerns in debates in the development community and wider society. Part of the concern emanates from the perceived and actual escalation in urban violence across the globe since the mid-1980s and its impact on the economies of nations, the institutions of society and lives of citizens. This escalation in violence has occurred at the same time as the continuing urbanization of many countries in the developing world and the apparent entrenchment of processes of economic inequity and social exclusion in cities of the South.[1]

This chapter will examine the relationship between poverty and urban violence, both of which are complex multidimensional phenomena. Consideration is first given to defining violence and differentiating its varying nature and the levels at which it operates. A brief survey of trends in urban violence is then presented. Theories of violence are considered and an examination of the role that poverty plays in violence is then situated in this wider theoretical framework. It should be clear to most readers that the integration of a number of factors, both historic and new, yields a more thorough, nuanced yet complex understanding of the interplay between well-being and violence in the city. The final section outlines the future challenges in tackling emergent forms of urban violence.

UNDERSTANDING VIOLENCE

Violence is a multifaceted phenomenon, with competing definitions as to what it constitutes. War, conflict and crime can, for example, all be viewed as subsets of more generalized definitions of violence that see the direct and instrumental exercise of physical force against people, property and institutions. In other perspectives, violence is not necessarily manifest at the physical level but produces outcomes that have physical, social and economic effects. Threats to persons or implemented policies that affect the well-being of groups would constitute types of violence from this perspective. For the purposes of this chapter, however, violence is taken to mean *the exercise of physical force so as to cause injury or damage to a person, social groups or property.* Reflections on such physical violence, and the fear of it, bring into focus again the need to combine qualitative understandings of well-being into considerations of 'development' (Gasper, 1999).

Three immediate clarifying observations can be made. First, the nature of violence is diverse. Moser and Winton (2002) categorize violence into three predominant forms, namely political violence, social violence and economic violence, all of which have an institutional dynamic at operation. *La Violencia* in Chile, communalism in western India in the 1990s and the postwar conflict in Mozambique represent dramatic historical examples of these variants of violence. Although categorizations are helpful to allow us to begin to disentangle and analyse the particular roots and operation of violence in different contexts, they should not blind us to the reality that violence usually has multiple causes, expressions and consequences. The violence in the urban centres in Jamaica between the mid-1970s and 1980s, for example, was predominantly political in causation but had deep historical roots and long-term economic objectives. Urban violence should, therefore, be seen as a broadly social problem with an urban expression.

Second, perpetrators and victims of violence are diverse and sometimes conflated. States, para-statal organizations, non-state groups and private individuals may all use violence. A careful historical analysis of urban violence within particular country contexts allows for identification of the actual and main sources of violence at specific junctures. In Latin America during the 1960s and 1970s, states were responsible for much violence against their own people both inside and outside of the city, whereas the 1990s have seen the growing and possibly greater influence of criminal organizations in using violence to organize both local and global markets. Individuals, households and neighbourhoods may be directly affected by violence and cities, regions and nations indirectly affected by the physical, economic and organizational adaptations that emerge in response to violence. A corollary of this argument is that there is an inequity in the target and impact of violence, even when such violence is categorized as random and gratuitous social violence. When violent crime is entrenched in a city, young men are more likely to perpetuate it and suffer murder, whereas women may suffer reduced spatial mobility and social power in the household.[2]

Third, the site of violence and the increasing fear of violence are urban areas. The flight of better-off residents from the centre of cities to walled or gated communities (even in east Asia), the general fortification of urban space, the growth of the private security industry, the emergence and contested impact of vigilante groups are all signs quite apart from official police data of the increased prevalence and fear of violence in the city.

Democracy has replaced dictatorship, guerrilla wars are mostly over – but everyday life for Latin Americans has become far less secure. An explosive increase in murder since the 1980s has turned Latin America into the world's most criminally violent continent. In the big cities, fear of crime has pushed the rich into the segregated wall of walled condominiums.

(Economist, *8 March 1997*).

THEORIES OF URBAN VIOLENCE

Why is it that we increasingly associate urban areas with violence? Additionally, why are causal relationships drawn between poverty in particular and urban violence? The disparate theoretical roots purporting to connect the city and violence are deep and old. For ease of discussion, our analysis will focus on contemporary social and socio-economic theories and empirical findings. There has been much discussion of the biological, evolutionary and psychological explanations of violence. The main problems with such approaches are their unsupportable sociobiological determinism, their weakness of translating inherently individual analysis to the collective executed phenomenon of violence and their problem in incorporating the undeniable influence of the wider social context on violence.

Differential association theories stress that urban areas will have many different subcultures, with some of them developing criminal tendencies, with members becoming socialized into violent and criminal behaviour (Sutherland and Cressey, 1978). In such a context, becoming a violent criminal, in particular, is a learned process and a different means of achieving the same economic or status-oriented ends. Theories of anomie or alienation stress the problems of the shift from traditional societies to modern society in terms of rural to urban migration. There is an assumed concomitant shift from traditional norms and values to a place where there is no clearly established system. Rural migrants leave the countryside, where there are clear roles, agreed norms and a consensual sense of what is correct or acceptable, for urban areas that are places of contestation.

Furthermore, the city presents a greater choice between values, ends and means for groups that are clearly not equal. In a context where people accept values of material prosperity through the means of hard work, but in an urban context which prevents the achievement of this end, there is likely to be either an adjustment in the goal or an adjustment in the means. Urban violence represents one means of achieving goals, be they purely economic or linked to prestige and status. These theories from a functionalist perspective, would regard violence as being less extreme and disruptive in contexts where there are cross-cutting categories in the urban society between income, status/privilege and power.

Cultural theories see urban violence as resulting from a breakdown in a common set of principles for the settlement of disputes. Where rules (laws or customs), conventions, morality and sanctions become contested, fluid and/or ineffective, violence can assert itself as a means of social interchange. The city reduces the strength of customs and sanctions due to the increased individuation, social anonymity, relational complexities and spatial diffusiveness it brings.

Rational choice theories see violent behaviour as a chosen action to fulfil a particular goal-set. Cornish and Clark (1989) see people as assessing a range of possible actions to fulfil a particular set of goals. Violence is one particular action alongside education, social networking, formal sector employment and political organizing for achieving desired economic goals. When violence is being considered, other factors are referred to, such as the risk of getting caught, the likelihood of completed and successful prosecution, and the probable severity of punishment. In this conception, people are primarily seen as rational, calculating, economic beings with perfect information. In reality, this is clearly untrue but variants of the model still have value. Surprisingly, numerous authors with social scientist backgrounds are increasingly seeing this economic rationality as lying behind much violence and conflict. The exponential growth and strength of the narcotics business is associated with violence being used in an instrumental way to overcome inner competitors and state constraints to this industry. Urban areas have provided a context for the organizing principle of violence and the threat of violence to flourish. Successful economic criminals can use violence to organize neighbourhood strongholds, deter or undermine law enforcement agencies and to extend their local and global markets. Even lower-level criminals will use violence, such as kidnapping, in a context where it proves effective for securing financial gain with little chance of clear up.

Authors such as Keen (1997) and Duffield (1999) have made an interesting adaptation of this rational economic choice theory by suggesting that parties to violence deliberately maintain violence, and intergroup conflict in particular, because the continuation of disorder enables them to achieve goals they could not otherwise achieve in a settled state. Where violence is endemic, it is not to be assumed that the perpetrators of violence bear the cost of it. It is exactly because they as organized groups derive net benefits from a state of violence that they continue in perpetrating violent conflict.

There is a question of the expectations of urban residents and the possible impact on violence in urban areas. One of the impacts of globalization has been the issue of rising expectations, particularly in urban areas that function as centres for the conspicuous display and sharing of global identities, lifestyles and ambitions. There are a number of scenarios in which the likelihood of urban violence is increased as follows:

- rising expectations but static capacity to meet them
- rising capability but faster-rising expectations

- capacities match expectations but then capacities fall
- fall in expectations and capabilities, met with general economic collapse.

The pace of urbanization mixed with the institutional constraints of the state to meet even the basic needs of new urban residents, may incite individuals, families, groups or neighbourhood associations to explore options to self-produce outcomes to meet their expectations. These options may include the use of violence to obtain economic and physical resources from other actors external to the perpetrators.

> *Living in illegally occupied areas, deprived of basic services, having to use dangerous or inadequate transport, victims of urban speculation, forced to function in the informal sector, without proper leisure facilities, and surrounded by advertising that invites them to acquire everything, poor urban families in the South are a milieu permeated with social frustrations in which the culture of violence can flourish.*
>
> *(Vanderschueren, 1996: 99).*

POVERTY, GOVERNANCE AND URBAN VIOLENCE

Theories of rational choice, differential association and urban anomie suggest myriad factors that underpin the emergence of urban violence, that include:

- income poverty and income inequity
- low and inequitable access to basic services
- diminished social capital within and between groups in cities
- the inefficacy of criminal justice systems
- transformation of values, identities and behaviour in the city.

Poverty and inequality

Poverty plays a key role in explanations of urban violence, though there are divergent interpretations on the causal mechanisms linking the two phenomena. More importantly, there is a lack of clear and comparative empirical data establishing a robust relationship between poverty and urban violence. Washington, D.C., for example, has murder rates that exceed those of Johannesburg, Kingston and São Paulo despite the higher levels of average income. The rates of urban violence and victimization of the middle-income countries with strong urban economies exceed those of low-income countries. Even within sub-Saharan Africa, we see greater urban violence in more relatively prosperous urban centres such as Nairobi, Cape Town and Lagos than in poorer cities such as Lusaka, Addis Ababa or Dakar. Taking income poverty, even combined with inequality of wealth and urban growth rates, as critical, we would have expected to see higher levels of urban violence in urban India and China. There is no clear pattern in the relationship between poverty and urban violence when we look at the world's regions or even at comparative data within the same country.

Lederman and Loayza (1999) argue that a stronger relationship exists between income inequality and violence. Taking a large sample of countries for the period 1974–90, results from cross-sectional regressions 'show that the Gini index of income distribution has a significant positive coefficient in all the regressions, revealing that countries with more unequal distributions of income tend to have higher crime rates than those with more egalitarian patterns of income distribution'. They go on to suggest that changes in income distribution, not changes in absolute levels of poverty, are associated with changes in violent crime rates. Burgess (1998) goes further, suggesting that neo-liberal adjustment packages such as Structural Adjustment Programmes (SAPs) have tended to increase economic inequalities, and where these inequalities correspond to racial, ethnic, religious or cultural differences, the level of urban violence can be particularly high.[3]

Urban growth and the limited capacity of institutions

Is the problem the level of urbanization and the corresponding demand for services it brings vis-à-vis the inability of the state to meet these needs? Lederman and Loayza (1999) argue that the overall level of urbanization does not affect the rate of violent crime. Moser and Winton (2002) suggest that city growth rates rather than overall city size is a stronger indicator of crime rates.

> Households in cities experiencing high population growth are more likely to be victimised than are those living in cities with more stable populations. The tentative reason suggested for this is the self-perpetuating relationship between rising crime rates, and increasingly overloaded and ineffective institutions, due to population growth.

> (Moser and Winton, 2002: 8).

Gizewski and Homer-Dixon (1995) argue that the relationship is far from simple and that analysts need to further examine the contribution of urban growth to violence through a deeper exploration of its synergistic and/or multiplicative interaction with other factors. Such factors include the international economic recession, weak regulatory frameworks, the strength of organized crime, the availability of small arms, the vitality of entrenched ethnic or religious cleavages and the socio-political latitude for self-help organizing among different strata of urban society.

Weakening of social capital

Just as complex is the relationship between poverty, social capital and violence. The urban context is seen as providing less communally owned and managed resources, differential access to social and economic resources, and the inevitable need for the construction of multiple-identities, all of which are seen as weakening the cognitive and practical ties between people. Where impoverished slum-dwellers cannot fulfil hospitality obligations to kinsmen, for example, a slow splintering of obligation and reciprocity may emerge.

There is abundant evidence to suggest that urban poverty and urban growth may not weaken social capital but rather reinforce it. For example, self-help housing in the urban periphery of Latin American cities, financial cooperation among women in the cities of south Asia, the provision of pre-school education in the Caribbean, burial societies in southern Africa. Other authors contend that strong structural social capital is not necessarily a good thing, with Rubio (1997) speaking of the *perverse* social capital created by drugs cartels. The emergence of *area crews* in Jamaica, *commands* in Brazil and region-wide *maras* in Central America challenge simplistic notions of the conceptions of and wider social value of 'social capital'. Both Harriss (2002) and Beall (2002) argue that social capital is not necessarily positive or value-neutral, but may in fact reflect the existing power structures in society that further marginalize the very poorest. Such groups provide some form of social cohesion, have bonds with similar grouping, and bridges to distinctly diverse political and occupational groups (Nordstrom, 2000). Yet overwhelmingly they are labelled as being negative criminally oriented groups.

What is clear is that these so-called shadow actors are active belligerents and key social actors in violent contexts. Their initial genesis may have included strong defensive elements towards their base communities or neighbourhoods, and indeed may be seen as providing a net social and economic benefit to communities that would otherwise have been more vulnerable to external physical attack and economic shocks in the formal sector. The trajectories of development of these groups as social organizations are not clear. Chevannes (2002) makes the case for more research centred on the socialization process that takes place in such groups, whereas Feenan (2002) outlines the complexity of researching about and in such contexts of organized violence.[4]

Even if we accept the concept of social capital, it is clear that our understanding of elements, nature and transformations needs to be enhanced. It is too simplistic to assume the urban social complexity leads to a diminution of social capital and this allows for an upsurge in violence. Cognitive social capital, such as trust, can diminish, and in doing so trigger the emergence of structural social capital, such as more neighbourhood watch groups to guard against violence. It should not be assumed that social capital is less robust in the city or that there is an inverse relationship between social capital and violence. Rather, there is an emergent and interactive relationship between the nature of violence expressed in space and forms of social organization and adaptation.

Weak criminal justice systems

Much emphasis has been placed on the efficacy of the criminal justice system as a deterrent to urban violence. In one sense, this is the last and most costly fall-back position after the observation of customs, conventions and morality proscribing violence has failed. It should be borne in mind, however, that systems of criminal justice (including policing) have achieved low clear-up rates for crime. At best, their role is much more symbolic than real, offering the promise that crime will be investigated and where possible prosecuted. It is clear that much under-reporting of crime among the poor takes place because they do not believe in the efficacy or appropriateness of formal criminal systems for resolving urban violence and crime. A crucial question is whether people adopted violence in the light of a system that is clearly ineffective or is it that the system is particularly ineffective in dealing with urban violence?

> Overwhelmed by the number of cases, [the criminal justice system] is slow, expensive, overburdened with procedures, hampered by a language that bears no relation to the concerns or needs of inhabitants and is ill-suited to a rapidly changing environment. Most people have little respect for it; the urban poor may have no confidence in it or respect for it at all.
>
> (Vandershueren, 1996: 102).

There is some evidence to suggest that the urban poor do not trust the police. Some of this distrust stems from the police being used historically as organizers and perpetrators of collective violence in poor urban communities, particularly in times of political turbulence. Part of the distrust emanates from the legacy in certain countries of the police organizing extra-judicial killings, particularly of the young urban males. A more common element of distrust is associated with the actual and perceived corruption of certain police officers, special operational teams and internal organizational processes. This matrix of distrust creates a layered dynamic. First, it operates to keep the most vulnerable among the urban poor disconnected from police services through fear of poor treatment or assault by the police, or violent reprisals from the accused parties. Second, it leads to the emergence of contested informal justice systems within poor urban communities, which are often violent and conflict generating in nature. Third, it leads to the fortification of space and arming of ghetto soldiers against all violent intrusions by the police or any other armed grouping.

A factor related to and just as salient as the weakness of the criminal justice system is the erosion of the state's monopoly on the use of violence. Groups and individuals in urban areas have increasing access to small arms and light weapons, mostly illegally. In some countries, private ownership of arms is a legacy of civil war while in others it is an outgrowth of the Cold War or its collapse. Possibly most importantly, the market for crime and for 'security' goods in insecure urban settings is the most potent force drawing forth this supply. The numbers of arms and weapons in circulation in most urban settings is staggering and explains the rise proportion of intentional killings accounted for by guns.

FUTURE VISIONS OF URBAN VIOLENCE

There seem to be a number of future threats regarding urban poverty and urban violence. These are related to the following phenomena.

The continued evolution of organized crime

Despite some noticeable individual successes in countering organized crime, the general pattern in most countries is towards an increasing level of organization and more instrumental use of violence among groups. Transpatial networks, which are flexible in structure, semi-autonomous in action and expansive in societal reach, seem to be more common. While many nation-states have special teams tackling organized crime, they often lack the financial and human resources, intradepartmental legitimacy and interorganizational capacity to effectively pursue, capture and prosecute transnational criminal organizations. At present, fewer than 15 per cent of cases of murder are cleared up. The continued growth of the internal and international markets for drugs and small arms is but one indicator of continuing trouble here (Nordstrom, 2000).

The Balkanization of secondary cities

The entrenchment of the feud-dynamic on ethnic and religious violence in cities remains a distinct possibility, as continuing incidents of collective violent outbreaks in south Asia, west and central Africa and eastern Europe make clear. If this element of feud becomes a part of the violence dynamic, theorists suggest that even the alleviation of the original causes of violence will have no constraining effect on the violence (Black-Michaud, 1975; Sandle, 1999; World Bank, 2003,). There are significant implications for urban planning, spatial mobility, stable economic investments and redistributive mechanisms in contexts where violence will increasingly lead to spatial segregation and fortification.

State failure to provide security and welfare

There is increasing debate about the phenomenon of state failure (Milliken and Krause, 2002). State failure, that is the failure to provide security, representation and welfare, obviously creates contexts where the likelihood of a slide to violence is increased. This may be particularly a problem in secondary cities and towns outside the symbolic or economic centre of power, but not necessarily so. The centre can act as a crucible and magnifier to the process of state failure and the resultant impact on unrestrained social competition and violence may be significant. Extra-state organizations may be expected to employ the use and threat of violence to secure influence in communities before legitimacy is enhanced through the provision of security, welfare and opportunities for economic activities.

Terrorism in urban areas

Finally, recent events in Madrid, Istanbul, Casablanca, Baghdad, Delhi, Seoul, Riyadh, Moscow and New York indicate the emergence of cities as renewed sites of terrorist activity. Terrorist events in this new millennium have been increasingly urban, focusing on key transport, commercial and political targets with high-kill and symbolic potential. This has implications obviously for all those concerned with contemporary debates around urban governance, planning, compactness, poly-nuclearity, architecture and transport.

CONCLUSIONS

Violence is not a clean, discrete phenomenon that appears and disappears, mediated only between a lone perpetrator and direct victim. Rather, it is a phenomenon that affects the well-being of many individuals, diverse social groups, entire neighbourhoods and the state itself. In participatory analysis of poverty, respondents frequently rate violence as the most pressing factor affecting their access to entitlements, their agency to exploit economic opportunities and their ability to claim their rights.

Violence and the fear of violence have immediate and direct practical effects on people's spatial mobility, the delivery of basic services to their neighbourhoods, their access to security and justice, and the success of their economic livelihood strategies. The more indirect consequences include a diminution in the quality and equity of education services, the emergence of extra-state crimogenic governance systems, a reduction in local economic investment and growth.

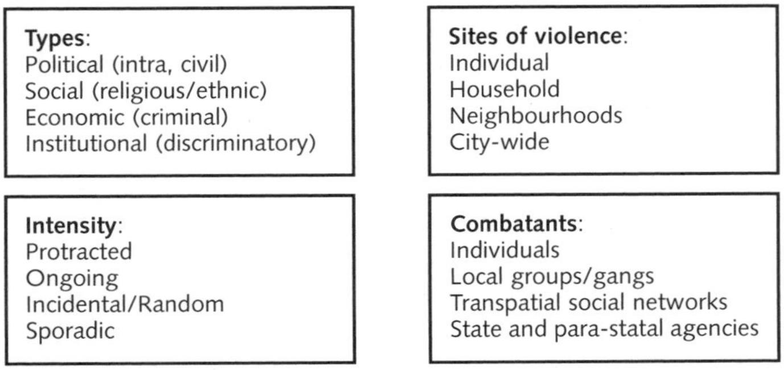

Types: Political (intra, civil) Social (religious/ethnic) Economic (criminal) Institutional (discriminatory)	**Sites of violence:** Individual Household Neighbourhoods City-wide
Intensity: Protracted Ongoing Incidental/Random Sporadic	**Combatants:** Individuals Local groups/gangs Transpatial social networks State and para-statal agencies

Figure 4.1   Dimensions of violence

PART II

THE DYNAMICS OF URBAN SYSTEMS

CHAPTER FIVE

A question of voice: informality and pro-poor policy in Johannesburg, South Africa

Steven Friedman, Kenny Hlela and Paul Thulare

INTRODUCTION

Is the battle against urban poverty purely a matter of finding appropriate technical solutions? Or is the political context more important?

For international financial institutions and many scholars, the problem is primarily technical. The literature abounds with studies discussing the technicalities of social policy and programmes, a plethora of research and writing on how to design interventions so that they reach the poor more effectively and have more enduring welfare effects (van der Gaag and Lipton, 1993; World Bank 1996, 1997). This view is the social policy equivalent of a mainstream economic policy approach which sees growth as the consequence of appropriate policy interventions designed by specialists with the requisite skill and training to understand what is required. Politics is not necessarily ignored – but it tends to be seen as a constraint, not an opportunity, as an intrusion of sectional interests and prejudices into the making of technically effective policy rather than a key to poverty erosion. (Raczynski, 1995).

While few scholars would entirely deny the role of technical responses, there is another view of the problem, which sees politics as a vital resource in the quest for growth and the fight against poverty. In the social policy realm, this view has pointed out the degree to which political circumstances or choices have produced social policy outcomes with significant positive welfare effects. Thus Skocpol and Katznelson (1996) show that a political consensus among power holders on the need to compensate Union civil war veterans and their families produced a generous, enduring and relatively effective poverty reduction programme in the United States during the nineteenth and early twentieth century. Comparative international work by Esping-Andersen (1990, 1996) demonstrates how a variety of political coalitions and traditions shape the choice of differing social policy regimes, which have significantly different impacts on the distribution of resources. Przeworski (1987) shows how labour's living standards were raised in democratic welfare states by coalition formation and bargaining which ensured that outcomes enjoyed wide social support and that poverty could be eroded without harming business confidence. And pioneering work by Rodrik (1999) suggests that, in countries of the global South, the ability to resolve conflict prompted by external shocks or domestically initiated economic reform is the key precondition for growth, a thesis which invites debate on and inquiry into the political context in which economic policy is made. The work of Douglass North (1990, 1991, 1995) has, of course, drawn attention to the pivotal role of political institutions in creating the preconditions for economic growth.

None of these approaches should be seen as an attempt to reduce the quest for policy and programmes which promise significant advances in poverty reduction to a purely political exercise. Clearly the social and economic policy design and that of the programmes which flow from them, do help to shape outcomes. But the evidence marshalled in the works cited here does argue for an approach which recognizes that politics shapes the environment in which social and economic policy and programmes are devised and that, in the absence of appropriate political conditions and institutions, anti-poverty interventions are likely to be frustrated. This may be agreed by those who see politics as a constraint as well as those who view it as a resource in the fight against poverty. But the consensus may be short-lived, for the stress on political preconditions also suggests that differing solutions may be necessary in different political contexts, that 'suboptimal' technical responses may be most likely to be effective if they are politically appropriate because they encourage cooperation between economic and social actors. The political is thus in this view not only a factor that policy-makers must acknowledge when they seek to implement policy, but when they design it too. If politics is a crucial underpinning for technical policy-making, then policy design needs to adapt itself to the political as well as to the technical challenges posed by a particular context.

More specifically, the historical and comparative evidence suggests that effective pro-poor social and economic policy is likely to emerge under one of two conditions. The first is the presence of what de Swaan (1988) calls 'social consciousness' – a widespread perception among economic elites that all social groups are interdependent, that elites bear some of the responsibility for the conditions of the poor, and a belief that efficacious means of assisting the poor exist or might be created (de Swaan et al., 2000). This may develop where a trigger to national solidarity, such as a perceived or actual external threat or the aftermath of conflict, prompts elite consensus that the poor, or a specific section of the poor, need public support. Examples include the already cited post-bellum US as well as, more recently, the East Asian 'tigers'. The second, analysed most notably by Przeworski (1987), is perhaps more common, particularly under democratic conditions. It is a product of political organization, coalition-building and compromise: the poor – traditionally represented by labour movements and parties – organize, build alliances with other sections of society, and then bargain with business and the affluent to fashion a pro-poor policy agenda and ensure its adoption and implementation.

THE SOUTHERN AFRICAN CASE

A recent study of civil society's role in Southern African poverty reduction (Centre for Policy Studies, 2002) found that, while most, if not all, countries in the region have an official poverty reduction agenda (either Poverty Reduction Strategy Processes (PRSP), introduced as part of the Highly Indebted Poor Country (HIPC) initiative, or home-grown initiatives), this is diluted by their often vague nature, weak implementation and evidence that programmes designed for the poor are not reaching them – or are failing to hear their needs and likely responses.

Thus only a few plans to address poverty show sufficient knowledge of the circumstances of the poor to accommodate the reality that poor people cannot be seen as homogenous because they are poor for different reasons. This insight is so commonplace to some grassroots understandings of poverty that it is embedded in language. Thus in Malawi, grassroots understandings of poverty are more varied and less narrow than the official treatment of the problem. In local languages, 'poverty' translates into four terms which encompass differing types ranging from lack of basic necessities to temporary need for material goods, and differing causes from lack of family ties through external shocks such as disease, to consequences of the business cycle. Its absence from some plans suggests a very tenuous link to the poor. Effective intervention may require not an undifferentiated concept of 'the poor' but an analysis of the specific constituencies that are poor. Even where plans acknowledge this differentiation, it is rarely built into the design of programmes. The importance of voice in shaping policy is shown by the fact that South Africa's poverty reduction agendas do tend to notice difference, at least rhetorically: this is a consequence of the role of active and influential women's organizations as well as associations seeking to speak for the disabled. Where this voice does not exist, difference remains unrecognized. But nowhere does difference seem to be strongly enough acknowledged to shape concrete programmes.

On implementation, most countries fare even worse. With some exceptions, pro-poor programmes are often very limited in their aims and in the number of people they reach, and rarely seem to be a priority. While it may be too early to conclude that some of the countries have no interest in concrete poverty-reduction programmes – many of the plans are quite recent – a substantial increase in activity would be needed to generate a working poverty-reduction agenda and the evidence does not suggest that this is likely. Critics insist that lack of implementation in the region betrays a 'commitment' to poverty reduction among its governments which is purely rhetorical. There is thus no strong evidence in most countries that the delivery of services is designed to give priority to the poor. Mozambique's PRSP, for example, gives priority to road construction not in the poorest areas but in those said to have the highest economic potential. Rural extension and agricultural research are also targeted to areas with higher growth potential. It is worth noting here that it has taken a sustained public investment programme over decades to achieve Botswana's fairly modest gains in poverty reduction.

The failure to implement stated policy may be seen as a managerial or technical problem. But programmes may not be implemented because there is no will in governments to implement them. While a clash between good intentions and low capacity may play a role, enthusiasm for poverty reduction in deed rather than word seems limited. This weak political will is a consequence of the absence of strong organizations of the poor which could press for more appropriate policy and more vigorous intervention – and of an influential social coalition which could make poverty reduction a political imperative.

In South Africa, where our urban case study is located, the link between lack of voice and inadequate policy and practice is even clearer. Government critics concerned about poverty repeatedly argue that the poor are being starved of badly needed services by ideologically generated fiscal stinginess. But some two-thirds of the budget is devoted to social spending and, according to the Minister of Finance, 57 per cent of spending is allocated to the poorest 40 per cent, under nine per cent to the wealthiest 20 per cent (Manuel, 2001). Larger budgets would not ensure more vigorous programmes since at present key development departments fail to spend their annual budgets.[1] This suggests that the chief obstacle to effective action against inequality is not the level of public spending but a failure to spend the government budget effectively. Further examination invites the conclusion that this failure is significantly linked to a mismatch between the needs and preferences of the poor on the one hand and the mainstream policy agenda on the other – and that those organized interests who seek to champion the interests of the poor show no greater understanding of their preferences than government politicians and officials.

Housing policy offers an illustration of the point. During the early 1990s, a dozen social and economic forums were established during the political negotiation period to address social and economic policy – the national housing forum's participants included important 'pro-poor' groups in civil society and one of its focuses was a lengthy negotiation between them and business on ways to ensure that mortgage finance reached the poor: none of the participants questioned the assumption that mortgage finance was a resource which the poor desired (Tomlinson, 1997). Research, however, suggests that several years were spent seeking ways of offering poor people something they did not want. Far from seeking mortgages, poor people who participated in nationwide focus group interviews insisted that they associated this form of housing finance with evictions and therefore were anxious to avoid mortgage commitments (Tomlinson, 1996). (The perception was largely based on experience – when home ownership was first opened to black people in the cities in the mid-1980s, housing was 'over-sold' and many of the purchasers proved unable to meet their obligations.)

This and other examples suggest that the 'pro-poor' formal organizations have also been out of touch with the preferences of the poor and that people living in poverty have been, therefore, without a voice in the policy debate. The result is ineffective policy in which housing subsidies are, for example, used to finance dwellings which their recipients sell to more affluent buyers (Tomlinson, 1997), or electrification programmes are based on inaccurate diagnosis of the consumption patterns of the poor (White et al., 2000). Whether the funds currently available for fighting poverty would be enough if the poor were heard accurately is not clear. At present what is evident is that money is being spent far less effectively than it could be, either because programmes do not respond to the needs of the poor or because the lack of a voice for the poor means there is no effective citizen pressure to ensure effective implementation.

In sum, the lack of an effective voice for the poor is a primary constraint on the formulation and implementation of effective pro-poor social policy in Southern Africa in general, and South Africa in particular. And a prime reason is that many of the poor no longer live in formal mass production workplaces – informal workers are said to account for some 30 per cent of the South African workforce now and, perhaps more importantly, their number is estimated to have almost doubled between 1995 and 1999 (Bhorat, 2003: 4). This means not only that they may be dispersed, making collective action more difficult, or engaged in forms of casual labour in which they have little bargaining power, but they may also be engaged in activity which, because it is not formally recognized, may encourage avoidance of the authorities responsible for pro-poor policy and programmes rather than engagement with them. These are the realities that shape attempts to address urban poverty, to which we now turn specifically.

CITIZEN VOICE AND POVERTY REDUCTION IN THE CITIES

Poverty trends in cities are, of course, consequences of the national trends discussed thus far. While poverty does manifest itself unevenly, geographically as well as among social groups, and poverty levels therefore differ both between cities and between them and the countryside, cities are, of course, not insulated from national trends and are to a significant degree a consequence of them.

Similarly, the governance approaches which affect urban poverty cannot be reduced to those pursued by local government. This may be particularly so in South Africa where, partly because of the desire and capacity of national political elites to impose strict party discipline on elected subnational government representatives, provincial and local government, while enjoying significant formal autonomy, often acts merely as an implementer of national government decisions (Götz and White, 1997). Much of the analysis thus far can, therefore, simply be assumed to apply to the local context. However, local government does possess some leeway to address poverty and aspects of local governance do shape the nature of poverty and

responses to it. An examination of responses at the municipal level confirms the proposition that the poor have no effective voice and that this
reduces the degree to which local governments are able to address poverty.

First, the strength of party discipline at the local level is itself a significant
factor since it ensures that local councillors are likely to see the national
leadership of their parties as at least as important a reference point as their
electorates. It also deters responsiveness to constituencies since party discipline can be used to expel councillors who champion the views of their
electorate. Councillors have suffered expulsion because, for example, they
supported shack dwellers whose homes were demolished by a council.

Second, one form that discipline takes within the governing African
National Congress is considerable encouragement to councillors to see
themselves not as representatives of their electorate, but as agents of 'service delivery', implementers who can assist the government to 'roll out' its
programmes.[2] In one sense, it is appropriate to see councillors as contributors to effective service delivery. They can play this role by speaking
effectively for their constituents and lobbying, where voters want this, for
different services to be delivered or for existing programmes to be implemented. But the context suggests that councillors are expected primarily
to assist the administrative arms of the council, not to express voters'
preferences.

Third, the structure of metropolitan government plays a role in dulling
the voice of the poor. A demarcation board which conducted its inquiry in
the months leading up to the local elections of 2000 dramatically consolidated the number of local authorities from over 800 to less than 300. Its
chief criterion was economy of scale rather than quality of representation
(Sutcliffe, 2000). This meant, inevitably, that the new councils were larger
and more remote from voters. Also, the insistence of national government,
and of the governing party, on the 'unicity' model – a single local government structure for entire metropolitan areas[3] – deprived voters of a tier of
representation more accessible to them, such as a borough system. As a
concession to the need for another level of voice, metropolitan councils
are permitted to establish ward committees, which are meant to be representative of citizens in the ward or local electoral district.[4] There is, however, no requirement that these be elected committees: members are
selected by the councillor. It seems trite to point out that representativeness may not be the only criterion employed. And even where a range of
organizations are represented on the committee, the lack of organization
among the poor makes their inclusion very unlikely. National government
does compel councils to consult citizens – legislation mandates municipalities to 'encourage, and create conditions for, the local community to
participate in the affairs of the municipality' through 'appropriate mechanisms, processes and procedures to enable the local community to participate. . . .'[5] In the recent past, the most significant vehicle for
participation has been the stipulation that all local governments develop
Integrated Development Plans (IDPs) spelling out their development

plans for the city,[6] and that residents participate in this process. But again the bias is clearly towards the organized – and, therefore, exclusionary of the poor.

These trends may not be exclusively responsible for national survey findings which suggest that local government is the most unpopular tier among voters (Idasa, 1998). Citizen hostility to this level of government may lie to a large degree in a history in which the black majority experienced local government as an unrepresentative, corrupt and hostile agent of a national government which denied them the vote (Giliomee and Schlemmer, 1989: 129ff), while whites, who did enjoy the vote, saw local councils as relatively powerless agents of national government. However, almost 10 years of democratic local government has done nothing to rectify this impression. It seems fair to conclude that councils are thus complicit in maintaining a pattern in which citizens, the poor included, do not see local government as a means to participate effectively in policy-making.

Johannesburg: a case study

All these trends are visible in Johannesburg, South Africa's most prosperous city and still its industrial hub despite trends over the past decade suggesting that its status might be in jeopardy.

The city is governed by the Greater Johannesburg Metropolitan Council, whose area of jurisdiction is estimated by some to be home to around 5 million people, although the council insists that the figure is just below 3 million, with an economically active population of 1.366 million (GJMC, 2003: 18). According to the council, 53 per cent of the economically active population are formally employed, while 17 per cent work in the informal sector or in domestic service (GJMC, 2003: 18). The other 30 per cent are classified as unemployed. The 2000 demarcation enlarged its borders markedly despite objections from the council itself. While this already ensured a greater gap between the council and voters, a senior city manager probably reflected thinking among the upper echelons of Johannesburg officials when, anticipating the demarcation outcome in late 1999, he argued strongly for a smaller elected council than the law was expected to allow, on the grounds that a larger council was an unnecessary expense.[7] Representation is, therefore, seen as at best a secondary priority to cost control. This, with the ruling party's firm hold over the council, may explain voter indifference – despite housing Soweto, the celebrated township reserved under apartheid for blacks which led the protests against apartheid in the mid–1970s, Johannesburg has tended to record percentage polls in local elections lower than the national average.[8]

Like other councils, Johannesburg has completed an IDP and has sought to bridge some of the representation gap discussed here by seeking to include citizens in identifying priorities. However, the Metropolitan

Council's own description of this process is instructive. It insists that consultation is not simply an exercise required by law: 'The City of Johannesburg is committed to strengthening and extending public participation of stakeholders in all aspects of the life of Council' (GJMC, 2003: 25). However, according to the council, a strategic agenda and 'indicative budget allocations' were agreed some five months before the consultation process began – in effect, citizens were allowed to comment on an IDP which was largely a *fait accompli*, rather than being invited to contribute to the IDP's content before its drafting (GJMC, 2003: 26). Nor were citizens directly invited to comment on the document – time constraints ensured that not even the metropolis's 109 ward committees were directly able to learn of the contents of the draft IDP. Instead, ward councillors were given the responsibility 'of cascading the information to their committees and communities . . .' (GJMC, 2003: 26) In addition, a meeting was held with 'non-governmental organizations, community-based organizations, labour and other service-oriented groups' as well as a 'representative group of socio-economic development and cultural organizations' at which the council also tabled its 'final draft policy for social funding'. Business organizations were briefed and invited to comment at a special meeting and 'a grand finale', a 'stakeholder summit' in the city hall, was convened at which interest groups submitted comments and received a response from the Executive Mayor (GJMC, 2003: 26–7). Notice of these meetings was posted in various newspapers and 14 'stakeholder sessions' were convened, although it is unclear who attended these.

It is difficult to see how the poor could have participated to any degree in these exercises. In principle, councillors are indeed the most appropriate conduit of communication to citizens, but there is no evidence that the briefing to councillors went beyond ward committees whose limitations as a source of voice for the poor were noted above. The negative citizen evaluation of local government noted above suggests that councillors are not very active in communicating with voters in any event. Since the other meetings were convened for organizations, and we have noted that the poor are, in the main, not organized, it seems unlikely that many poor residents were represented at these gatherings. Indeed, there may be no more revealing aspect to this exercise than the council's acknowledgement that it advertised the meetings in English and Afrikaans language newspapers. The print media are the least effective communication medium in South Africa since low literacy levels and, in may cases, unfamiliarity with English (or Afrikaans) make vernacular language radio the most effective medium for reaching the poor. Since the council seems unaware of or unwilling to use the medium most likely to reach poor residents, it seems highly unlikely that the stakeholder meetings which it advertised included many representatives of the poor.

The policy agenda that emerged from this process seems to reflect this lack of voice for the poor. To place it in context, it is important to note that the council's approach to development is heavily influenced by an aspiration that Johannesburg become a 'world-class (African) city'.[9] A critique of this aspiration to 'world-class' status by a co-author of this paper argues that Johannesburg policy documents do not offer a clear account of what a 'world-class' city is, or what seeking to become one impels the metropolitan council to do which would otherwise not have been done. Nor, beyond an apparent misreading of the urbanist Saskia Sassen and much fashionable rhetoric about the impact of the global context, does the council build a coherent argument for why it is necessary to become 'world class'. The critique argued that enthusiasm for 'world-class' status had far more to do with the aspirations of the new city elite than with a strategic imperative (Friedman, 2002). Of course, Johannesburg's planners are not alone – the 'competitive city' idea, which suggests that cities need to compete with each other for footloose investment, is common in the South and the 'world-class' notion is an application of that assumption. Many specialists would also want to take issue with the critique's contention that this is not an appropriate way of understanding the preconditions of local economic growth.

Whatever the merits of the council's aspiration, however, the important point for our purposes is what the choice of this motif says about the milieu in which urban policy is made. Planners who strive to achieve world-class status do not necessarily ignore poverty – indeed, some of Johannesburg's documents which stress the need to become 'an African world-class city' contain copious references to it and the need to tackle it (GJMC, 2003). But they are unlikely to derive either their information about the poor or their preferred solutions to poverty from the poor themselves. Their 'reference group', those from whom they derive their information, is far more likely to be the arbiters of 'world-class' status – other urban specialists. And they are far more likely to see the solution to poverty as an application of fashionable 'world-class' principles rather than an understanding of the concrete circumstances of the poor derived from direct contact. The analysis of national development policy and its failure to understand the poor, offered above, suggests that this is likely to ensure strategies unsuited to the circumstances of Johannesburg's poor.

That policy is about but not of the poor is confirmed by the documents produced by the planners who embrace these notions. They talk of a 'participatory process aimed at empowering the poor and marginalized'. But what does the word 'empowering' or its corollary 'empowerment' – ubiquitous in contemporary South Africa – mean? It could simply be intended in a procedural, facilitative, sense: a process may bestow upon people the formal power to participate. But it may also imply that power is, somehow, a capacity that can be transferred from those who have it to those who do not[10] by some sort of technical process. People lack power unless it is bestowed upon them by some official process; this implies that the 'poor and marginalized' can attain power only if the technicians find the appropriate 'participatory process' to grant it. But the 'power' bestowed in this way is far more likely to try to remake the poor in the planners' image than to open the frontiers of choice.

The 'world-class city' documents display great enthusiasm for 'new' management techniques such as 'performance management systems' (GJMC, 2002), some of whose features include:

- the signing of fixed-term contracts with top managers
- 'regular reviews, performance contracts and management development'
- exhortations to 'develop best practice standards'
- exhortations to 'investigate and implement the concept of "best value"' (which is nowhere defined)
- benchmarking targets.

While more effective public management techniques would surely be welcomed by most city residents, including the poor, it is noteworthy that technique, not responsiveness to citizens, is considered the key to effectiveness. This eagerness to reduce the process of governing to a managerial exercise equivalent to running a corporation is not exclusive to South Africa's elite, let alone that of Johannesburg. It has become pervasive in the approach of many donor agencies and governments as well as that of multi-lateral institutions such as the Commonwealth. Besides creating an illusion of order and governability, it also offers donors an excellent excuse to reduce governance to a managerial process on which donor and beneficiary government can agree. In South Africa, the desire of a new elite to defuse racial prejudice by demonstrating that a black-led government is as technically competent as its equivalents in Northern countries creates a community of interest between it and donor agencies, in which the desire of the former to show that it can reshape the society in a 'world-class' mould reinforces the latter's enthusiasm for reducing the process of governing to a laboratory for the latest management fads.

Despite the continued enthusiasm of Johannesburg's strategists and planners for fashionable governance theories, they have responded to current challenges with profoundly 'old-fashioned' responses. They rely on centralized control, management technique and a shopping list of goals from which working with citizens is noticeably absent. The presumed ability of the officials and technicians in council offices to 'deliver' to a grateful citizenry continues to be assumed. It is hard to imagine where an attempt to respond to the voice of citizens, poor or otherwise, might fit in this vision. Action against poverty is assumed to be the outcome of 'international best practice', not of allowing the poor to identify their needs and then relying on partnership between city government and local interests, including the poor, to generate widely acceptable remedies.

This approach, with the inaccessibility of public participation vehicles discussed earlier, may explain why the voices the council hears in its IDP consultation process do not seem to be those of the poor. While it reports a series of responses to its consultation exercise, it does not indicate who offered them. Some may reflect the concerns of the poor, but they are also entirely consistent with those of better-resourced groups who always participate in the public policy debate – a desire for better debt management, the imposition of safety standards in buildings, access to free services, pleas for better protection from crime or controls on urban sprawl, and concern at tariff increases (GJMC, 2003: 30–31). These responses are regular features of the public policy debate on the city, in which the poor do not participate – there is no evidence that the poor stamped a particular imprint on these understandings of the city's needs. And, while some of the reported responses clearly showed that they had been initiated by particular constituencies – such as business's complaint that regulatory approval for transactions was slow or southern suburbs' residents complaint that the north received all the development – none could be linked to the poor.

Perhaps the clearest confirmation that the poor were not heard is the 'Vision and Strategy' which emerged from this exercise (GJMC, 2003). In sharp contrast to other Johannesburg planning documents, it does not even mention poverty explicitly. Only one sentence could be construed to apply directly to the poor: 'The City's social package includes a minimum amount of free electricity and water for those people who are not in arrears, and rates rebates for indigent households' (GJMC, 2003: 36). 'Lifeline tariffs' for bulk services such as water and electricity which require more affluent users to cross-subsidize the poor are the city's primary anti-poverty strategy. It is worth noting, however, that the R450 million (US$70 million) which it says it spends directly on supporting the poor[11] is only some three per cent of its budget. For the rest, the city's vision spells out commitments to promote economic growth, improve public safety, serve the public better and combat HIV/AIDS. Again, while the poor might benefit from some or all of these outcomes, they cannot be seen as anti-poverty measures – still less can they be viewed as a product of an attempt to gauge the needs and circumstances of the poor.

The conclusion that the poor remain unrepresented in Johannesburg is, therefore, illustrated by the IDP exercise. The consequence is a city plan that largely ignores the problem of poverty even if some of its stated goals might benefit the poor. The result will inevitably be modest or no progress against poverty. The problem lies not only in the choices of the city elite but also in the reality that they are not being made in dialogue with the 47 per cent of the city's economically active population who are said to be working informally or not at all. Until people working outside formal workplaces become part of the policy debate, it is likely to continue ignoring or misapprehending their needs, and anti-poverty measures will remain largely ineffective. But how plausible is it that their organized voice may begin to be heard?

ORGANIZED INFORMALITY?

It is one thing to insist that people working outside the formal workplace need to organize so that they can be heard in the search for solutions to poverty, quite another to say how that might occur, particularly since informality[12] makes organization more difficult and so ensures that the poor face considerable barriers to collective action.

Of course, new circumstances may not have made organization of the poor impossible (or even, perhaps, more difficult). They could, rather, have created an environment in which new types of organization are needed. But current literature seems to give little cause for optimism that organizations of the informal poor capable of articulating their concerns can emerge.

A review of the literature shows that the severe limitations on democratic organization among people working informally is a constant theme: 'community leaders dominate the organisations that they belong to, reinforcing the belief among residents that they have little control or influence over their lives and their local organisations' (Mitlin, 2001). This may ensure low turnout at meetings and limited visible support. Inevitably, it prompts a pessimistic view of the ability of these organizations to represent the interests of the urban poor. Organizations in the informal economy are found to be dominated by leadership figures, to provide limited opportunities for participation and representation, and to enjoy a very short life span. And some organizations do not exercise a voice because they choose not to. Mitlin (2001) notes that: 'Despite the enthusiasm of development agencies and other professionals for civil society, many grassroots organisations are more concerned with poverty alleviation than with poverty reduction; with maintaining existing social relationships rather than with securing ones that are more equitable'. The South African literature reports similar findings. Informal traders said to be represented by associations claim that they do not belong to any association, because they do not know them (Lund, 1998). Informal trader associations are said to be unable to produce consistent membership numbers or claim to represent specific constituencies. Some are said to become members in an involuntary way, by virtue of where they are located.

Scholars such as Thornton suggest that organizations of the informal kind also have little desire to engage with public authorities because workers in the informal economy are engaged in economic activities for which the state plays no supportive role (Lund, 1998). But the assertion that associations of the informally employed wish to avoid the state has been challenged – Widner (1991) finds cases in which participants in the informal economy have a commonality of interest with some government officials. Indeed, relations with politicians and officials are said to be key causes of the associations' weaknesses. Mitlin argues that problems of leadership and participation within these organizations are linked to state officials' and politicians' relations of patronage with 'community leaders' who are sustained not by the support base among citizens, which is often assumed to be the key source of influence in democratic systems, but their ability to establish strong links with politicians or officials. Local governments may, for example, recognize one association and ignore its rivals. In Pretoria, near Johannesburg, the council is said to have a close relationship with one street trader organization and to have been instrumental in establishing it, making it responsible for selecting those who were to be given trading sites (Skinner, 2000). In some cases, municipalities may confer power on associations simply because they are eager to show that they are consulting their constituents – in South Africa, legislation mandating consultation with citizen groups may increase incentives to boost undemocratic leaderships. Fluency in English, for example, is crucial for those who want to take up leadership positions because this provides access to official decision-makers.

Divisions among the informal poor are not always created by external agents such as local government. But evidence that government actions influence organization among the informal poor raises the possibility that their voicelessness might stem not from deep-rooted structural problems, but from arrangements chosen by government actors who give some in the informal economy a powerful hold over others. Governments may thus have more scope to influence the associational life of people in the informal economy than is often assumed. But, if government intervention seems able to influence propensity to organize, it seems highly unlikely that the authorities are capable of initiating democratically run organizations of the poor. Current literature suggests that governments may have more influence over whether people in the informal sector organize than on how they do so. Where, then, might a catalyst to organization emerge?

One possibility is an attempt by the trade union movement, the cradle of organization of the poor in a previous period, to organize the poor outside the formal workplace. There is a growing recognition among unions that informality is likely to remain a constraint to organization for the foreseeable future (Gallin, 2001). South African unions, like those elsewhere in the world, have thus been debating the recruitment of informal workers: failure to do so is seen to be detrimental to their survival because the pool of formal workers is shrinking (Naidoo, 2003). But how possible is this? Gallin, a strong advocate of union efforts to organize informal workers, admits that the heterogeneous nature of employment relations, the difficulties of locating and contacting workers in informal employment and – in some instances – obstacles created by legislation make organizing informal workers difficult (Gallin, 2001: 531). He goes on to claim that unions underestimate the capacity of informal workers to organize. This does not, however, seem to be borne out by South African evidence.

Recent research here has highlighted obstacles to organizing the informally employed by the traditional unions, as well as by unions established solely for informal workers (Bennett, 2003). The Self Employed Women's

Union (SEWU), an association formed specifically to cater for women working in the informal economy, and the Southern African Clothing and Textile Workers' Union (SACTWU), which has taken a particular interest in organizing people working in informal conditions, find it difficult to recruit members in the informal economy. One of the most daunting tasks has been to solicit membership fees – SEWU lost 35 per cent of its members when it shifted from accepting cash for membership fees and introduced debit orders, thus simulating unions' reliance on automatic deduction of union dues from pay packets. One reason cited was the inability to open and maintain bank accounts because of the lack of steady income. SEWU has cited another reason for its limited success in organizing informal workers – it reports that some are reluctant to join because of their previous experience of union membership (Bennett, 2003). SACTWU has thus realized that recruiting informal workers needs more resources than those usually devoted to formal workers. The diversity of interests in the informal economy and the lack of a clear employer–employee relationship emerge from the literature as some of the reasons that make organizing difficult.

Optimistic assessments of potential for organizing the poor outside the formal workplace also tend to neglect the role of informal power holders: powerful groups – in business or politics or government – benefit from informality. To some authors, these obstacles do not mean that organizing the informal is impossible for unions – merely that it needs to be approached differently (Sandoval, 2001). But, while these analyses establish that some informal sector workers may be interested in organizing, they do not show why they should consider unionism an appropriate vehicle. An analysis suggests that informal workers who live or work in the same area may be available to unions (Sanyal, 1991), but empirical work questions this.

Some analyses suggest that, even if unions prove unable to organize informal workers, union experiences may play a crucial role in shaping organization outside the formal economy. Thus it has been argued that retrenched union members are likely to be the key initiators of collective action in informal settings (Desai, 2002). Logic would tend to support this claim – the poor usually lack the resources to organize in a way that would enable them to take part in formal democratic politics, and this explains why movements of the poor are so often initiated by people who are themselves not poor. Retrenched workers would be expected to possess skills and experience of organization which most of the poor do not have – and, because they are retrenched, to have developed a common interest with the informal poor. Our current field research in an informal settlement finds that retrenched unionists are indeed leaders of organization: they facilitated a land invasion. But experiences of unionism do not, it seems, translate smoothly into support for democratic methods of organization. Initial evidence suggests that the type of organization favoured by retrenched workers may not be the structured procedural democracy favoured by trade unions, but a reliance on charismatic, undemocratic leadership. A style demanded by the need to express voice in the formal workplace does not, then, necessarily remain the preferred option when the formally employed are forced into informality.

Contrary to the claims of analysts who suggest that the informal poor are available to be organized if only unions would organize them, the constraint may lie not in a failure of union nerve but in structural conditions. One author finds that the poor are rarely in a similar life situation to their neighbours: informality has meant that they are 'differentiated by the type of employment, by stage in the life cycle, and above all, by the importance of the individual household and its labour resources as a means of survival'. Social and economic fragmentation in this environment tends to encourage 'vertical, rather than horizontal, political relationships as individuals sought patronage and protection from above as a means of securing what little they had gained in housing or as a means of obtaining more benefits for themselves and their neighbours' (Roberts, 1996).

The informal economy is also characterized by various interests that are not easily identifiable. Widner notes: 'People move in and out of the informal sector for a variety of reasons . . .' (Widner, 1991: 34). The difference in reasons, and thus circumstances, makes it difficult to organize these individuals because they appear less likely to share interests with other informal workers – many key issues may affect them differently, making united action impossible. And people who expect to be engaged in informal work temporarily are also unlikely to be willing to act to change their circumstances. Informal business people are more likely to organize politically to demand lower licence fees, more amenities, less regulation or other benefits if they believe themselves trapped in a particular occupation or income level (Widner, 1991). Our field work suggests that there is still a strong perception by those participating in the informal economy that they or their children will find formal jobs despite the overwhelming evidence to the contrary.

A further constraint may be power relations to which the poor are subject and which might prompt resistance to development if programmes threaten existing arrangements that benefit local power holders. This mobilization to maintain the status quo may be initiated by leaders seeking to preserve their dominance where scarce resources prevent self-organization (Sihlongonyane, 2001).

In sum, the literature and some preliminary field work suggests that, despite the enthusiasm of analyses which indicate that a change in trade union strategy would ensure an effective voice for the poor, prospects of democratic organization for people working outside the formal economy seem limited. That may not be a permanent condition: after all, unions may find new ways of addressing these constraints. And studies have shown that when the poor participating in the informal economy have accepted the reality that these arrangements are likely to be permanent, they are likely to attempt to change their circumstances. In those countries where there is the longest history of informality, informal sector workers appear to be more organized (Widner, 1991). This, of course, makes it possible that many of the impediments to informal organization identified in the literature are temporary. But the 'temporary' may endure for quite some time: current scholarship leaves little cause for optimism that the conditions for effective pro-poor urban policy will emerge soon.

TOWARDS A VOICE FOR THE POOR

Field work in Johannesburg reported elsewhere (Thulare, 2004) confirms many of the more sceptical prognoses about organizations of the informally employed. But it also raises questions about the assumption that these organizations are inevitably incapable of providing a route into democratic decision-making.

Are there, therefore, interventions that might strengthen impulses in this direction, speeding the injection of the poor into policy debate in alliance with like-minded interests and in negotiation with others? The task cannot be achieved by simulating organization of the poor. But intervention can create opportunities for it to emerge and express itself – in itself a great challenge since it entails a detailed knowledge of grassroots conditions, which is a rarity in government and development agencies.

Strengthening and deepening representative institutions, including local government, is a key goal. This task must be distinguished from the planner's usual response to the need to enhance public participation – the establishment of forums or public participation vehicles to that end. These attempts to hear 'the voice of the people' invariably ignore the reality that, in a free society, there is no single voice because 'the people' are divided by interests and values which may often contest or conflict with each other. A key feature of democratic systems, therefore, is that they provide channels for these conflicts which prevent them becoming destructive and allow alliances and compromises to form in response to need. Forums or participation exercises – such as the PRSP exercises mentioned above – tend to minimize difference and seek common positions in a way that prevents contest. The effect is usually to suppress views that might be vital to a solution. The voices of the poor may not be suppressed – but only because it is unlikely that they ever get to the table at all. Structured participation exercises are biased against the poor because they require capacities that they often lack and direct discussion into channels in which the poor are likely to make little impact. But even this critique assumes, usually inaccurately, that the poor are party to the discussion at all.

A workable consensus on development priorities would need to be the outcome of an approach which acknowledged conflict and then sought to channel it through hard bargaining between independent interest groups, all of whom brought something to the table which offered them some negotiating power (mass membership, skills and capital, power to influence public opinion are but three examples). A comprehensive anti-poverty strategy might not emerge quickly, if at all: only agreement on some specifics may be possible. But the outcome would be far more likely to express a real process of engagement between social groups and, rather like an industrial agreement reached after bitter bargaining between owners and labourers, far more likely to accurately reflect the possible and to be capable of implementation because it is the outcome of a process of genuine engagement. Crucial to that engagement is an organized voice for the poor – which is likely to be suppressed by reliance on participation exercises. Encouraging closer links between elected representatives and their constituents – and, more generally, coming to see the flowering of open political contest as a crucial means to acquiring the capacity to address urban poverty – is a surer route to providing a voice for the poor than seeking more effective ways of including poor people in participation exercises.

Beyond this, a new approach by officials and the politicians they serve may be the key to a greater voice for the poor and therefore greater effectiveness. The first change needed is one in which, instead of attempts to simulate democracy by creating forums, anti-poverty programmes should concentrate instead on informing all vested interests, particularly the poor, of their options. Instead of the current approach, in South Africa and elsewhere, in which government plans and programmes are subject to consultation or public participation exercises (such as the Johannesburg example discussed above), strategies that ensure that all citizens are sufficiently informed of their development options in ways that allow them to choose may be more appropriate.

This attempt is crucial, but not nearly as simple as it sounds. First, ensuring that those who are usually denied access to information by their lack of literacy and English fluency, and by their distance from the places and media where and through which information flows are informed, may require capacities to reach the grassroots of society that have thus far eluded most governments and development agencies throughout the South. In South Africa, the narrow view of communication thus far is perhaps best summed up in the fact that local governments are mandated to communicate with citizens only through newspapers and radio.[13] There is no provision for direct contact with voters (and, indeed, no evidence, if Johannesburg is a guide, of much enthusiasm for radio, the most powerful medium in the society). Indeed, bringing adequate information to the grassroots may be viewed as a goal and a medium-term orientation of governance and development strategy. Second, officials of governments and agencies that communicate with beneficiaries of development programmes usually succumb readily to the temptation to 'explain' options in a way that predetermines the choice by stressing the advantages of the preferred route and the disadvantages of the others. The temptation is at its greatest when technical information is being conveyed to lay people. Since government and development agency officers are meant to be serving or working in the interests of the poor, they should be striving towards an attempt to convey choices in ways that enable listeners to understand their options but leaves the choice to them. The more official approaches begin to hold this out as a norm and an aspiration, the more likely is it that the poor will be permitted to choose rather than be expected to endorse the choices of others.

If more information is made available to the poor, the chances that poor people may choose to respond by expressing a view are enhanced. But much may depend on the way in which information is disseminated. The more officials are able to form links with, and remain in contact with, those they inform, the more likely it is that they will receive a coherent response. Thus a set of pamphlets dropped over a neighbourhood or an announcement made on radio, while in themselves important advances on current practice, are likely to have far less effect than direct contact. The key here is an attempt to establish a link between officials and the (poor) citizen, in which the latter is better able to respond to the former.

Finally, if this approach were to be adopted, and poor citizens began responding, the response of officials to their expression of voice would be crucial. While channelling response into administratively neat channels such as the forums mentioned above or other forms of structured discussion with officialdom might best suit administrators and the politicians they serve, this may not, for reasons suggested above, suit poor citizens who might prefer less structured forms, including the expression of democratic rights through peaceful public protest. If anti-poverty programmes are to be informed by the voice of the poor, it is essential that this not be stilled by straitjacketing it into forms that prevent it being expressed. Thus, both the form and the content of the response by the poor would need to be taken seriously. While this certainly does not mean automatically adopting them – since society is composed of a variety of interests which must be at least willing to accept anti-poverty strategies – it does mean helping to inject them into the debate so that they may prompt both the alliances and the compromises from which viable policy and implementation emerge.

In sum, a new orientation from officials of development agencies and governments is needed. One that recognizes the organized, politically effective voice of the poor, and the open, often conflictual, politics it would prompt as indispensable assets to poverty-reduction strategies, and which seeks not to create organization of the poor artificially, but to act as a catalyst to its emergence and to engage seriously with it if it does indeed emerge.

CHAPTER SIX

Begging, requesting, demanding, negotiating: moving towards urban poor partnerships in governance

Mary Racelis

INTRODUCTION

Virtually every self-respecting development non-governmental organiza-tion (NGO) or social action group today promotes the participation of poor and marginalized people in decisions and programmes affecting their lives. Empowerment is the word of choice. Similarly, international agencies and donor groups are urging governments to carry out participatory gover-nance, highlighting the benefits of accountability, transparency, efficiency and citizen participation. Even governments in developing countries have come around to seeing – or saying they see – the advantages of bringing their more disadvantaged constituents into decision-making processes.

This change in orientation over the past decades from authoritarian, top-down urban governance styles has not come easily. It stems from decades of determined community organizing among the urban poor citizenry, aided by NGOs and other concerned civil society groups. For the past 50 years thousands of urban informal settlers faced with demolition squads bent on forced evictions, have fought back with sticks, stones and block-ades manned by angry protesting crowds. Sometimes they win a stay of execution; other times, overwhelmed by baton-wielding police and even tear gas, they surrender and 'voluntarily' dismantle their rickety shacks in preparation for relocation to a distant out-of-city site usually devoid of income-earning opportunities. While today's informal settlers still encounter these assaults on their rights to housing and secure tenure, an increasing number are experiencing more enlightened postures on the part of government. The result: new partnerships of people and government.

In the Philippines, this shift stems in no small measure from over 30 years of NGO community organizing in urban informal settlements. The goal was to create autonomous, empowered people's organizations (POs) capable of asserting their rights. Although the institutional changes needed to sustain these positive changes in governance have come agonizingly slowly to over 4 million urban informal poor, observers are now seeing the beginnings of real improvements in urban poor people's lives.

These have come about in fits and starts through land proclamations, moratoriums on eviction and distant relocation, and titling or other forms of secure tenure. Improved basic services, like health, education, clean water, sanitation, electricity and information dissemination, are gradually reaching poor communities. Infrastructure projects have featured paved roadways and pathways, bridges and community buildings serving as early childhood, health or multi-purpose centres. All this came about not so much through suddenly enlightened political leaders, but from the relentless prodding of the organized poor. Instrumental in their conscious-ness raising and increased sense of efficacy have been NGO community organizers and advocacy groups.

Given the more positive orientation and readiness of some national and city officials to take action for the benefit of urban poor groups, organized communities have moderated their more aggressive forms of demand, like mass protests and marches, in favour of dialogue and negotiation. But they remain ready to stage a rally or march if officials move too slowly or go back on their word. On the government side of the negotiating table, some for-merly recalcitrant city and national officials are now beginning to recognize that they must respond in new ways if the problems of mass poverty are ever to be solved. The still-all-too-few enlightened ones are experimenting with some creative approaches suggested by the organized poor and NGOs, and fostering policy frameworks, laws and ordinances, and institutional support structures more conducive to their well-being.

How communities or clusters of urban poor households gained the capacity to move from a passive to active stance through NGO community organizing is still not sufficiently appreciated in government circles. This stems in part from the relatively low priority given by NGOs and POs to documenting and disseminating information on their activities. Moreover, in principle, NGOs resist taking credit for their organizing efforts, prefer-ring to throw the spotlight on the victories achieved by the POs. Recogniz-ing this vacuum of information, academic social scientists, public administration professionals, research institutes and NGO research units are now actively recording and analysing these empowering processes for transformative development.

This chapter examines four Philippine cases of how once-powerless urban poor groups have metamorphosed from a begging or requesting mode in dealing with officials and elites, to a demand mode which high-lights poor people negotiating confidently with powerful figures as equals. On the government side, initial responses reinforcing the dole-out welfare recipient mode have shifted toward more consultative, even collaborative ventures with multiple PO–NGO partners. The evidence of this change of mentality and political will emerges in the revitalization and creation of bureaucratic and political structures and procedures supportive of poor people's perspectives and people–government partnerships.

The case study presentations are followed by an analysis of community organizing processes and the resulting institutional structures that were created or modified by government in response to poor people's demands. These mutually reinforcing linkages have enabled once powerless urban poor settlers to make their voices heard in the corridors of power. Finally, some implications are presented as to how these reforms in people–government interaction may affect current and prospective interaction among multistakeholders.

PARTICIPATION: DIFFERENTIAL UNDERSTANDINGS

While 'participation' has long been a codeword in the lexicon of NGOs, POs and most recently government, a common understanding of what 'participation' entails has proven far more elusive. The diverse meanings of contending parties has led to confusion on all sides and added to distrust and disillusionment between civil society and government. Plummer (2000: 52) illustrates this ambiguity in the context of urban services and infrastructure delivery, listing the varied ways in which 'participation' is articulated.

1. *Manipulation*: government interacts with communities with a view to obtaining free labour, cost recovery and political gain, keeping in mind also donor conditionality; improving people's lives is considered secondary or even ignored.
2. *Information*: government announces its intentions to communities but controls the amount and type of information released; it does not encourage changes in its decisions. Its objectives aim to get services in place and used, achieve cost recovery and minimize community resistance to plans.
3. *Consultation*: government favours community participation and group formation, organizes forums for feedback and promotes some capacity building on an ad hoc project basis; but it does little to institutionalize these processes. Its objectives, in addition to those in (2), are to enhance community ownership, project sustainability and efficiency, and target vulnerable groups.
4. *Cooperation*: government promotes community decision-making, some institutionalization of processes, and incipient community empowerment. Its objectives include those under (3), plus community capacity building and a degree of empowerment.
5. *Mobilization by the community*: government accepts that communities control decision-making processes, responds favourably to initiatives defined by the community or encourages their controlling their own initiatives. Its objectives focus on community empowerment and community-managed service delivery, which in turn reinforces ownership, sustainability, efficiency, targeting vulnerable groups, and achieving cost recovery, all done by the community itself.

All five forms of participation occur in the Philippines, with wide variations across the NGO–government landscape and frequently even in the same community. Thus, government officials criticized for not engaging in a participatory process will emphatically state that they did in fact do so, citing a community consultation at which they outlined the steps to be taken in connection with a planned resettlement scheme. The community, on the other hand, will deny that participation took place, alleging that only community members favourable to the government were invited, or that only a few token groups were present from the community, or that the meeting in question featured one-way communication in which the government initiators dismissed as irrelevant the people's objections and counterproposals. Alternatively, the manipulative mode of certain government officials, so common in earlier non-participatory days, has, after extensive organized community claim-making, been transformed over the years into more consultative or cooperative modes. Nonetheless, the 'best practices' being identified remain the equivalent of a few small boats bobbing in a vast sea of 'worst practices' still favoured by governance entities.

Other observers have described continuum frameworks, visualizing participation as ranging from passive at one end, to catalysing change in the social relations of power at the other (KALAHI-CIDSS-KKB, 2003). One of the earliest of these formulations was Arnstein's ladder of participation, with non-participation (manipulation and therapy) lodged at the bottom rung as most exploitative and disempowering, tokenism (information, consultation, placation) occupying the middle steps and citizens' power (controlling and empowering) surfacing at the top. Moser emphasized the important distinction between participation as a means of mobilizing people for desired outcomes, e.g. water supply or drainage, versus participation as an end in itself. In the latter case, participation becomes a process in which mobilized poor groups gain greater control over resources and regulative institutions, thereby fostering redistribution (Plummer, 2000: 3).

Fowler (1997: 102), on the other hand, concentrates on NGO relations with the community, citing functional stages in people-NGO interaction, namely:

1. NGO entry into the community
2. partnering and building sustainability
3. planned withdrawal with sustainable impact.

A Philippine-derived continuum emphasizes the varying modes of participation utilized by community groups and government in handling, endorsing or counteracting government-derived or community-initiated projects or actions. The emphasis here is on the locus of power and decision-making, that is, Who decides?:

1. 'solid citizen' educated professionals
2. local government leaders
3. planners in *ex post facto* consultation with people
4. planners in consultation with people from the beginning of plan formulation

5. decision-making local boards with one or two people, and occasionally even half, representing the interests of disadvantaged groups
6. decision-making local boards on which the mass of heretofore
   excluded people holds majority representation (Racelis
   Hollnsteiner, 1977: 14–15).

This continuum model flourished during the dictatorship period under
President Ferdinand E. Marcos (1970–86), when the rise of technocrats
made modes 1–3 the prevailing choice of government. In contrast, community groups organized by grassroots NGOs opted and struggled for
modes 4–6. The former embodied elite decision-making 'for the people',
while the latter sought genuine people-led decision-making aimed at
shifting power relations in their favour. Given the belief in technocrat-led
development and the authoritarian structure of the political process, the
Marcos government did little (except for the Tondo Foreshore) about put-
ting in place institutional structures to support, much less sustain, community initiatives modestly aiming for at least mode 4. People were only
too well aware that threatened bureaucratic and elite interest groups
could easily impute 'Communist' leanings or Party membership to any
groups that challenged prevailing governmental decisions or advocated
modes 5 and 6. The latter could lead to summary arrest, possibly torture
and even 'salvaging' (the Philippine term for 'disappeared'). At the same
time, a few resourceful POs backed up by NGO community organizers
managed to come close to mode 5 and continued their advocacy towards
mode 6.

With the 'people power' overthrow of the Marcos dictatorship in 1986, in
itself a triumph of civil society organization and networking, a new era of
democratic openness opened up. The experience of community organizers
and activist leaders, who had couched their Saul Alinsky conflict-
confrontation mobilizing style in the martial law era under the safety net of
the Philippine Catholic Bishops' liberal wing support of the theology of liberation and Paolo Freire, would now inspire the creation of thousands of
active, secular grassroots-oriented NGOs towards community organizing.
This combination of open political space for POs and NGOs brought by a
new democratic leader, President Corazon C. Aquino, and the participatory
policy and legal frameworks her administration put together, allowed civil
society's engagement *with* instead of chronically *against* government
(Racelis, 2000: 172–5).

These incipient partnerships evolved, however, with great caution and
often consternation on both sides. Lingering distrust of government and
fear of co-optation by the elite-oriented bureaucracy remained high among
civil society groups. In the same vein, most government officials resisted
ceding any of their decision-making powers to what they saw as unedu-
cated, ragtag groups of poor people audaciously acting as though they had
the right to expect, or even worse, demand certain prerogatives. High on
the latter's roster of undesirables were the PO supporters – NGO 'bleeding

heart do-gooders' – or perhaps they were Leftists. The thought of sharing power became even more repugnant to these government figures when poor people acted assertively rather than being meekly respectful. Nonetheless, urged on by civil society leaders now occupying high government positions in the Aquino and Ramos administrations (1986 to 1998), NGOs cautiously tested the government waters through 'critical collaboration'. For their part, bureaucracy officials slowly and often reluctantly, legitimized increased power-sharing with people under the rubric of 'good governance', a new buzzword on the development and donor scene.

Let us examine some actual cases of people–NGO–government interactive engagement to ascertain how once antagonistic and adversarial relations have metamorphosed into mutually supportive partnerships. These models illustrate the possible when poor people organize and government listens and responds positively. Yet, it must be recognized that these examples of participatory governance still represent exceptions far more than they do the rule. Mutually rewarding and reinforcing partnerships still remain few and far between in a country of 85 million people, of whom an estimated 29 million (33.7%) – and probably more – fall below the poverty line (National Economic Development Authority, 2003: 2).

GETTING TO PARTICIPATORY GOVERNANCE: FOUR CASE STUDIES

Zone One Tondo Organization (ZOTO), Manila

ZOTO was formed in October 1970 on Manila's Tondo Foreshore, when 30 000 informal settler families, or 180 000 people, were faced with impending demolition, eviction and distant, out-of city relocation to make room for a new container port. Some 65 community leaders representing 20 local organizations responded to the offer of the Philippine Ecumenical Council on Community Organization (PECCO) to help build a mass-based democratic organization powerful enough to resist outside manipulation and act on behalf of local people and their priority concerns. The first mobilization arose out of the aftermath of a severe typhoon that hit the community. Contributions were coming from donors as far away as Germany. Residents were convinced from long experience that if the relief items went through government channels, large portions were likely to be diverted for the personal benefit of officials and their cronies and followers in and outside the community, rather than to the neediest.

PECCO community organizers quickly realized that they had a ready-made issue for arousing people's indignation, even anger, against corruption that would deprive needy people in the Tondo Foreshore of their just due. Motivating the people to take action looked promising. ZOTO negotiated with the German donor to invest the entire US$10 000 contribution in new galvanized iron sheets to replace the roofs blown away by the typhoon winds. The PO guaranteed that the supplies would carry a delivery time of no more than two hours from the time they arrived at Slip Zero. Recipients in turn agreed that if they had not nailed their new roofs in place by the following day, they would forfeit the items to someone else for use. The scheme worked so well that a few days after the typhoon, the Foreshore was gleaming with hundreds of shiny new roofs.

ZOTO wrested a further concession from the German donor: henceforth, the latter should shift all its emergency relief efforts directly to the PO rather than through the government. This was accomplished through a rally mounted against the relief agency in the elite neighbourhood housing its office, much to the discomfort of well-to-do neighbours. When the donor capitulated, ZOTO went into high gear to sustain its record of fair, honest and efficient relief goods distribution. Given this track record, it subsequently initiated community actions that pressured government officials to take people's protests against evictions seriously, as well as their demands for land titles, jobs, water, health and other basic services. Increasing numbers of member organizations which affiliated with ZOTO enabled it to claim some 60 000 urban poor members its first year.

ZOTO felt strong enough to hold its first convention seven months later, drawing 750 delegates, many of them women, from 52 organizations. Having mounted a number of mobilizations that targeted the appropriate government officials and wrested concessions from them, members now knew from experience who among their own ranks could handle the challenges of democratically leading and managing so large a federation. Formal elections of permanent officials and the planning of a new constitution were thus timely. A year later, their second annual convention attracted 1300 delegates from 85 organizations, waving placards proclaiming their member organizations: Voices of the Poor, Organization of Men, Women's Association, Mothers' Sewing Group, Tenants Association, Sons and Daughters of Sweat, Lucky Teenagers, New Generation Circle, Organization of Protestors, Garlic Peelers Association, and many more. After two years of successful operation, ZOTO registered itself as a legal entity with a constitution and by-laws (Murphy, 1972: 1).

Its long struggle for the land moved into high gear in the next two decades as the Philippine government obtained a World Bank loan that earmarked the Tondo Foreshore for port development and envisioned distant relocation for the 180 000 'squatters'. Under pressure from ZOTO, the original government plan was substantially modified to highlight on-site upgrading with tenure security, and the acquisition of additional land and housing only a few kilometres away for those displaced by roads and other infrastructure development. This was the product of numerous PO–government meetings, committee sessions and an occasional rally to highlight bureaucratic inertia. ZOTO members could track the trajectory of participation, since they now sat on a number of committees organized by the Tondo Foreshore Development Authority.

Soon ZOTO members were joining training sessions in settlement planning, and financial and credit management, led by professional architect-planners and business experts invited through NGOs to contribute their talent *pro bono* on behalf of their community clients. Technical topics were demystified and members developed the knowledge, skills and confidence to discuss, argue and negotiate with the authorities in complex areas of government planning. Friendly journalists reported sympathetically on the people's demands for security of tenure through land acquisition, housing provision and settlement improvement. They were impressed by ZOTO President Trinidad Herrera's speeches asserting that, 'No Filipino should be a squatter in his own country', a slogan later co-opted by President Ferdinand E. Marcos as his. ZOTO added: 'We are Filipinos. This is Filipino land . . . therefore the only squatters are the outside oppressors who have their own corrupt interests' (Murphy, 1972: 3).

Hundreds of mobilizing and linked activities took place before the Marcos government grudgingly agreed in principle to the People's Plan calling for most of the residents to remain on-site. As General Gaudencio Tobias, who was in charge of the Tondo Foreshore Development Authority, admitted to this author many years later, 'I commanded the Philippine Corps of Engineers in Viet Nam and believe me, I felt braver tackling hostile Vietnamese than I did facing strong and determined residents of the Tondo Foreshore confronting me on a local issue.'

Participatory planning came in many guises. Community members sorted out varying levels of rights, using their criteria to ensure that the longest-residing owner-occupant families had higher priority claims to remain than, for example, recently arrived migrant renters. ZOTO drew on local knowledge to ascertain this, along with a review of the kinds of household receipts for electricity or water delivery payments that households could present as evidence of their tenure. Amounts and collection schemes for amortization payments were hotly debated. The possibility of leasehold for the first five years followed by land title issuance was proposed and accepted by the government as a viable option. Those living on sites affected by port construction, road building and road widening agreed to move voluntarily once those households were identified in the new Tondo Foreshore plan.

ZOTO's many victories gaining government concessions in the 1970s and 1980s stemmed from its effective organizing. Its non-violent mass protests centring around a local issue were a far cry from the more violent demonstrations mounted by Leftist parties aimed at the overthrow of the government and the dissolution of private capitalism. After years of struggle, debate and confrontation, and with the strong urging of the World Bank, the government agreed to turn over the land to the residents, who were now amortizing owners paying modest installments over a 25-year period.

A twin accomplishment was the government's willingness to develop Dagat-dagatan as an overflow site, where people would also get rights to land and ready-made low-rise housing. Government trucks would transport the latter not to the notorious Carmona relocation site 40 km to the south, but to Dagat-dagatan, a rehabilitated fishpond site identified by ZOTO as suitable for a new landfill community. It could absorb with a minimum of strife the spillover families from Tondo 8 km away. These were the people on the roadways and adjacent to the new port, ultimately totalling 7000 families. For the 20 000 who remained onsite in the Foreshore, government would initiate a slum upgrading scheme involving a reblocking process, build more schools and health clinics, install potable water systems and provide livelihood opportunities. Ironically, the Parola Compound intended for port use and fenced off after its inhabitants had moved to Dagat-dagatan has since been invaded by 10 000 informal settler families, double the former population. Twenty-five years later, they in turn have resumed the struggle for land rights along the Pasig River.

The Foreshore and Dagat-dagatan communities stand out as tributes to participatory planning and development, all the more astonishing because their struggle took place under a martial law regime. Possibly the somewhat benign attitude was initially taken by the Marcos administration because ZOTO was known to be affiliated with PECCO, an ecumenical group of Catholic and Protestant priests, pastors, nuns and laity. Marcos avoided Church retaliation as much as possible. Moreover, because in the early years, ZOTO had avoided Marxist dialectics and related action, preferring PECCO's more peaceful philosophy of 'let the people decide', it looked comparatively non-threatening to the political set-up. The ideological balance had shifted by the late 1970s, however, as political organizers from Communist-Party-linked National Democratic Front organizers infiltrated the Foreshore and trained new political cadres. PECCO moved its organizers to less violence-ridden areas.

The twenty-first century has seen a new and resilient generation take over the ZOTO leadership. It is pursuing a wide range of programmes to access basic services, ensure gender equity, information and communication, good governance and non-traditional politics. Its area of coverage now encompasses members in 11 resettlement sites. (CAPWIP, 2003: 3). Its first president, Trinidad Herrera, remains active in Dagat-dagatan, as a local government (barangay) councillor. She is proof that partnerships between people's organizations and the government form more easily when NGO leaders move into the government bureaucracies, or when PO–NGO leaders win election to government posts. They help form the institutional arrangements needed for participatory governance.

Sama-sama, Quezon City

Sama-sama (Joining Together) on Commonwealth Avenue in Quezon City, the site of the National Government Centre, was initially organized in 1975 as a Basic Christian Community under the aegis of its parish priest. The shift from largely spiritual concerns to active fear of demolition and eviction, and chronic anxiety over their insecure tenure status, gradually exposed the mostly women members to broader social perspectives. In the early 1980s, the Community Organization of the Philippines Enterprise (COPE, formerly PECCO) was called in to help the people organize their resistance to eviction in non-violent ways, shore up their claim to land rights and learn how to deal as equals with powerful officials (Murphy et al., 2001: 1–3).

Again, despite the repression of the martial law years, Sama-sama managed to mount protest actions targeting those officials with the authority to respond to their demands. Since they were usually well prepared with their arguments, having gone through role-playing sessions with COPE organizers, and skilled at bringing in the media to dramatize their cause, government officials had to take note and ultimately make concessions. Marches to the housing authority or water district office gave Sama-sama credibility by demonstrating to neighbours the members' willingness to struggle for the land and basic services rights of *all* the informal settlers in the National Government Centre, not just Sama-sama members. They also demonstrated concrete gains in securing regular supplies of potable water, streetlights, a day-care centre, and land-fill for rutted streets and pathways. Deeper learning among community members was enhanced by the ratio of one community organizer to 700 families (Murphy et al., 2001: 4–5).

Aside from steadily resisting eviction and insisting on land titles, Sama-sama's greatest victory was the proclamation in 1986 by newly installed President Aquino of 150 hectares of land to be turned over to their occupants. Moreover, Sama-sama was designated the official representative of the people in the National Government Center (NGC) Development Committee overseeing the development of the 150 hectares (Racelis, 2001), an amazing breakthrough.

That was the beginning of a long struggle, however, only now reaching its conclusion 17 years after the presidential proclamation. Government delays in obtaining the funds needed for the Commonwealth land reform programme and plan for a commercial cross-subsidizing Control Zone along the highway prevented any upgrading and construction activities from getting underway. This hiatus in turn encouraged an additional 24 000 families, often supported by syndicates selling 'rights' illegally, to settle in the NGC. The number of families jumped to 42 000 by 1994 and 60 000 by 2001, rendering obsolete the original People's Plan meant for 18 000 families in 1986.

No longer possible either was the goal of moving 9000 families from the right side of Commonwealth across the street to the proclaimed area so that the government could use the vacated land for the originally intended government buildings. In retrospect, the organizers believe they should have spent less time in planning and simply resettled the eligible families so as to claim the spaces before outside competitors with limited or no rights appropriated the land. To ready the households for the titling process, Sama-sama actively worked with the government to inform, survey and tag over 25 000 households eligible for a Certificate of Land Transfer (Murphy et al., 2001: 4–5).

While the land issue remained paramount, the leaders took steps to maintain organizational loyalty by involving the people in activities whose benefits were more visible. Sama-sama, with the help of COPE, developed its own slum-upgrading programme. This entailed voluntary reblocking to make way for drainage canals and wider roadways constructed on a self-help, voluntary labour basis. In the first pilot area alone, community improvement costs came to nearly PhP1 million, with urban poor residents contributing one-fifth of the cash input and nearly all of the sweat equity labour. City Hall furnished the cement and other materials, along with technical advice (Racelis, 2001: 17). Some 22 neighbourhoods benefited from a Sama-sama-initiated scheme that allowed over 2000 families to obtain a lease on the land they occupied, with the option to buy it after 15 years.

A saving cooperative of around 500 members contributing about PhP20 (4 US cents) a month rapidly increased its loan funds in a decade to PhP1 million. Borrowers can now obtain loans up to PhP10 000 (US$200). Socially bonding activities coupled with fund raising have included an annual Valentine's Day party at a local restaurant complete with a Mrs Valentine beauty contest, participation in city-wide Lenten protest procession portraying Christ being beaten by his captors, and at Christmas-time the Holy Family's search for a room in light of the impending birth. The messages, respectively, of oppression and 'no room at the inn' resonate with poor informal settlers. A major source of income for the organization is the annual Christmas raffle, where wealthier friends and supporters contribute items like a 12 cubic foot refrigerator or television set as first prize, followed by a washing machine, a steam iron, smaller appliances and gift checks to well-known restaurants.

Sama-sama had to go to the barricades again in 1993 when the Ramos presidency planned to build large numbers of medium-rise buildings in their area (and all over Metro Manila) on sites designated for land transfers in the People's Plan. Because the funding for such an ambitious project and the insistence of NGOs and POs that the poor for whom they were intended could not afford the amortizations, the plan was ultimately shelved, but not before a few demonstration units were built in Commonwealth.

This was also the period when Sama-sama lost its right to represent the entire NGC on the government-community panel, owing to the critical stance of the new Housing and Urban Development Coordinating Committee (HUDCC) chair. He and his associates in fact further undermined Sama-sama's authority by installing competing local association heads on the committee in what appeared to be divide-and-rule tactics often favoured by government figures. The resentment of barangay local officials at Sama-sama's success, factional fissures within NGC groups, rapid turnover of NGC project administrators, confusion as to which government housing agency handled community development loans and what procedures applied for loan releases all plagued the populace struggling to establish their land claims (Racelis, 2001: 18).

Demoralization struck the membership starting from the time the government failed to respond to Sama-sama's objections to the rapid influx of new settlers that was destroying the validity of the People's Plan. Moreover, they suspected that the police and city officials were in cahoots with land syndicates interested in controlling the terrain. Internal management problems also afflicted the organization: fewer consultations between leaders and members and a weak set of second-line leaders. The predominance of women among the leadership and membership was highlighted when their husbands objected to the amount of time their wives were spending on community matters. These conflicts were exacerbated by jealousy at their interaction with other men in the course of community work. Finally, the murder of two Sama-sama leaders greatly heightened tensions and disunity.

The organization weathered these storms with continuing pressure for the issuance of Certificates of Lot Entitlements, to be followed by Certificates of Land Transfers, or titles, upon full payment of the land. It joined coalitions with other informal settlers whose areas had recently been proclaimed by President Macapagal-Arroyo and before her, President Estrada. These newest claimants benefited greatly from Sama-sama's long experience in this field. Actual titles are now being issued not only to members but to all qualified residents of Commonwealth's 150-hectare proclaimed area. Sama-sama is once more being recognized by government-community committees as the leading and most knowledgeable organization on land titling and self-help development in the city.

Pasig River Rehabilitation Programme, Metro Manila

The Pasig River runs through four Metro Manila cities and one town before emerging during high tide at Laguna de Bay, a tidal lake to the east, or during low tide, at the opposite end in Manila Bay to the west. Once a major thoroughfare for boat traffic before World War II, over the years it has become so polluted and filled with waste and garbage that fish can no longer survive in its murky depths. In 1998, the Pasig River Rehabilitation Commission (PRRC) was established by the national government as part of a 15-year development plan 'to improve environmental management of the Pasig River basin within Metro Manila, particularly for wastewater management and to promote urban renewal'. The first five years of the plan called for relocating several thousand informal settler families to decent settlements, according to a set of strict guidelines prepared by the Asian Development Bank (ADB).

The massive demolition of stilt houses and relocation of 5000 poor informal settler families on the riverbanks began in earnest in 1998. The following year another 3000 households were transferred to resettlement sites over 40 km away. To make matters worse, the government announced that it would enforce the 10-metre easement rule, which prescribed eviction for any household within that space – an estimated 10 000 families along the river. Parts of the areas they would vacate were to become ribbon parks and recreational areas, which would in turn stimulate commercial development.

Even though they were offered land and core housing in the resettlement sites, the vast majority of displaced families faced great difficulties. Employment and other income-generation activities were virtually nil, and skills-training programmes largely ineffective for employment purposes. Water taps were few and far between and the water trickling from them often looked suspiciously dark and undrinkable. Electricity was limited, adding a security problem to the area. Public transport out to the road was limited and the fare back to their earning places in the city unaffordable.

The house itself was sometimes only a roof on four posts, awaiting completion by the new resident. Although the prospect of owning a piece land was enticing, too many informal settlers could not afford to live so far away from their livelihoods in the city. Alternatively, the family could opt for a strategy of having the wife and the younger children remain in the relocation sites, while the husband and the school-aged children moved back to the city during the week to be near work and school. The women feared, however, that if left to themselves in the city, their husbands would find another woman and eventually abandon their families in the resettlement village.

To help riverside and adjacent urban poor communities assert their rights in the transfer and insist on better resettlement conditions, organizers from the Community Organizers Multiversity began working in the riverside communities. A series of mobilizations and dialogues by newly organized community groups, notably the Powerful Alliance of Affected Families along the Pasig River (ULAP), led to their discovery that the ADB-PRRC plan shown to them had not highlighted the provision for a large slum renewal component along the river. This changed their entire formulation of ULAP's position. From then on, its leaders insisted that rather than move thousands of families to distant resettlement sites at great expense and trauma, the government should take steps to allocate the land to them or acquire adjacent land, enhanced by upgrading and housing schemes. Also under contention was the 10-metre easement, the product of a martial law era Executive Order that the riverbank dwellers challenged in court.

The media play an important part in adding to the pressures on government, especially when something dramatic happens. This became clear when a demolition team descended on Barangay Pineda to force the people out. The PO had asked the government to delay or cancel demolitions beyond the three-metre easement line (the 10-metre rule), and to recognize that in any case, the resettlement sites were not ready for this move.

When the demolition crew arrived, the people, along with the CO Multiversity and Urban Poor Associates organizers, had formed a line of resistance, placing negotiating tables with a statue of the Blessed Virgin Mary in the way of the team. Community members were praying and singing hymns. The police waited for the prayers to end, then moved into the area to start tearing down the houses. The scene was a media paradise. Some 300 demolition personnel were dismantling houses, protected by 35 policemen, including black-clothed SWAT teams, and fire engines, with an ambulance standing by. Soon a fight broke out between the crew and residents, culminating in the stabbing of a demolition worker.

The story made the headlines and attracted more television, radio and press reporters. PO members told the story of how the government had rejected their People's Plan and was forcing them to move to a resettlement site whose conditions did not meet minimum standards. The ADB's involvement gave further importance to the story, especially when officials visited the Metro Manila Development Authority to inform them that the ADB would not support a resettlement programme that generated such violence. The senator heading the Housing Committee visited the area to size up the situation, again drawing media attention. The struggle continues.

In the intervening five years, numerous meetings have taken place between ULAP groups and the national government. A Resettlement Committee set up by the HUDCC chair, a former NGO leader, featured regular meetings at which representatives of ULAP and other affected POs could raise their problems with national and local government officials in regard to resettlement – the location, timing, amortizing costs, transfer allowances, transportation, employment, water, sanitation, electricity, safety, and many such issues. This Committee lost its clout after the HUDCC chair resigned because of a disagreement with the President, and once the POs turned away from resettlement as their prime approach.

The results are still to be assessed for the entire Pasig riverbank residents, but a number of positive developments have taken place. The Pineda community on long-abandoned railroad tracks in Pasig City has won its struggle to acquire the land, gone through a planning and reblocking process under NGO auspices, in order to start a Community Mortgage Programme loan programme for title acquisition. Punta Sta Ana has convinced the PRRC to look seriously into purchasing an adjacent nine-hectare private property for low-rise housing accommodating even the 10-metre easement dwellers. If the land is not obtained, they intend to remain right where they are. Resettled families in the distant sites have managed to pressure the authorities to make good some of their promises in response to the people's demands for subsidized transport, more water and schools. And the 10-metre easement is now being discussed in government circles, with a strong possibility that it will no longer be enforced.

Playing a key role here has been the Asian Development Bank as the loan source for the Pasig River Rehabilitation Programme. Its anti-poverty stance over the past few years, promotion of participatory governance and stringent guidelines for resettlement sites have had a strong impact on government policy. This is partly because the NGOs and POs involved have built fairly strong bonds with ADB project personnel and quickly convey complaints about government handling of the situation to them. While the ADB has been generally cautious about 'taking sides' vis-à-vis the government, its progressive approach encourages much greater flexibility in the conceptualization and implementation of ADB-funded projects like the PRRC. As for national and local government officials, most have learned a great deal about participatory governance, starting with listening to the people's views and desires. While Metro Manila mayors in particular, along with national officials, continue to resist these voices, others have shown their interest in carrying out more such projects with maximum benefits to poor people.

Naga City Urban Poor Federation, Bicol Region

Founded in 1575, Naga City, is a medium-sized city of 96 square kilometres located 400 km south of Metro Manila with a population of over 140 000 people. The Bicol region of which it is a part is recognized as one of the poorest areas of the country. Soon after the people power revolution of 1986, which ousted President Marcos and brought in President Aquino, COPE organizers began working with several urban poor groups occupying land adjacent to abandoned railroad tracks. The issue immediately before them was the scarcity of clean, potable water in the community. After several meetings and visits to the old mayor, the community's pressure tactics succeeded and they managed to get the local water district to install a water tap. From this victory, they went on to address security of tenure and other basic services needs (Murphy, undated).

The elections of 1998 brought in young Mayor Jesse Robredo, who had strong socially oriented leanings. When on day one, he found the urban poor and COPE organizers at City Hall waiting to discuss their issues with him, he immediately saw the value of joining with rather than fighting them. As he states (Robredo, 1999:12):

> The best way for local governments to tackle poverty is to share the task with civil society. This means opening up the process of priority setting, decision-making and resource-allocation to representatives of civil society making them as much responsible as the officials of the local government.
>
> Government need not give everything to the poor. The poor are more than ready to help themselves if only they are involved in the decision-making process early on.

Government cannot do the task alone, insisted the mayor. Accordingly, soon after he assumed office, he set up the Naga Socialized Programme for Empowerment and Economic Development (SPEED), which provided multiple channels through which city groups could identify development priorities and their views on policy issues. Among these were neigh-bourhood-level consultation, sectoral dialogues, city-wide referenda on major projects or policies, and surveys. Disadvantaged groups were brought into the priority-setting and decision-making process of the city government. Their inputs brought them a fair share of the annual budget. 'Naga SPEED put in sync people and government, an unstop-pable synergy that focused resources towards uplifting the plight of its impoverished sectors.'

A second major innovation was the Naga City Empowerment Ordinance, which institutionalized the Naga City People's Council (NCPC). This non-partisan body was composed of NGOs, POs and private sector groups, who could propose legislation and carry out additional duties. Soon Council-designated NGOs were sitting on boards, councils, committees, task forces and other special bodies of the city government. The Ordinance also pro-vided for representation in the city legislature of elected non-agricultural labour, women and urban poor.

In essence, the Empowerment Ordinance deconcentrated political power and shared it with civil society through non-government organizations and community leaders who participate in the various aspects of local governance. Equally important, it safeguarded public resources from being dissipated in politically attractive but developmentally irrelevant projects . . .

(Robredo, 1999: 6).

In 1989, the urban poor, now organized into the Naga City Urban Poor Federation (NCUPF), promoted the adoption of the Community Mortgage Programme (CMP) in the city, the creation of the Urban Poor Affairs office, and the passage of the Comprehensive and Continuing Urban Poor Ordi-nance of Naga, or the Kaantabay sa Kauwagan Progam (Angeles, 1997). Mayor Robredo envisioned this Partners in Development Programme as primarily empowering the 25 per cent of city residents who were informal settlers and slum-dwellers. It featured on- and off-site development for poor urbanites to obtain land and improved housing. To help implement these programmes, he readily acceded to the NCUPF's proposal for a sepa-rate urban poor window under the comprehensive livelihood programme of the city government. There, applicants could get loans for economic empowerment. A separate urban poor trust fund account enabled the accumulation of CMP fees, amortization for the resettlement sites and the sale of other government properties for socialized housing.

With the NCUPF as a close ally, 33 hectares of private and government-owned land have been turned over to 2017 urban poor families, encom-passing over half of them. A tripartite mechanism for settling land tenure issues between landowners and land occupants has been established. To reduce the migrant stream to Naga City from surrounding areas, the mayor created the Metro Naga Development Council, a partnership between the city and 14 surrounding municipalities, later joined by national government agencies and local NGOs. The framework is one of integrated area development highlighting urban–rural linkages.

The much-awarded mayor invariably cites his indebtedness to Naga City's NGO and civil society partners for what is considered the best-run city in the Philippines and one of the most vibrant in terms of citizen participation and satisfaction. Indeed, Mayor Robredo won the next two elections by an overwhelming vote. Genuine participatory governance is good politics and good politics gets good politicians re-elected. The community organizers and PO for their part keep the government accountable and transparent by staying true to their educational and empowering processes of action–reflection–action–reflection. Naga City POs have learned to do this because trained community organizers take them through the following steps.

1. Integration: data and information gathering (action).
2. Social investigation and analysis; issue identification (reflection).
3. Tentative planning and strategizing (reflection).
4. Legwork, groundwork, agitation (action).
5. Caucuses, meetings (reflection).
6. Role play (reflection).
7. Mobilization (action).
8. Evaluation (reflection).
9. Reflection, consolidation (reflection).
10. Organizing the People's Organization (action) ... and the cycle continues.

(Angeles, 2000: 12; also NCR-COs, CO-TRAIN, UPA, and PHILSSA, 2001: 21)

At the same time, NCUPF engaged extensively in networking with other activist groups, participating in protest rallies and other mass actions spearheaded by different political blocs. Although its members recognize the value of having a socially aware and supportive mayor, they also know that they must keep the pressure on to ensure that ordinances are implemented and that funds are actually released, and that important agreements achieved from the government by the urban poor sector need to be protected (Angeles, 2000: 20).

INSTITUTIONAL STRUCTURES FOR PEOPLE'S EMPOWERMENT

Because urban poor settlers have been targeted for demolition, resented for taking over land illegally and derided for their unsightly surroundings, the institutional arrangements of governance that should respond to their needs have not developed as quickly as needed. Just as microfinance approaches have filled in the interstices between regular banks and informal moneylenders, so too do the particular needs of the urban poor need

creative adaptation. It is not until a problem is raised to the level of consciousness, examined by those affected by it, and transformed into a new
set of understandings conducive to practical action, that the institutional
repercussions can be devised.

That is what organized urban poor groups have been doing for decades.
Their resistance to eviction and refusal to return to their home town
despite a one-way ticket home has forced governments to construct more
humane and acceptable resettlement sites. The low priority the urban
poor accord distant resettlement or high- and medium-rise housing compared to on-site or nearby relocation and upgrading has meant that after
years of strife, government is coming around to seeing the picture in
terms of the lives the poor actually live.

Some of the newer or revitalized institutional structures and mechanisms illustrate the timeliness of this creative effort. Most cities now
have an Urban Poor Affairs Office with a staff specifically expected to
listen to and address the needs brought up by that constituency. Listening to the urban poor is becoming more possible because their representatives sit on government committees, or meet with their mayor
and even the President with some regularity. City leaders hold public
meetings and hearings, organize referendums and open up city council
meetings to interested parties. They publish their budgets for greater
transparency and encourage the citizenry to examine them critically.
The Social Security System and PhilHealth, in consultation with NGOs,
is making headway in developing systems that enable low-income
earners and informal settlers to obtain social security and medicare.
Computerized records now enable even less-literate clients to obtain
access to information on land titles in one visit. On the national level,
urban poor representatives elected by their sector sit on the National
Anti-Poverty Commission and propose ways in which national agencies
can reach the poor more effectively.

A movement that has brought this turnaround in government about is
community organizing. Building People's Organizations – democratic,
autonomous, self-actualizing and able to make demands of those in
authority – creates the pressure from below so necessary to make slowly
moving bureaucratic processes move and recalcitrant officials listen. Only
when poor people are able to overcome apathy and fear through taking collective action and then reflecting for renewed action, can they make the
leap forward. From small, community-focused issues, many go on to
expand their horizons and participate in the metropolitan-wide, national
and international debates.

However, many urban poor settlers who mobilize to acquire land often
relax once that has been accomplished, leaving to others the continuing
search and struggle for new issues and broader systems to tackle. Labour
organizer Honculada reflects on community organizing, '. . . organizing
has empowered people on a micro-level; developed an awareness of
democratic processes; offered alternative actions for people's organiza-

tion and brought about personal transformation in the sense of collectivity and commitment'. In stressing 'process and peoples power', she adds, 'community organizing may constrain organized groups from rising above the level of issues in order to grapple with the deeper causes of social contradictions'.

In the same vein, Karaos (2003: 35) comments that by focusing on local benefits and linking with politicians eager to co-opt slum dwellers through patronage benefits, urban poor groups never move beyond particularistic concerns to challenge unjust social structures through systemic urban land reform, for example. She observes:

> *Populism and clientelism . . . share a common tendency which is their abhorrence for institutions and institutionalized channels of interest representation. Because of this, both of them end up reinforcing existing power relations. They do not encourage the formation of independent organizations with stable linkages to political institutions; instead they cultivate the dependence of subaltern groups on politicians who then act as their exclusive access to the political system.*

The challenge therefore is to find a way to connect the autonomously organized urban poor communities to either civil society formations or political parties that can provide institutionalized channels of access to representation in the power structures of society. If civil society groups and the progressive political parties cannot perform this role, the advancement of a social reform agenda by the progressive movement stands in danger of being subverted by autonomous community organizations acting solely on the basis of self-interest.

This sobering reflection is certainly apt. It suggests that a larger number of autonomous, democratic groups linked together in networks and alliances is still needed to reach the critical mass that brings about structural reform. When the key stakeholders – government, POs, NGOs and the private sector– converge around a common challenge, that is when the need to design the missing institutions becomes compelling.

LOOKING TO THE FUTURE

The implications are clear. Organizing disadvantaged communities must continue on an expanded and accelerated basis to cover all major urban poor clusters in our cities. Only then can one speak confidently of a democratic people–government–civil society partnership. NGOs and other grassroots-oriented groups are instrumental in helping people deal with the aspirations or threats about which they feel strongly and for which they are willing to go to battle. It is time that donors committed to partnerships with people that go beyond the 'project' orientation that favours pre-ordained outcomes, like child nutrition, poultry raising, micro-enterprise, early childhood centres or house construction, to supporting community organizing around issues that people in chronic states of human insecurity identify and about which they feel passionate enough to take action.

Although the above types of economic and social project benefit may also come out of community organizing efforts, the mobilizing process accomplishes far more. It moves empowered groups into the centre of the political process of demand-making and participatory governance, and into the social psychological realms of motivation, self-realization and self-confidence. For perhaps the first time in their lives, they actively pursue the core principles of human security – freedom from want, freedom from fear and the freedom to take action on one's own behalf (Commission on Human Security, 2003: 10).

When as a result of citizen pressure, government agrees at last to a moratorium on evictions and negotiates with embattled residents to provide security of tenure; when it acknowledges people's rights to information by releasing a heretofore 'secret' list of qualified land claimants; when it accepts on-site upgrading as preferable to eviction and distant relocation; when it dismantles police-protected trafficking syndicates that prey on women and children; when it prioritizes 50 slots in a construction project for workers hired from the community – that is empowerment. And that is how institutional infrastructure responsive to people's demands gets created and sustained. Serious government officials thus come to appreciate the win–win situation before them. It soon dawns on them that their work is considerably simplified and even enhanced because of people's interest, experience and knowledge. This is the stuff of which enlightened governance is fashioned.

But even community organizing is only a start. For organized poor groups to transform their victories and new partnerships into a mobilizing force for social reform, they need a critical mass linked through alliances, coalitions and federations. This marks the beginnings of an 'urban poor vote', which future candidates for election must court if they want to win.

In this vein, Filipino POs and NGOs with an eye to the future are examining with great interest how a trade union leader in Brazil has managed, after years of struggle, to carry his party to an electoral victory and capture the presidency. Perhaps the next step in the Philippines is to transform alliances and federations of people's organizations into a workers party centred around the interests of the urban and rural poor. Tapping the insights of trade union leaders may prove fruitful in this regard. Thus, new partnerships may evolve, even as organized groups continue to work with more familiar partners in government and the private sector.

The struggle will be long and difficult. But poor people are used to that. Partnerships with government and the private sector that allocate marginalized communities their fair share of material and non-material resources and, in the process, form responsive, pro-poor institutional structures, can transform currently unacceptable urban disparities into the equitable cities most of us want. For government and the private sector, the handwriting is on the wall.

CHAPTER SEVEN

Migratory flows, poverty and social inclusion in Latin America[1]

Mona Serageldin, Yves Cabannes, Elda Solloso and Luis Valenzuela

INTRODUCTION

In the past decade, but particularly since the mid 1990s, Latin America has experienced a dramatic increase in migratory population flows across national boundaries regionally and internationally.

Disparities in the distribution of wealth have generated and sustained such massive movements in Asia and the MENA (Middle East North Africa: Thailand, India, Pakistan, Philippines, Egypt, Sudan, Yemen, Jordan) since the mid–1970s, when workers from poorer areas sought jobs in the oil-rich countries. The vast majority were employed as lower-skilled labour in construction and services, graduates were hired as mid-level technical and managerial personnel, and some experienced professionals secured senior positions in the face of competitors based in the West.

These migratory patterns have been well studied in terms of labour dynamics and the impact of remittances on the economies of migrant-sending countries. In contrast, the impacts on rural areas and on the dynamics of urban growth were not addressed until their magnitude could no longer be ignored.

Attempts by national governments in need of foreign exchange to tap remittances through control measures, including taxes, transfer fees and mandatory contributions to various government funds, predictably failed. These measures only managed to divert transfers to informal channels and curtail potential investments by expatriates. Offering incentives to attract remittances to formal institutions and investment purposes proved a more productive approach. These incentives included foreign exchange accounts and preferential treatment of investors in real estate and development projects.

The massive migratory movements taking place in Latin American countries (LAC) today share some similarities but also display differences with the MENA/Asia experience.

Categories and levels of migratory flows

The LAC migration is also fuelled by growing disparities in the distribution of wealth in a region where disparities are already very wide and have been aggravated by globalization, restructuring of national economies and a succession of financial crisis, since the mid 1990s. The ECLAC (Economic Commission for Latin America and the Caribbean) estimates that from 1998 to 2002 poverty increased from 42 per cent to 44 per cent, an increase of 20 million persons. Of the 220 million poor, 90 million live in extreme poverty mostly in the rural areas.[2]

Wars and natural disasters have generated overlays of migratory flows of a more or less temporary character usually confined to cross-border movements or rural-urban and intercity movements within the same country. In the 1980s, Bolivians and Paraguayans flocked to Argentina, and Colombians to Venezuela. Today a reverse migration out of these two countries prevails with Argentinians and Venezuelans themselves moving to the USA and the EU. In Central America, during the decade of conflict, Nicaraguans migrated to Costa Rica and Honduras, and Guatemalans, predominantly ethnic Mayans, to Belize.

Since the mid-1990s expatriate workers from the Caribbean, Central America and South America have flocked to the USA and to a lesser extent to the EU countries. Spain is the preferred destination of migrants from Ecuador, Colombia, Peru and the Dominican Republic. Brazilians go to Japan and Portugal, Peruvians and Argentinians to Italy, and migrants from the Caribbean countries to the UK and Canada. According to recent studies by the IADB (Inter-American Development Bank), remittances from these migrants to their home countries have grown by 40 per cent since 2000, reaching US$32 billion in 2002. This increase has propelled Latin America to the forefront as the largest recipient of remittances, accounting for 31 per cent of the volume of remittances in the developing world.[3]

There are no less than 12 million LAC migrants principally in the USA, from where 70 per cent of LAC remittances in 2002 originated. Another US$1 billion were transferred by migrants in each of Canada, Spain and the rest of EU. Although dwarfed by international migration, intra-regional migration involves an estimated 3 million workers who remit US$1.5 billion. There are established migrant communities of Dominicans and Nicaraguans in Costa Rica, Bolivians in Argentina and Haitians in the Dominican Republic. In addition, there has been a large influx of people from all of Central America to Mexico and the US border towns, a region that boomed after the North American Free Trade Agreement (NAFTA) was enacted but has experienced a loss of 300 000 jobs in the past few years as a result of the slowdown in the US economy (Hinosa Ojeda, 2003).

Key economic impacts and levels of migratory flows

Recent studies of migration in LAC focus on the volume of remittances and their impact on the national economy, the modalities of transfers and the ways by which financial institutions can tap this potentially lucrative market. Because individual transactions typically involve amounts of US$100 to US$300 (usually on a monthly basis), banks have largely left this market to money-transmitting companies and postal services, in addition to various categories of informal actors.[4]

Some studies include surveys of migrants that do not presume to be representative samples but nevertheless give interesting information on the characteristics of migrants, the motives underlying emigration, remittances and the choice of mode of money transmission. Some studies, and in particular the work of Manuel Orozco, look at the links to families and communities of origin and the transfer and use of remittances.

As the number of migrants increases and remittances grow in volume, the number of formal or informal intermediaries seeking to capitalize on the migration process, the money transmission market, and the sale of good and services to migrants and their families also increases. These intermediaries reap substantial profits while migrants and other household members are mostly unaware of the real charges and fees that they are actually paying. The information on these different categories of intermediaries is scanty and, in the case of informal intermediaries, of questionable reliability given the reluctance of those directly concerned to discuss their business and the structure of their operations.

EXTERNAL MIGRATION

Brief review of studies on remittances in Latin America and the Caribbean

Accurate estimates of transnational migration are difficult to come by because of the predominance of extra legal movements and undocumented migrants. Unrecorded transfers probably account for about 20 to 30 per cent of remittances originating in the USA. Since 2000, Central America, the Caribbean and the Andean region are the major recipient areas, exhibiting above-average annual rates of increase of 18.6 per cent, 20.7 per cent and 19.8 per cent respectively.[5]

Remittances are a major source of income for migrant sending countries. According to the IADB studies, remittances account for 25 per cent of gross domestic product (GDP) in Nicaragua and bring in an infusion of foreign exchange equivalent to half the value of exports. In El Salvador, this contribution is greater than the totality of the country's exports. Mexico is the largest recipient of net remittances in Central America and accounts for about one-third of the LAC total. Remittances grew from US$2.4 billion in 1990 to US$10.5 billion in 2002. While this value is equivalent to only 10 per cent of Mexico's exports it amounts to 80 per cent of foreign direct investment. In Brazil, net remittances of US$15 billion in 2002 make a vital contribution to the balance of payment as the country struggles to recover from the 1998 financial crisis.[6]

A study of remittance senders in the USA conducted by D.C. Benavides for The Pew Hispanic Centre (PHC)/Kaiser Family Foundation in 2002, shows that:

- 60 per cent are male
- 63 per cent under the age of 40
- 59 per cent have not completed high school
- 64 per cent are employed as unskilled labourers
- 54 per cent can either barely understand English or do not understand it at all.

Average age at migration is 25 years and 45 per cent plan to eventually go back. Seventy-two per cent live in rental accommodations, which they share with four others on average.[7]

Because of the priority placed on saving and remitting, migrants willingly endure difficult living conditions and accept exclusion in one location in order to acquire assets, usually land and housing, or start a business and achieve inclusion at another location in a different country. In the case of floating populations, similar patterns prevail, with migrants working in one locality and investing in another.

Migrants differentiate between remittances sent for subsistence or basic expenditures, including health and education, and remittances sent for savings and investments purposes. In poorer households, the bulk if not the totality of the transfers are spent on necessities. Receiving members of the household spend as needed to pay for their daily living expenses. Transfers intended for investment are jointly managed and are part of the household's strategy for self- improvement. Decisions regarding the timing and sequence of the investments are carefully planned according to needs and means.

Links between transnational migrants and place of origin

Manuel Orozco's (2001) work on immigrant Latino communities in the USA highlighted the emergence in the 1990s of home town associations among expatriate communities and their growing role in maintaining links to places of origin. These associations combine social functions in the USA with coordinated efforts to support home towns in Latin America.

Home town associations are still quite small, private voluntary organizations lacking formal organizational structures. They raised on the average of US$10 000 per year to send to their home towns in 1999. They rarely have institutional counterparts in their home countries. Between 20 and 30 per cent of migrants contribute to these collective remittances. An interesting feature is the evolution of the support they fund, from charitable activities mainly linked to the church to investment projects to improve infrastructure and services in their home towns and villages.

Mexico has taken the lead in recognizing the potential of these associations and in attracting their investments by offering incentives to finance joint projects. Special home town development funds are created to leverage association funds with grants by state, federal and, more recently, municipal governments. Zacatecas, Jalisco and Guanajuato – a region of high out-migration – were the first states to set up such funds. In the latter two states the joint ventures were used to finance 'employment-generating projects', mainly garment factories. Jobs were created and relatives of migrants were given preference in hiring. Nevertheless the projects perpetuate the deplorable features of the *maquiladoras'* system.

The associations' community-wide development projects are of greater interest since they finance infrastructure (potable water, sanitation, street paving) and community facilities (school, health centres, parks). These projects can lead to productive partnerships between the associations, local authorities and CBOs (community-based organizations) to meet community needs.

Migration and remittances in Ecuador

Ecuador is a particularly interesting case to consider in view of the explosive growth of external migration fuelled in large part by the economic crisis of the 1990s. The crisis was exacerbated in 1996 by falling oil prices and the impact of the shift in oceanic currents that gave rise to the *El Niño* climatic conditions affecting agriculture and fisheries.

The deepening economic problems throughout the decade are reflected in key economic indicators.

- The stagnation of the GDP per capita, which remained unchanged in dollar terms at about US$2500 (Solimano, 2003) while the consumer price index climbed from under 100 to close to 1000 (Banco Central del Ecuador, 2001: 11).
- The growing inequalities as the share of income accruing to the poorest 20 per cent of the population fell from 4.6 per cent to 2.5 per cent, while the share received by the richest 20 per cent grew from 52 per cent to 61.2 per cent. Consequently, the proportion of people living in poverty doubled to reach 71 per cent in 2000 and the proportion living in extreme poverty almost tripled reaching 31 per cent.[8]
- Rising unemployment, which doubled to peak at 20 per cent (Banco Central del Ecuador, 2001: 11).
- Rampant inflation, which stood at 104% by the end of the decade, and rapid depreciation of the currency.

The pace of out-migration picked up in the mid–1990s then shot up exponentially from 1998 on. Official data reflect that Ecuador's total migration between 1990 and 2000 was 550 000 (Banco Central del Ecuador, 2001: 16).

However, it is estimated that between 1999 and 2003 around 600 000 to 1 million Ecuadorians left the country. Until 1995, the USA was the main destination for Ecuadorians, receiving 65 per cent of all migrants from that country. However, from 1995 to 2002 Spain became the preferred destination, receiving 53 per cent of the migrants while the US share decreased to 30 per cent.[9]. This flow peaked in 2002 when the total number of Ecuadorians registered by the Spanish Ministry of Interior reached 132 628, a 156.6 per cent increase over 2001.[10] In 2002, Spanish immigration regulations were revised as a consequence of new EU guidelines. Enforcing the new regulations is expected to contain if not stem the influx of migrants and, as a result, the USA may become again the main destination of Ecuadorian transnational migration.

Today, 14 per cent of the Ecuadorian population relies on remittances as a source of income.[11] The total volume of remittances soared from US$65 million in 1990 to US$1.4 billion in 2002, accounting for 7.4 per cent of the GDP and 24.5 per cent of exports, despite the recent increase in oil prices (Solimano, 2003). With a foreign debt standing at 60.8 per cent of GDP and 36 per cent of the 2003 budget allocated to debt service, foreign exchange earnings are critical to the stability of the country. Remittances have become the second source of foreign exchange after oil exports and exceed by ten times the foreign aid received by Ecuador and by five times the International Monetary Fund (IMF) loans disbursements.[12] According to a survey commissioned by FOMIN (Multilateral Investment Fund at the Inter-American Development Bank) and the PHC in 2003, Spain is the prime destination of migrants from Quito and Guayaquil, who generate 44 per cent of the remittances, while the USA was until very recently the preferred destination of migrants from the Cuenca rural areas and the Andean region, whose transfers account for 38 per cent of remittances.[13]

Migration is a key component of household self-improvement strategies. It is a carefully considered and planned family decision. This is a characteristic shared by migrants in LAC, MENA and Asia. Households have to cover the cost of travel and subsistence for members they send abroad until the latter have secured work and are able to start remitting. It is a significant commitment of funds that can only be generated through the depletion of savings, the sale of assets (real estate, cattle, jewellery, etc.) and indebtedness. It is viewed as an investment that the household makes with the expectation of future benefits.

The FOMIN/PHC survey also documented the characteristics of Ecuadorian migrants and their families. The survey showed that the migrant member is the one with the highest wage-earning potential. Households able to finance migration are those with a monthly income of US$250 to US$500, that is at or just above the poverty line. About two-thirds of the families receiving remittances fall in this income bracket compared to 27 per cent for the general population. No less than 57 per cent of Ecuadorian households earn less than US$250 per month and are as yet unable to benefit from migration.

The average amount remitted is US$175 per month transferred through money-transmitting companies (Western Union, Moneygram, Delgado Travel, Prontoenvios, etc.). The bulk of families receiving remittances earn less than US$500 per month. Each migrant supports an average of three persons, mostly women, children and elderly family members. Indeed 66 per cent of receivers are females in the 18 to 49 age groups.

Remittances are mainly used for basic expenses including food, housing, health and education. Expenditures on household appliances and investments in housing and micro-enterprises increase with family income. While many migrants plan to return, it is estimated that only four out of ten actually do. In time, migrants either bring their immediate families to the destination country or get married there. At that point remittances decrease substantially.

THE IMPACT OF REMITTANCES IN MIGRANT SENDING AREAS

Impact of migratory and floating populations on urban development and social inclusion

Azuay province is the area with the highest rate of out-migration in Ecuador. Between 1990 and 2002 some 249 000 people left the province accounting for 45.3 per cent of the national total (Banco Central del Ecuador, 2001). A major source of information is the government passport office in the province. There were 22 000 migrants from the Cuenca canton, of which 36.9 per cent came from the rural areas. Detailed data in terms of people per parish and the evolution of flows are not known with precision. Most of the migrants are working-age males, principally in the 25–34 age group. The majority are single, in contrast to migrants from urban areas, who are typically married. The bulk live in family residences or in 'villas' attesting to their economic level above the poverty line. In 2000, Ecuadorian migrants remitted US$1.3 billion of which US$600 million went to the Azuay province. The municipality of Cuenca receives around US$400 to US$500 million annually, that is US$1.5 million per day.[14]

Massive migratory movements inevitably affect the urban economy. Since 1999, prices have increased dramatically in Cuenca, making it one of the most expensive cities in Ecuador. Cuenca's inflation is reflected in the increase of the Basic Basket price, which is US$370 for Ecuador and US$470 for Cuenca, that is around 25 per cent higher. Several indicators that measure the impact of migration on poverty were identified through field research and interviews with public officials and citizens.

The average remittance received by households residing in Cuenca is US$185 per month. Cuenca's Chamber of Commerce states that most remittances have been used to finance new housing construction, and purchase vehicles and home appliances. Yet interviews indicate that about

50 per cent of remittances flows are directed towards migration-related services to service the debt incurred with formal agencies and informal facilitators referred to as 'coyotes', and to facilitate the return and visit of expatriate family members. The major beneficiaries of these expenditures are the intermediaries in the migration business. The cost of migrating to the US with false documentation provided by 'coyotes' is around US$12 000 to US$14 000. In many ways, 'coyotes' stand out as the main beneficiaries from migration in the canton, together with the networks of public employers who issue fraudulent passports, visas and authorizations for the different countries.

Remittances used to purchase status goods such as cars, household appliances and imported clothes do not benefit local production, and benefit Ecuadorian merchants in a limited way only. They generate new consumption patterns and do not address the structural factors causing poverty that foster migration. Moreover, the increasing arrival of goods manufactured in China, particularly house wares, shoes, clothing and toys, is impoverishing local artisans. The contraband of these products lowers their price even more and fuels migration of unemployed and impoverished workers.

Due to its location, Cuenca is becoming a specialized centre for migration-related services, legal and extralegal. The city has become a magnet acting as a gateway for those who want to leave the country and the Andean region. Assessing the impact of this function on the urban fabric and the quality of life in the city is critical to understanding issues of social inclusion.

Impact of migration on the local real estate market

According to the Construction Chamber, just before the dollarization of the economy approximately 50 per cent of the remittances were directed towards the construction sector. Land acquisition and housing were safe investments for migrants, particularly those in the US. Consequently, the price of urban land skyrocketed. Serviced land in the city reached US$300 to US$350 per square metre, sometimes higher, two years ago, compared to US$250 to US$300 per square metre for a well-located parcel in Quito.

The dollarization and the subsequent freezing of savings accounts undermined the confidence in the banking sector. Low interest rates in the US further eroded the attractiveness of investments in new housing construction in Ecuador. As a result, real estate values tumbled. A well-located plot acquired by the Cuenca Chamber of Commerce recently for US$180 to US$200 per square metre was priced at US$600 per square metre and US$1000 per square metre two and three years ago respectively. The Chamber estimates that there is a market for housing whose cost including the serviced lot does not exceed US$30 000. It seems that today migrants prefer to invest in a more urban, more functional and less ostentatious type of housing (see Figure 7.1).

Figure 7.1   Street and sidewalk upgraded through the 'Improve your Neighbourhood' programme
Source: Yves Cabannes

Moreover, due to the significant differential in land prices within the canton, construction activity has tended to decrease in urban areas and to increase in the urban centres of rural parishes or in more distant rural areas. Serviced land in the city costs around US$120 per square metre and land in the rural outskirts of Cuenca costs US$90 per square metre. Land that can be serviced is priced at US$25–30 per square metre, while rural land that can be supplied with water and electricity costs about US$5 per square metre. The higher affordability of land and living patterns accounts for the marked preference of migrants, particularly those from rural areas, for building new housing in rural communities mostly on agriculture and pasture land. New buildings reflecting imported North American models abound. Still lacking basic infrastructure (access roads, potable water and sewerage), these new assets stand as symbols of increasing incomes and social inclusion (see Figure 7.2).

For migrants, investment in real estate in the place of origin is part of a broader strategy of asset building. In the early years abroad or while their status is not yet legalized, they tend to invest more in their communities of origin. As they settle in their country of destination, or their status is legalized, investment in their home communities tends to stop. Rather, they may sell the assets they have previously acquired. These strategies may account for the fact that in some parishes where migration started in the pre-dollarization period, there are houses for sale, whereas in more recent out-migration areas there are houses being built.

Figure 7.2   Large house financed by migrant remittances in Cuenca peri-urban area
Source: UMP–LAC

Table 7.1   Annual variation in housing construction in Cuenca

Year	Built m²	Annual variation	No. of building permits
2001	510 895		
2002	522 842	+2%	1713
2003	505 327	−3.4 %	1686

Source: Municipalidad de Cuenca, Colegio de Arquitectos y Cámara de la Construcción.

In some localities, housing that was worth US$60 000 a few years back is put on the market today for US$45 000 and still finds no buyers.

These trends have led to a decline in housing construction in Cuenca. The increase in the floor area added in 2002 was minimal and a decrease of 3.4 per cent was recorded in 2003, resulting in a decline of US$3.6 million in construction activity in the housing sector, as shown in Table 7.1.

According to the Construction Chamber, the sector suffered from the migrant's lack of interest rather than from a decrease in remittances per se. In contrast to the decline of housing construction activity in Cuenca, the floor area added in the rural parishes increased by 2 per cent in 2003 to reach 90 000 square metres.

Intra-regional migratory flows

The departure of large numbers of persons from the labour force has led to a decline in the unemployment rate and an increase in the wages of labourers. Agricultural and artisanal production has declined due to a shortage of labour and the higher wages commanded by the remaining workers.

Labour shortages have in turn generated secondary patterns of intra-regional migratory movements. Cuenca is today an immigrant-receiving region, which is a new phenomenon in Ecuador, typically a land of out-migration. There is no system in place to monitor this phenomenon, and laws and policies regarding the newcomers are lacking. Peruvians and to a much lesser extent Colombian migrants are coming to Ecuador to work in the trades where labour shortages are most acute. Their willingness to work for lower wages makes them attractive to employers and their availability prevents further decline in production. Because of the relative importance of out-migration in the area, this feature is more evident in Cuenca than in Quito or Guayaquil.

- *Peruvians.* Economic policies during the Fujimori administration led to a marked increase in poverty, prompting out-migration. In the past few years, the flow of migrants from Peru has increased significantly fostered by the Peace agreements signed between the Province of Azuay and the North Peruvian region on 26 October 1998. At present, Peruvians are estimated to number about 3000 to 4000 in Azuay Province. They work as street vendors, construction workers and domestic workers. Lack of reliable statistics, unregistered deportations and corrupt immigration controls make it difficult to arrive at accurate estimates of these migratory movements. In Cuenca, the Construction Chamber points out that there are currently 2200 Peruvian workers who are hired by local firms. The number of street vendors fluctuates, but there seems to be no fewer than 300 at any one time. Unfortunately, there is no available information regarding domestic workers, who are mostly females.
- *Colombians.* The Colombian armed conflict is fostering the arrival of immigrants and refugees to northern Ecuador. From October 2002 to January 2004, 5700 Colombians requested to settle in Cuenca as refugees mostly seeking political asylum. Furthermore, some young Ecuadorians are being hired as soldiers in the various guerrilla and paramilitary armies. They leave the rural areas, receive minimal stipends and are unable to support their families. This situation contributes to creating instability in this part of the country and to accelerating internal migratory movements.
- *Ecuadorians from other regions.* The dollarization of the economy and the subsequent appreciation of the currency have exacerbated the low external competitiveness of local products leading to the closure of enterprises in the non-technology-intensive sectors. Unemployed workers constitute floating populations in search of survival. In the first migratory explosion, just after the economic crisis, workers from the poorer areas such as Chimborazo and Guamote in the Andean region came to Cuenca to work. They lived in shacks close to the construction sites. However, both their level of skill and salary demands could not compete with Peruvians and this flow of migrants is today

virtually insignificant in Cuenca, as many Ecuadorians sought and found alternative destinations abroad.

Irrespective of their origin, immigrants came to live and work in the urban parishes, particularly in the city centre.

Impact of migration on housing affordability

In the housing construction sector, prices jumped due to the combined effect of labour shortages and increased demand. The evolution in the cost of construction labour is probably one of the indicators that best illustrates the impact of migration on housing affordability. Construction labour is in short supply and commands high prices, with local masons competing with builders, architects and engineers for a share of the building activity. The hourly wage for a master mason in 2003 was US$1.29, while in Cuenca it was US$3.00, up from US$1.00 in 2001. Masons are paid US$2.00 per hour in Cuenca, whereas the minimum wage is US$1.27, while mason assistants receive US$1.50 versus US$1.26 and labourers US$1.25 versus US$1.24. Following the sharp rises of 2000 and 2001, construction costs stabilized in 2002 and declined in 2003, partially due to the supply of Peruvian labour. According to the Construction Chamber, construction costs for single-family housing fell from US$190 per square metre in 2002 to US$175 per square metre in 2003.

In contrast, rents in Cuenca multiplied by a factor of 3 to 4 in the past four years. The field interviews showed that middle-income groups were hard hit as rents that ranged between US$60 and US$70 per month skyrocketed to US$250. Investment in rental housing has become a lucrative option for international migrants as well as local developers. In some cases, rents are set according to the opportunity cost of a similar investment in the US. According to some informants, it is more profitable for a migrant to contract debt in the US or Spain and buy or build rental accommodations for Ecuadorian migrants to these countries.

The arrival of Peruvian and Colombian migrants has also led to an increase in the cost of lower-end rental accommodations, further adding to the complexity of the dynamics of real estate markets at a time of rapid change. Rent prices increased particularly in urban areas and especially in 'conventillos', the traditional housing typology in the historic centre, due to limited supply and immigrants' demand for accommodations in central locations. The rents increase in relation to the degree of marginalization of immigrant population. The fieldwork showed that the poorer immigrants paid the highest per floor area cost. Monthly rents in rooms with no sanitary facilities cost US$20 to US$40 and reached up to US$70. These are rooms mostly without windows, unfurnished, infested with rats, lacking natural light, ventilation and water supply. Migrants often sleep directly on the floor, on cardboard. Up to 10 people can share a room. In this case, the landlord charges additional per person fees and can make US$140 per month per room, that is over US$10 per square metre, a price comparable to the best-located apartments in Quito. These landlords generally do not pay taxes.

The increase in housing prices has eroded the affordability of housing for families who do not have members outside of the country, or households with members abroad but who do not receive remittances, as well as for the immigrants to Cuenca, particularly Peruvians.

These effects were also felt in the Middle East and North Africa region in the mid-1980s when the construction labour was siphoned off to the Gulf region to work on massive development projects. In the labour-sending countries, construction prices doubled in 1974 in one of the worst inflationary trends experienced in the area. The huge volume of remittances pumped capital into real estate, driving the cost of land and housing beyond the affordability of the middle classes, a situation which has not been remedied since. While of a lesser magnitude, the situation in Cuenca exhibits similar features.

Impact of migrations on the profile of poverty

In 2000, Cuenca's extreme poverty rate stood at 30 per cent, a level lower than the rest of the country due to the high levels of out-migration and remittances. According to the mayor of Cuenca, this rate has increased to 44 per cent today despite the sustained migratory flows. To assess the impact of migration on poverty four categories of poor and excluded groups were examined.

- ■ *Families with members outside Ecuador but who do not receive remittances.* They are probably the most affected group, having lost working-age members and resources as well as prestige within their communities. They are viewed as abandoned families, cast outside the traditional values and social networks, and their youth have no role models and no support.
- ■ *Families with no migrants.* They suffer from the effects of the dollarization of the economy and the price inflation in Cuenca. New consumption models affect their children. It increases their fascination for the American and European lifestyles and it fosters their desire to emigrate. However, families in this group have retained their wage earners and are more integrated in the community and its solidarity networks.
- ■ *New immigrants.* It has been reported that some of the Peruvian immigrants who live under bonded labour conditions on the outskirts of Cuenca endure open xenophobia, exploitation, theft of documentation and violations of their rights by the police. Deportations of around 300 to 500 people per week are frequent. Many of these deportations are organized in collaboration with

the employers so that workers are evicted just before the end of work periods without receiving their wages for several months of work. The erosion of community links under the Fujimori regime may account for the lack of solidarity among migrants and the lack of organization within and across occupational categories (street vendors and construction workers) despite being subjected to the same abuse and exclusion. Colombians are a more formally educated group, and include students leaving areas of armed conflict but intending to continue their education and middle-class families wishing to settle and invest in a place that is both physically and culturally close. They do not constitute a visible population group. They must have had an impact on driving up prices in the rental market, but there is no documentation of this impact.

■ *Families receiving insufficient remittances.* Although remittances may not allow them to significantly improve their living conditions, they are better integrated in the community.

Interviews with local NGOs and the municipality and research fieldwork and documentation converge on a key issue: the dramatic consequences of migration on families staying in Cuenca. Adverse impacts observed in Cuenca canton include the breakdown of the traditional family structure, the social marginalization of the youth, leading to school drop out, alcoholism and gang formation, and the social exclusion of migrants' children stereotyped as lazy, drug addicts and satanic. The adverse consequences created by the absence of key male family members in a culture imbued with strong patriarchal traditions based on family and kin group ties, functions and obligations, illustrate the difference between exclusion and poverty. On average, the income of migrants' children has increased significantly, yet in particular urban areas their level of social exclusion was never higher.

Municipal initiatives to address the impact of migration

Cuenca municipality has adopted strategies and launched major initiatives to address the impact of migration in partnership with NGOs, CBOs, churches and other civil society groups, some of whom received technical support from UMP-LAC. The action plan includes initiatives targeted at migrant populations as well as cross-sectoral interventions targeted at specific geographic areas.

■ Developing and mapping indicators of social inclusion to identify concentrations of poverty and exclusion and setting up a system to monitor change in these indicators.

■ Establishing the 'House of Migrants' to foster social inclusion of families without remittances and 'The Centre of Attention to Migrants and their Families' to give legal support to migrants from the Andean region, predominantly Peruvians at this time.

■ Organizing 'The Network for Economic Solidarity', included in the Cuenca Strategic Plan for Investments in order to:

  – develop proposals for projects affecting vulnerable population. One of the first initiatives is to promote community-oriented tourism in the rural parishes in order to bring revenues to impoverished communities without disrupting indigenous customs and ways of life in particular among the Quechua community
  – foster the development of a network of organizations interested in promoting a system of fair exchange and trade among local producers to minimize the number of intermediaries involved in the marketing process
  – organize fairs in different market areas in the city to promote rural, artisanal, agricultural and fisheries production. These sectors have been adversely affected by migratory movements and are usually excluded from prime commercial locations in the city.

■ Providing micro-credit for housing and productive activities in order to enable families to improve their income and repay the debts incurred to finance migration of some of their members.
■ 'Improve your Neighbourhood' programme in the urban area.
■ Participatory budgeting in the rural parishes.

The latter two initiatives deserve to be highlighted in view of their ability to mobilize social capital and create a space for social inclusion within the communities, helping mitigate some of the negative consequences of migration.

'Improve your Neighbourhood' programme

This interesting infrastructure improvement programme functions as a partnership between the local authorities, the private sector and civil society. It is in many ways structured to capture remittances and generate benefits for the city as a whole as well as to the individual property owners.

The programme services 'consolidated' neighbourhoods with a high density of privately owned housing. Basic infrastructure provision, tree planting and street paving raise property values, benefiting both the city and the homeowners. Neighbourhood residents submit a request for improvements to the municipality, directly or through their neighbourhood organization. For the selected neighbourhoods, the municipality undertakes the technical studies, calculates the costs of the project and the charges to the beneficiaries. Infrastructure and paving works along each street are divided according to the block layout into 'public works packages' of US$30 000 to US$40 000 for which construction permits are not

Figure 7.3   'Improve your Neighbourhood' programme public works
Source: Yves Cabannes

required. The packages are distributed among Cuenca engineers who operate as small construction firms, hire the labour and deliver the public works within 60 days (see Figure 7.3).

Property owners are charged a share of the cost in accordance to the length of their lot frontage, payable over five years plus a management fee of 12 per cent. A 15 per cent discount is offered to those who prepay the full amount of the charges. To date, the payment rates are close to 98 per cent thereby confirming willingness to pay for access to services. The long waiting lists point to the need, effectiveness and success of this programme. The municipality has also set up a system to reschedule repayment in case of hardship and provide subsidies to economically distressed families (single individuals, retired persons or women-headed households) that account for less than 15 per cent of the total. The ability to tap remittances allows the municipality to work with the banks that agree to issue loans at slightly lower interest rates (around 11 per cent in 2003). In most cases the funds go directly to the engineers or builders undertaking the public works. Property owners make their payments directly to the bank or, in some cases, to the municipality.

The programme has achieved impressive results. Between 2000 and 2003, more than 700 engineers were retained to deliver works valued at about US$21 million. Over 90 km of urban roads/streets (158 000 square metres) have been paved and serviced with infrastructure. Additional projects totalling US$18 million are planned for 2004. The impact of the programme on property values is dramatic. A house originally valued at US$20 000 could sell for US$35 000 following an investment of US$1 500 in public works. This valorization accounts for the enthusiasm of property owners and the long lists of applicants.

The benefits for the city are clear: not only is the quality of the urban environment enhanced as homeowners invest in their properties and neighbourhoods, but the sheer visibility of the public works contribute to sustain the mayor's popularity. The municipality does not incur any outlays as the management fee charged seems to cover its cost, while the increase in revenue generated by property taxes collected on the valorized property will make a significant contribution to the municipality's finances. Assessments are updated every five years, roughly corresponding to the time it takes a family to repay the public works. However, running such a programme requires excellent managerial capacities, and Cuenca municipality has assembled a dedicated and enthusiastic team having the needed capabilities.

Participatory budgeting in rural parishes

Cuenca municipality has been experimenting with decentralization in the 21 rural parishes of the canton. Since 2000, a share of the municipal budget is transferred to these poorer areas to fund capital improvements. Parishioner committees comprising five elected members prioritize the projects to be executed during each budget cycle with the rural communities. The projects selected are mainly public works such as sports and community facilities, access roads, wells and electric power supply. Since 2000, around US$5 million has been transferred to the parishes. The communities have matched these transfers on a 1:1 basis. Participation is high and reaches 100 per cent in some communities. In the rural parishes most affected by migration, 70 to 80 per cent of the families have at least one member in a foreign country. Migrants contribute funds or construction materials. Their participation helps maintain ties to their communities of origin, reactivates traditional bonds and social relations, and recognizes the value of the 'international family' to the community at large (see Figure 7.4).

Figure 7.4   Community participation (Minga) in a parishioner committee of the Cuenca canton. Retaining wall financed through the participatory budget
Source: Parishioner Committee

Community representatives noted that the participatory budget has opened up opportunities for the inclusion of migrants' children in the execution of public works. Participation provides them with a space for socialization, which they can no longer find within their dispersed families. Sometimes, members of a youth gang help with the public works. In these cases, the perception the community has of them changes, and they become identified as positive elements. The sport facilities financed by the municipality also contribute to social inclusion. Alcoholism and gangs reflect in part the lack of leisure activities available in the parish for those having some pocket money and looking for another way of life. Traditionally, sports generate social and community recognition and cohesion. The new sport facilities financed by the municipality have opened up an important space for social inclusion of male and female youngsters alike.

Local economic development is key to alleviating the hardships endured by households who do not receive remittances.

The municipality, with the support of Urban Management Programme (UMP) is encouraging families not to limit their priorities to infrastructure works but demand resources to finance community economic activities and is developing a Strategic Investment Plan funded in part by the Cities Alliance.

Recent urban development patterns

As more Ecuadorians leave for the US and Spain, Cuenca will become an increasingly multicultural and multiethnic city in the Andean region where Ecuadorian, Colombian, Peruvian and perhaps Bolivian communities will live and work. A long-term vision and a strategic plan to address the needs of a city with around 50 000 foreigners have yet to be formulated. Preventing 'ghetto' formation is imperative in a city that has so far been able to avoid spatial segregation.

Cuenca's physical structure is characterized by three major components.

- The 'consolidated' urban area where mutually reinforcing micro-projects are improving the urban environment. Paved and serviced neighbourhoods are allowing an increase in densities and property values in the city, as well as the infill of vacant lots. The urbanized area is expanding towards Ricaurte, which can now be considered part of Cuenca's urbanized zone.
- The historic centre with its invaluable architectural, urbanistic and cultural heritage that has earned Cuenca international recognition as a World Heritage city attracting foreign and national tourists. The marked increase in the number of poor households, particularly migrants and street vendors, and the conversion of 'conventillos' into tenements have resulted in rapid dilapidation in various parts of the centre. New approaches are needed to safeguard and preserve Cuenca's cultural assets. The development of touristic facilities and

infrastructure should be supplemented by a concerted effort to arrest the progressive deterioration of the historic urban fabric. Involving all stakeholders in the preparation of an action plan to transform 'conventillos' into decent low-cost accommodation and to address the needs of floating and immigrant populations is a first step in this direction.

■ The rural parishes within the first belt road and the small urbanizing centres on the fringe will continue to grow and the municipality intends to rezone these areas as urban zones, thereby allowing them to benefit from the 'Improve your Neighbourhood' programme. Channelling of funds to rural communities through the participatory budget will foster the transformation of these parishes into development nodes. However, the uncontrolled proliferation of new housing funded by the remittances is endangering the environmental sustainability and the scenic beauty of the region. There is an urgent need for adequate planning and the formulation of enforceable environmental regulations.

As he reflects on the future of Cuenca, the mayor notes that the concept of 'diffuse city' or 'discontinuous city' is the spatial dimension conducive to promoting a multicultural perspective and respecting the urban identity of Cuenca's different components. This spatial configuration provides the integrative setting needed to build a truly 'inclusionary city'.

CONCLUDING REMARKS

Migratory movements are creating a complex web of interlinked economic and social processes with overlays of different primary and secondary flows and patterns in the same geographic space. From a social perspective these processes have introduced new parameters of social inclusion and exclusion in urban areas with large migrant and floating populations.

In Latin America, migration has come to be viewed as the best avenue for improving living conditions and upward mobility. Households are willing to deplete savings, sell assets and contract debt in order to finance migration of one or more of their members.

State and municipal governments have understood the contribution that migratory movements can make to the local economy. They are devising strategies and methods to attract remittances and capture a share to finance development projects, and some are becoming increasingly adept at it. However, the focus on these joint projects should not obscure the need to address the plight of poorer populations, who can neither participate in, nor benefit from, migration. Poverty-alleviation strategies and action plans in Latin America and the Caribbean should address the plight of the groups most affected by migration, namely: families unable to finance migration of some of their members; families with members abroad but who no longer receiving remittances; and immigrants from neighbouring countries.

In the case of Cuenca, disparities among the poorer strata of the population have increased sharply. The income gap and social distance between those households who manage to send a member abroad and those who are unable to do so have widened markedly. This social fragmentation is in turn reflected in changes in the dynamics of urban growth and development, altering the fabric of neighbourhoods and the spatial incidence of poverty and exclusion. The influx of Peruvians and transients is adding overlays of complexity to these dynamics.

Assessing the multidimensional impacts of migration requires setting up of a system to monitor change in the regions and towns that are experiencing out-migration and the urban areas that attract floating and transient populations. The use of remittances has to be traced and their impact on local real estate markets and cost of living assessed in order to fully address issues of poverty and their spatial manifestations. Similarly, the social impacts of migration should be monitored and assessed in order to address the social and spatial dimension of these new patterns of exclusion. This is critical to the formulation of public policies addressing the challenges of poverty alleviation and social inclusion, and to the assessment of their performance. As local governments seek to attract remittances to finance economic and social development projects, monitoring these changes becomes an important component of urban planning and management, and a fundamental input shaping policies, strategies and action plans.

CHAPTER EIGHT

Room for manoeuvre: tenure and the urban poor in India[1]

Sunil Kumar

INTRODUCTION

Tenure concerns involving the poor in developing world cities have and continue to focus on the legal status of low-income settlements (see, for instance, Fernandes and Varley, 1998; Durand-Lasserve and Royston, 2002). Insecure land tenure exacerbates the vulnerability of the poor to the extent that it has justifiably become the focus of an international Campaign for Secure Tenure (UNCHS, 1999). However, there is an another set of tenures, unrelated to questions of legality or land, that have not received the same level of attention: namely owners, tenants and landlords.[2] The importance of this set of tenures in terms of poverty and housing is now more significant because of two interrelated yet unconnected developments that have taken place since the 1980s.

The first is a change in the conceptualization of poverty. There is a growing consensus that poverty is more than just the proportion of individuals who fall below a defined poverty line. For example, the *World Development Report 2000–2001: Attacking Poverty* (World Bank, 2000b) broadens the definition of poverty by adding ill treatment by institutions of the state and powerlessness to influence key decisions (World Bank, 2000b). Although this change in understanding poverty derives from work in rural areas, it is gradually beginning to permeate urban poverty as well (Moser, 1995, 1996, 1998; Wratten, 1995). Second, there has been a growing interest in tenants and landlords specifically, and rental housing markets in general. However, much of the research on tenants has focused on housing choice and mobility, whereas a significant amount of research on landlords has concentrated on the scale of their operation. Only recently have issues relating to housing tenure been linked to current understanding of urban poverty in terms of vulnerability and livelihoods (Kumar, 2001). Despite this understanding of tenure and poverty, and recent suggestions as to how governments can support rental housing (UN-Habitat, 2003a), most national housing policies[3] show little sign of deviating from home ownership as the preferred tenure choice.[4] Some may argue that the focus on owner-occupation is justified because a significant proportion of the poor do not own their housing. Although it is true that most low-income households aspire to own their housing, it must be recognized that aspirations for ownership are end-goal expressions – they are based on the location of rental accommodation currently occupied by tenants and projected into the future (Gilbert, 1991). The reality is that ownership is not affordable to many tenant households in the places they reside. Rental housing therefore becomes important in 'poverty-risk periods' (Pugh, 1995). It is clear that a primary focus on ownership makes current housing policy myopic to the realities of how individuals and households negotiate access to housing. In short, the emphasis on ownership is a unidimensional policy response to the multidimensional nature of urban poverty and results in a mismatch between policy and the role that housing plays in the lives of the urban poor (see Kumar, 2002).

Rental housing has both opponents and proponents. Opponents view tenants as disenfranchised individuals and households whose social and economic mobility is hampered by their tenure.[5] As will been seen in the next section, this is a limited view as there is evidence to show that a significant proportion of landlords were once tenants and that residential mobility does take place over a period of time. Opponents also view landlords as monopolistic and exploitative, a view that is far removed from reality, as research has shown that it is individuals and households who primarily produce housing for rent and that a large proportion of landlords are as poor as or even poorer than their tenants. Notions of exploitation also implicitly equate rental housing with poor quality. While some rental housing is of poor quality, it is important to question why this is so. Is it primarily the result of exploitative landlordism? Or, is it the result of either the nature of local demand or unsympathetic urban regulations.

In contrast, while proponents support greater tenure choice, their thinking has had little impact on housing policy. Why does support for rental housing and its inclusion in national governments' housing policy remain rhetorical? Is it primarily due to the politicization of rental housing which would mean that bestowing ownership rights is an astute and effective means of garnering support from tenant constituencies without losing the support of landlords, except in circumstances (such as the illegal occupation of land) when landlords are required to give up a share of the land in order for tenants to be housed. Or is it related to a lack of understanding of the complexity that underpins the production of rental accommodation as well as the fact that most low-income rental housing markets in cities in developing countries often operate outside formal legal and institutional frameworks?

This chapter focuses on both landlords and tenants.[6] It argues that pitting landlord against tenant is unproductive. A more constructive approach would be to explore the 'room for manoeuvre' that rental housing provides both tenants and landlords in their pursuit of urban livelihoods. This requires: (a) unpacking the economic, social and political processes underpinning the relationships between tenants and landlords; and (b) an understanding of the exogenous (the local economy, politics, land and finance systems and varied social networks) and endogenous factors (life-cycle potentials and constraints, employment and livelihoods) that characterize the operation of low-income rental housing markets.

Drawing on recent research on rental housing markets in two Indian cities – Bangalore (capital of Karnataka state) and Surat (the second largest city in the state of Gujarat) – this chapter shows that intra- and inter-city differences (for example in size, demographic characteristics and their economies) influence the nature and operation of rental housing markets. Nevertheless, on the whole, rental housing markets are important to well-functioning cities, while specifically they are:

- an important part of the portfolio of individual and household livelihood strategies for tenants as well as landlords
- influenced by and respond to local conditions
- less exclusionary than ownership markets
- shrouded by insecurity as a result of government attitude.

It is common practice for studies of housing to be based on housing or settlement typologies. The main limitation of using settlement types as a unit of analysis, is that it masks the multiple layers of interaction between:

- the local economy
- service levels
- local demand for rental-housing
- the operation of local land markets
- the role of local councillors and unelected community leaders.

The poor live both within and outside settlement boundaries and thus the electoral ward was used as the unit of analysis.[7] A qualitative inquiry was adopted to identify the social relations embedded in the production, exchange and consumption of rental housing. Limited data on rental housing, especially on landlords, necessitated a city-wide rapid appraisal of landlords and tenants at the ward level and the subsequent collation of this information to gain a city-level understanding. Wards were then 'purposively selected' (to reflect variations in rental housing arrangements) and a range of landlords, owners and tenants were interviewed to develop a picture of the social relations that underpinned the operation of rental housing in the chosen ward (for more detail see Kumar, 2001).

Before expanding on the key findings, a brief review of the literature on tenants, landlords and rental housing is followed by an overview of the similarities and differences in the operation of rental housing markets in Surat and Bangalore.

TENANTS, LANDLORDS AND URBAN RENTAL HOUSING MARKETS

In the rental housing literature, disproportionate attention has been paid to why individuals and households rent accommodation. The renting of accommodation and its role in the life course of individuals and households was recognized as early as the late 1960s. Turner (1968), in analysing changing 'social situations' (bridge headers, consolidators and status seekers) and their relationship with the 'dwelling environment' (location, tenure and amenity), highlighted the importance of tenure choice. However, an implicit assumption of the model was that tenure choice was a linear path, with home ownership becoming the final destiny. Work by Gilbert and Ward in Bogotá, Mexico City and Valencia argued that residential mobility among poor migrants was 'less the outcome of migrant choice' based on stage theories and more the 'product of constraints imposed by the land and housing markets' (Gilbert and Ward, 1982: 146; see also, Edwards, 1983). Thus, although individuals and households aspired to own, and despite the fact that a significant proportion of poorer households began their housing histories as tenants and following a number of tenancy moves managed to become owner-occupiers (see, for instance, Green, 1988; Gilbert and Ward, 1982; Gilbert and Varley, 1989a), this progression was not automatic. Gilbert's (1983) 'choice or constraint' thesis, which posited that individuals and households who did not choose to rent did so as a result of constraints at the city, settlement and household levels, became a key research theme in the 1980s (see, for instance, Coulomb, 1989; Edwards, 1982; Gilbert and Varley, 1989a, 1990; Gilbert and Ward, 1982; Gilbert, 1983, 1987, 1991; Gilbert et al., 1993, 1997; Grant, 1996; Green, 1988; Tipple and Willis, 1991; Wahab, 1984).

International development institutions found it difficult to ignore this body of work. Although the first World Bank policy paper on housing, entitled *Housing*, made no mention of rental housing (World Bank, 1975), fleeting references to rental housing only appeared in later policy papers, *Learning by Doing* (World Bank, 1983) and *Housing: Enabling Markets to Work* (World Bank, 1993a). It is interesting to note this limited attention despite the fact that a World Bank report in 1987 made a strong case for a balance housing policy in terms of tenure (see, for example, Lemer, 1987). Of late, however, there has been an explicit recognition of the importance of rental housing by the United Nations Human Settlements Programme (UNCHS, 1989, 1990, 1993).

With a few notable exceptions (for example, Amis, 1984; Bryant, 1989), studies during the 1980s focused on tenants as *consumers* of rental accommodation. It is this 'demand' side understanding that underpins most UN-Habitat (previously UNCHS) documents. Kumar (1996a) has argued that unless there is a similar understanding of the 'supply' side or the *producers* of rental accommodation, efforts to encourage and support the rental housing option are likely to be unrealistic.

Most writing on landlords in developing world cities only began to appear in the late 1980s (Aina, 1990; Angel and Amtapunth, 1989; Bryant, 1989; Datta, 1995; Edwards, 1990; Gilbert and Varley, 1989b; Grant, 1996; Ikejiofor, 1997; Pennant, 1990; Watson and McCarthy, 1998). Much of this literature was concerned with describing the scale of operation of landlords and landlord–tenant relationships. Little attempt was made to conceptualize why landlords undertook the production of rented accommodation (Kumar, 1996a; for an exception, see Hoffman et al., 1991 who categorize landlords as incidental, petty and small developers). Kumar (1996b) provides a conceptual framework of why landlords undertake the production of rental housing at the household level. Three points on a continuum of landlords are identified. At the poorer end are 'subsistence landlords' who rent rooms in order to supplement income and meet basic consumption needs, and at the richer end are 'petty capitalist' landlords who either possess a number of rental properties or seek to expand their ownership of landed property. If holdings become sizeable, such landlords are able to depend on rental income as their main source of income. In between these two points are 'petty bourgeois' landlords who do not need the rental income to survive, but are unable to make any improvements to their dwellings or the material quality of their lives (for example, consumer durables) without the supplementation of household incomes with rental income. These forms of landlordism are not static – landlords move upwards as well as downwards along this continuum as a result of exogenous or endogenous factors. For example a petty bourgeois landlord could decide to invest in a second property and therefore move into becoming a petty capitalist landlord. Or, a petty bourgeois landlord could lose a principal income earner and become a subsistence landlord (also see Kumar, 1996c). In today's poverty terminology, movement along the continuum can be associated with risk and vulnerability – depletion signifying a move backwards and reproduction a move forwards.

RENTAL HOUSING MARKETS IN BANGALORE AND SURAT

Rental housing markets in Bangalore and Surat contain inter-city as well as intra-city similarities and differences. Inter-city similarities can be observed in:

- the operation of rent control
- the segregation of rental housing markets
- the responsiveness of rental housing provision to local contexts.

Inter-city differences arise mainly as a result of variations in:

- the nature of local economic activities and opportunities
- differences in the social structure of the population between the two cities

- the extent or lack of planning interventions
- the operation of land markets and industrial development
- the dominance of social networks versus economic purchasing power
- the range and influence of local power brokers.

Intra-city variations in both cities are linked to the following:

- opportunities in accessing land
- differing levels of service provision (especially transport, water and sanitation)
- the nature of demand for various forms of housing tenure and rental housing investment patterns.

Intra-city similarities are, in the main, related to the importance of rental housing for a range of income and social groups.

Inter-city and intra-city similarities

Rental housing markets in both Bangalore and Surat are segmented by the legal status of the settlements they are located in and by the income group that live in these settlements. Thus, changes in the demand and supply in high-income rental housing markets do not directly influence demand and supply in low-income rental markets. Within low-income rental markets, local employment opportunities and levels of services (transport as well as water and sanitation) have a direct impact on the forms of economic and social transactions within these submarkets. In both cities, state-led planning processes have reduced opportunities for the development of rental housing markets, as a result of which renting is most prevalent where state intervention is limited or non-existent.

Although rent control legislation in both cities is designed to benefit low rental properties, in practice the benefits accrue mostly to middle and high-income residential tenants, especially those who occupy inner-city rented accommodation. While landlords and tenants in rental housing markets that cater for poorer groups have heard of 'rent control', they do not know what its legal provisions are nor have they made use of it. Landlord–tenant disputes are often arbitrated and resolved through the intermediaries that brought landlord and tenant in contact with one another or by local power brokers when this is not the case.

In both cities rental housing markets are responsive to local demand and adapt to meet changes in local employment structures. In Bangalore, for example, growth in home-based block printing on '*sarees*' (traditional south Indian female attire) has resulted in some landlords building rooms that are long and narrow for rent to accommodate this activity. In Surat on the other hand, the predominance of single migrant men in the textile and diamond industries has given rise to a range of rental housing options both in terms of their quality and level of services, as well as allowing the multiple occupancy of a single room by male migrants.

Inter-city and intra-city differences

In comparison with Bangalore, much of Surat is largely unplanned. In Bangalore, the initial focus on facilitating the growth of public sector industries in the 1950s led to large-scale land acquisition by the government. In addition, the delegation of planning responsibilities to the Bangalore Development Authority in 1976 led to large parts of the city in the south, southeast and the southwest being developed into plotted residential layouts for middle and high-income groups. In Surat, the Surat Municipal Corporation, through the implementation of town planning schemes, has provided serviced land for middle and high-income groups. Its activities in relation to low-income housing have been restricted to slum clearance and resettlement, especially after a suspected outbreak of the plague in 1993. The growth of the diamond industry and the development of industrial estates for textiles by the Gujarat Industrial Development Corporation (GIDC) prompted the private provision of housing for those employed in these industries. Private developers have either converted agricultural land into plotted sites or built row-housing units.

Surat is a city of migrants, Bangalore less so. It is estimated that 60 per cent of Surat's population (Shah, 1997) and 80 per cent of those living in squatter settlements (Das, 1994) have been born outside Surat District. In comparison, only 13 per cent of Bangalore's population are migrants (Census of India, 1998). In Surat, the superimposition of the place of origin of migrants with niche employment markets in the diamond and textile industries gives rise to the 'principle of particularism', where access to jobs is determined by kinship and ethnic linkages (Harriss et al., 1990). In addition, the fact that some textile *masters* (supervisors or managers) have gone into land development (on a part-time or full-time basis) and have targeted their workers as clients has given rise to a number of inclusionary and exclusionary outcomes. Land transactions have become an extension of particularistic relationships and are largely predicated on notions of trust because of the quasi-legal nature of housing development. Levels of trust are strengthened through membership of kinship associations or *sanghas* (local political and apolitical associations) which also act as conduits of information about the new residential developments. One outcome is that of negotiated transactions – for example, many developers in Surat provide their clients with the opportunity to pay for land in instalments. In Bangalore, such social links between traditional land-owning communities have gradually eroded largely due to changes in the economic and social structure of the city's population. Transactions are now predominantly based on the capacity of buyers to pay upfront. Moneylenders and the leasing of property to raise finance have become the norm. It is interesting to note that the large presence of migrants in Surat requires tenants to pay rental deposits to insure landlords against rent defaults. In Bangalore, landlords were found to ask for deposits to smooth problems, for example, to pay off debts.

Another aspect of the demographic structure of the population of the two cities in terms of the sex selectivity of migration is its implications for gender relations. In Surat, the sex ratio of 839 is the lowest in urban Gujarat, which averages 907 as a whole. While sex selectivity of migration is initially biased towards males in both the diamond and textile industries, only the diamond workers have managed to bring their spouses and children to Surat over time. In comparison, Bangalore Urban Agglomeration has a sex ratio of 902. Not surprisingly, the predominance of both *de facto* as well as *de jure* women-headed households is much greater in Bangalore than in Surat. Gender relations in Surat lie between the city and the place of origin of migrants, whereas in Bangalore they are played out in housing submarkets as evidenced by the existence of female tenants and landlords.

Differences in access to land and services in the two cities have given rise to different roles for local councillors and unelected community leaders. In Surat, the dominance of quasi-legal housing layouts gives the private developer greater control over a potential constituency of buyers. The developer also attempts to further strengthen his (most developers were found to be men) position by representing demands (such as the provision of services) of his client group to local councillors. In comparison, Bangalore's poor depend more on local councillors in accessing land and services. This variation also has a bearing on attitudes to rental housing. In Surat, developers often hold on to a small proportion of plots in the housing layout they develop. This is speculative and the plots are rented out in the short term. Given that developers themselves are in favour of renting, they generally do not prevent those who have purchased land from them to build rooms for rent. In Bangalore, the picture is mixed. The power of local councillors is greatest when they are able to get squatter settlements legalized, as this benefits all the residents in the settlement. Residents of squatter settlements also have a keen interest in ensuring that tenants do not benefit from legalization (this is one of the most serious conflicts between landlords and tenants). However, once a squatter settlement has been legalized, the power of councillors gradually diminishes from having control over a group to that over an individual. This may, for example, take the form of helping an individual or household to get the necessary papers to access the public food distribution system or getting names transferred on title deeds. Some councillors attempt to retain this diminished level of control as far as possible by preventing the renting of rooms. Councillors seem to fear that they will not have the same control over tenants (as the original settlers) who, if there are sufficient numbers, may become a force to be reckoned with.

In Surat, allowing individuals to co-occupy rental accommodation enables the rent and deposit burdens to be shared. More importantly, it provides peer support in times of economic hardship or social calamities. This is not prevalent in Bangalore, resulting in the poor spending a larger proportion of their earnings on rent in comparison with Surat. In Surat, the comparative higher incomes that the rich can earn from the diamond and textile industries have resulted in rental housing not being seen as a business but a long-term investment. Contrast this with Bangalore where limited education hinders those in agriculture to enter into other businesses and makes rental housing a key part of their investment portfolio.

These inter-city and intra-city differences suggest that strategies to support and promote rental housing will have to take different forms. These may be issues relating to accessing land and finance, the role of kinship and ethnic networks, gender issues relating to landlord–tenant relationships, the nexus of local employment and the location of rental housing markets, and the role of land developers vis-à-vis local councillors and non-elected leaders.

FOUR KEY FINDINGS

The chapter now addresses the four findings outlined in the introduction. Due to the limitations of space, selected paraphrased vignettes from interviews with landlords and tenants are used to illustrate particular points.

Rental housing is an important part of the portfolio of individual and household livelihood responses of tenants as well as landlords

In both Bangalore and Surat, renting out accommodation is an important part of the portfolio of the livelihood responses and strategies of landlords. For most landlords, rents supplement other income-generating activities. Although it is difficult to isolate the final destination of rental income streams, its uses include:

- a safety net against precarious employment
- meeting household expenditure
- housing improvements
- a regular source of income when moving from waged employment to own account forms of employment
- capital investment and rotation in business
- a form of pension after retirement and old age
- investment for the next generation.

Landlord C is close to retirement. This prompted him to consider investing in a good-quality dwelling to generate a decent rental income. He borrowed Rs300 000 – Rs100 000 from a moneylender and the rest from four relatives – and constructed a two-storied, double-bedroom structure of brick walls and reinforced cement concrete roof. The ground floor has been rented for Rs1500 per month and an advance of Rs30 000, and the first floor leased out for Rs100 000 for a period of three years. The lease amount has been used to repay the moneylender and the deposit to repay part of the loan from his relatives. The rent is being saved in a chit fund and will be supplemented by his retirement benefit to repay the loan and the lease. He feels that will leave him a sizeable and steady rental income. [Landlord, Yeshwantpur ward, Bangalore]

Reasons for investing in rental housing vary and are influenced by a combination of factors. In Surat, short working lives in the textile industry mean there is a need to make a transition to other income-generating activities.

. . . [textile] contract job is very vulnerable to seasonal and market fluctuations. I had been fortunate enough to earn a high income till now but this trend is not likely to continue forever. Most textile workers try to start their own business, which I also tried, but was not successful. The first reason I invested in renting is to accumulate surplus . . . I can go back to my village in the event that I do not have much income. Over a period, I found that rental returns are much higher and regular. Bishi [savings and credit association] is useful as a short-term saving mechanism but risks are higher if the organizer refuses to give you the money. Whereas renting is safe as far as regular income is concerned and provides assets for my children. [Landlord, Surat]

In Bangalore, individuals seek to move to economic activities that are less precarious and better paid than the activities they are currently engaged in. Although access to institutional housing finance is problematic in both cities, social networks in Surat increase access to interest-free finance, making finance less of a problem than in Bangalore. In both cities, investment in rental housing is also determined by foreseen (for example, weddings) as well as unforeseen (for example, medical expenses) consumption expenditure.

P is a retired landlord who currently occupies one half of a resettlement site inherited from his grandmother. When he retired from a textile mill in 1994, he purchased half a site with a tile house in the same settlement for Rs50 000. He invested his retirement benefit of Rs25 000 and raised the rest from a moneylender. The dwelling was immediately rented for Rs500 per month and the deposit of Rs25 000 used to repay the moneylender. His daughter works in a garment factory and is the sole earner. She brings home Rs1400 per month. In the same year, he sold some property in his village and upgraded his grandmother's house. Soon after, his wife died and his son-in-law required urgent medical treatment. In order to meet these expenses, he has leased one half of his house for Rs80 000. He is not certain how he will repay the lease and might have to sell one of the plots. [Landlord, Dayand Nagar, Bashyam Nagar ward, Bangalore]

In all, the fluidity and multiplicity of these factors not only influences the destination of rent receipts but also decisions relating to the form and nature of accommodation that is produced.

R migrated to Surat from the sate of Rajasthan in 1977 and worked as a helper in a grocery store. In 1984, he started his own store in a rented property and two years later invested in a plot and constructed a house for his family and a shop for his business. He invested at a time when he was consolidating his business – as he would have regular income to clear his debts. In 1995, he invested in a second plot on which he has built ten rooms for rent – five on the ground floor (reinforced concrete cement roof) and five on the first floor (tin roof). This is because tenants from Maharashtra and Rajasthan look for this kind of rental accommodation. The rental income is equal to 75 per cent of the income from his provision store. He says that the regular rental income helps manage household expenses as his business income is constantly fluctuating. [Landlord, Shivhira Nagar, Dindoli ward, Surat]

In Bangalore, the bulk of migrant young educated professionals are initially dependent on rental accommodation as are a number of self- and casually employed poorer households. The fact that a majority of landlords in Bangalore and Surat were once tenants is testament to the 'waiting-room' function that rental housing plays.

GBP (aged 35) migrated to Surat in 1985 and through his caste network found work as a powerloom operator. The amount he initially earned was just enough for his expenses in Surat and to support his parents. According to GBP, the maximum that a powerloom operator can earn is Rs3500. He was not willing to work two shifts, like most of his fellow workers, and was also aware that he would not be able to bring his family to Surat as well as save money for the future if he continued in textiles. As many of those from his caste are already in the provision store business, he decided to start a small shop. The shift to a business meant that he might not be able to get regular income to pay the rent and meet other expenses, so he began saving and purchased land for a shop and house. Two rooms were constructed for rent. As he was planning to leave his job as a powerloom operator, he started saving the rent in a long-term bishi [savings and credit association] – Rs600 per month for 24 months. When he left his job in 1993, he had savings of Rs18 000. Until his provision shop stabilizes, he will use this amount for rotation as well as family expenses. [Landlord, Aribhav Nagar, Pandesara, Surat]

Rental housing can reduce the vulnerability both landlords and tenants. This is particularly the case for older and women-headed or managed landlord[8] households as it also provides a source of psychosocial security. It is also important for tenants who are newly married, women headed or elderly.

Mrs S (40) heads a household that in addition to herself includes her mother-in-law (50) and an adopted daughter (6) who is at school. Both women work as domestic help earning Rs500 and Rs300 per month respectively. S's tenant is a woman with two school-going children, who works in a tile-making factory and earns Rs60 per day. Apart from the rental income, which is saved and used to meet expenses during festive seasons, the tenant provides the family with security. Although there have been instances when rent payments have been delayed, Mrs S feels that the tenant will not create problems, which could happen if she lets it out to a 'strong family with a male head'. Mrs S feels that she and her mother-in-law are too weak to handle fights within the settlement. [Landlord, Rajendra Nagar, Koramangala, Bangalore]

Rental-housing markets are influenced by and respond to local conditions

Well-functioning rental markets are those that are articulated with local employment and provide affordable and well-located accommodation. Thus a successful enabling housing policy is one that seeks to ensure the co-existence of all forms of tenure with much greater attention paid to the links between local employment and housing.

In both Bangalore and Surat, the emergence, extent and nature of rental housing markets are locally determined. In the main, they reflect demand resulting from local employment opportunities. Changes in the nature and form of local employment have a 'domino' effect on rental housing markets resulting in either its upgrading to fetch higher rents, peripheral relocation or conversion to ownership.

> It is possible to find accommodation within Yeshwantpur layouts but it will cost nearly Rs1000. Hence within the slum, there is a great demand for houses between Rs300 and Rs400. Finding the advance amount is the main problem in the case of changing residence. Rent increases depend on the owners. My present owner has not increased the rent after a year. Only when he vacates the place she will raise it by Rs50. [Tenant, BK Nagar, Yeshwantpur ward, Bangalore]

Local politics also needs to be given consideration. In both cities, local councillors influence housing policy and local development indirectly. However, it seems that local politics in Bangalore influences access to land and housing for the poor more than it does in Surat. One possible explanation for this is that there are many more lucrative avenues through which economic status and political power can be gained in Surat than Bangalore. Since the main agent of housing provision in Surat – the developer – is involved in renting out accommodation, they are more supportive of their clients doing the same. In Bangalore, local councillors and unelected leaders seem to have more of a say as to whether accommodation, particularly in squatter settlements, could be rented out. This is possibly because they see themselves as patrons of those they have helped to squat and fear that if accommodation were rented out to tenants, they would not have control over this secondary group.

Rental housing markets are more inclusionary than ownership housing markets

Housing markets are both inclusionary and exclusionary. Exclusion occurs along both economic (rents and deposits) and social (religion, caste, regional association, gender and age) lines. However, rental housing markets, due to the temporary nature of the occupation of property, are found to be less exclusionary than ownership housing markets.

Exclusion in Surat is social in nature – kinship networks and ethnic ties determine access to housing, especially ownership.

C Ben, the landlady from Hitendra Nagar, has strong views as to whom she wants as tenants. She prefers 'Kandeshis' – she will never go for the 'seller community' as they are 'very powerful' and there is the possibility that she may lose her property. She says that she prefers tenants who have a permanent income or a 'good' job. She does not prefer tenants who earn daily wages. [Landlady, Hitendra Nagar, Jahingapura ward, Surat]

In Bangalore, the reverse is true. Being a city largely of third-generation migrants, the significance of social networks has been replaced by the capacity to make lump-sum payments. Surat, on the other hand, is a city of first-generation migrants where access to employment and housing is still strongly mediated on the basis of kinship networks and ethnic ties. The downside of this is that landlords are sometimes constrained in how much they are able to charge their 'fellow' tenants. Both cities, however, indicate a tendency to exclude and include along religious lines. As recent events in Surat and tensions in Bangalore have indicated, communal tension built on religious or ethnic cleavages can make the ownership of housing a liability rather than an asset as it provides a fixed target for violence and vandalism.

Of the six rooms [that are rented], newly married Muslim families occupy three. Bachelors who are unskilled construction coolies [workers] and welders share the other three rooms. He says that Muslim families find it difficult to find a place [to rent] across the road because a different regional and religious group dominates the area. He does not have any agreement with his tenants but all of them are connected to the same Masjid [mosque]. [Landlord, Limbayat ward, Surat]

Inclusion and exclusion on the basis of gender assumes different dimensions depending on whether one is a tenant or a landlord, and the way in which the female household is structured – namely, women-managed or women-headed households. In general it is easier for women-managed households and women-headed households with older male working children to gain access to rented accommodation in patriarchal social systems such as those that exist in Bangalore and Surat.

Mrs MM's husband, who was allocated a plot in a resettlement site in Surat, purchased an additional one. He has rented them both to Oryian migrants. His choice of tenants was because Oriyan's paid more rent than others as they find it difficult to secure rented accommodation. A month before the interview, he left her and she is not sure if he will return. She is in a vulnerable position vis-à-vis her tenants and is only consoled by the fact that her two older sons are aged 20 and 15 respectively and could deal with the tenants. Rent receipts are her only form of savings (Rs700 to Rs1000 per month). She is planning to occupy land at the back of the resettlement site and construct units for rent to Oriyan migrants as she finds that they pay good rents. [Landlord, Rasolabad, South-West Zone, Surat]

As noted earlier, gender issues in relation to rental housing assume greater significance in Bangalore than in Surat because the demographic structure of the population of the latter is more biased towards men. Where the relationship involves male landlords and female tenants, it depends on the ability of women to convince male landlords that they can pay the rent. Where women landlords were involved, 'introduction by a mutual contact' seemed to play an important part.

> *For a woman-headed household, recommendations are essential because if the tenant creates a problem, the person who recommended the tenant can be called upon to sort the problem out. [Landlady, Rajendra Nagar, Koramangala, Bangalore]*

Social planners need to be aware of the exclusionary tendency of rental housing markets. They need to encourage producers – individuals and organizations – to cater for tenants excluded from renting.

Rental housing markets are shrouded by insecurity as a result of government policy

Rental housing markets are rendered opaque by fear of government legislation such as property tax and rent control. Rental housing markets are also stifled by oppressive urban policies and norms relating, for example, to plot size and building regulations.

In Bangalore as well as Surat, the burden of 'ad-hoc' and inequitable property tax regimes treats landlords as an undifferentiated category in terms of their absolute and relative poverty. As a result, landlord responses range from labelling tenants as relatives to taking down temporary partitions between rental units when the tax collector calls. Not only does this drive rental housing underground but more importantly it results in poorly serviced units with landlords, for instance, refusing to build kitchens as they are the clearest indicator of multiple occupancy. Added to this is the fear of rent control by landlords, despite the fact that the poor in both cities have seldom used this avenue to seek redress through the due process of law.

Policies relating to intra-city resettlement or rehousing the poor have a major impact on how rental housing markets develop and the resultant impact they have on the livelihoods of the poor. In Surat, an implicit aim underpinning resettlement projects containing sites of 15 square metres is to prevent the construction of rooms for rent. Such attitudes are anti-poor on two counts. First, it is only the better off who benefit as they have the capacity to invest savings in the construction of an upper floor with units for rent. Second, it adversely affects those who depended on a rental income in the past and forces them to sell the allotted plot and relocate. Such displacement of the poor is often by the better off – the latter are presented with opportunities to increase the size of their landed holdings, and consequently the number of units they can build to let. Such 'predatory' forms of landlordism are of concern not only because they provide the opportunity for local monopolies to develop, but also because they increase inequalities.

In short, such anti-poor policies (which are the result of myopic perceptions that equate renting with exploitation) actually provide fertile ground for corruption and an increase in clientelist opportunities for local councillors and other power brokers.

ISSUES FOR SOCIAL PLANNERS AND POLICY MAKERS

Although landlords may not always treat tenants equitably for the reasons noted, it is clear that rental housing markets are important for landlords and tenants. It is impossible to imagine the state being able to successfully 'clone' the range of options and opportunities provided by private landlords. Thus, a key concern for policy-makers and planners is to identify ways in which the state can enhance the operation of rental markets without destroying the core of its success – namely, the supply of accommodation at various locations, of varying quality and levels of services, and at varying rents. A central plank of any enabling housing strategy should be greater openness and debate about the role and significance of tenure diversity. There is an urgent need to move from a preoccupation with ownership-based rights to the institutionalization of locally responsive mechanisms to ensure security of tenure. This means treating landlords and tenants equitably, with each being made aware of their respective rights and responsibilities.

The differential basis through which factors of production are accessed needs closer scrutiny. The research findings indicate that in Surat, kinship and ethnic ties are more influential, whereas in Bangalore a demonstration of economic ability predominates. One policy implication of this, for example, is the need to rethink the availability of and access to housing finance. What works in Bangalore will not work in Surat. Similarly, in relation to land, the supply mechanisms in Surat are very different from those in Bangalore. Thus, for example, greater cooperation between land developers and municipal authorities may be desirable in Surat, whereas in Bangalore, the role of the Bangalore Metropolitan Development Authority and its planning procedures need to be re-examined.

India's National Housing Policy, adopted in 1994, provides only a broad framework within which state governments may act. This is because the Indian Constitution stipulates that housing is a state subject and therefore it is the responsibility of individual states to formulate their own housing policies. The conundrum is in linking the national level to the state level, and more importantly the state level to the local level. A rental housing policy that does not contain the flexibility to be moulded by intra-city differentials is not likely to respond to the priorities of either landlords or tenants. Emphasis is often placed on local government and local governance in managing urban change. However, not only do municipal administrations have little influence on policy formulation, but also more importantly they have little say in why a particular policy (or parts of it) is not suitable to local realities. The anticipation that the 1993 Nagar Palika Act[9] will change the balance of state–local decision-making[10] is unlikely to happen unless there is greater devolution of financial and policy-making powers.

With housing policy in India being a state subject, little can be achieved if dialogue between researchers, international development agencies (both bilateral and multilateral) and governments remain at the national level. This might explain why support for rental housing in policy and practice still proves elusive. Development agencies such as the UK government's Department for International Development (DFID) and the World Bank can influence changes in policy and practice through their pro-poor agendas. UNCHS, on the other hand, has the potential to create awareness, especially through the instruments of its dual campaigns on 'housing rights' and 'governance'. However, both avenues must be locally grounded and dialogue established with appropriate levels of government if the role of rental housing as 'service provision' for tenants and a 'livelihood response' for landlords is to be transformed from rhetoric to reality.

CHAPTER NINE

Urban housing and livelihoods: comparative case examples from Kenya and India

Michael Majale

INTRODUCTION

The world is urbanizing at a very rapid pace – but it is in the South that urbanization processes are intensifying at a really disconcerting rate.[1] Three-quarters of global population increase is currently occurring in the urban South, causing hypergrowth in cities that are incapable of accommodating this unprecedented upsurge. Contemporary rural–urban transformation and urban growth in Asia and Africa, in particular, are taking place in a context of far higher absolute population growth, far lower income levels and with much less institutional capacity than was the case earlier in the North.

There is also an urbanization of poverty in the South, manifested most conspicuously in mushrooming and expanding slums and informal settlements characterized by a lack of basic urban services (water supply, sanitation, drainage, solid waste disposal, and roads and footpaths) and deplorable overcrowded housing conditions. In many cities, more than half the population live and work in these unhygienic, hazardous environments where they face multiple threats to their health, well-being and security. Not only are they vulnerable to disease, crime and natural disasters, but they are also largely disenfranchised. Moreover, most countries are unable to provide sufficient job opportunities for the rapidly growing number of new entrants to the urban labour market each year. A substantial proportion of able and enterprising women and men living and working in informal settlements are thus unemployed or underemployed in the informal sector, earning low incomes for long hours of work. And a majority are unable to afford the cost of adequate shelter.[2]

It is in light of the above that the Integrated Urban Housing Development in Kenya and India project (IUHP) was formulated. The purpose of the IUHP was 'to identify and promote a sustainable shelter-delivery strategy for the urban poor to be adopted by national and local government in Kenya and India'. The project was seen as a substantive step towards progressive realization of the overall project goal – 'to increase the access of low-income households and the poor to adequate, safe and secure shelter' – through integrated participatory and partnership-oriented housing development and income-generation initiatives. Funded under the Department for International Development's Engineering Knowledge and Research Programme (DFID–KaR) and coordinated by Intermediate Technology Development Group–United Kingdom (ITDG–UK), the project started in April 1999 and ended in September 2003. In addition to undertaking some of the worldwide research and analysis, ITDG–UK also supported the partners who conducted the research activities in Nakuru (Kenya) and Alwar (India), two secondary towns of similar size (250 000–350 000 inhabitants). Project activities in Kenya were implemented by Intermediate Technology Development Group–Eastern Africa (ITDG–EA), while the Society for Development Studies (SDS) was subcontracted to carry out the work in India.

The project aimed to research and act at the local level to inform and influence the wider debate among policy-makers, public sector bodies, donor agencies and non-government organizations (NGOs). In addition to the project experience and knowledge gained through implementation of project activities on the ground, reviews of the literature and practice contributed to a better understanding of the differences between single-sector, multisectoral and integrated development interventions linking micro- and small enterprise (MSE) development with improved housing for urban poor dwellers.

This chapter reviews project working papers and the findings of the research, as well as the findings of an evaluation of the project conducted in Kenya and India between 20 May and 16 June 2003. The presentations and deliberations of an end-of-project international workshop held in March 2003 are also reviewed. On the basis of the foregoing, and some of the current thinking on the same, the author seeks to establish if a case can be made for promoting an integrated approach to urban housing development as a sustainable shelter-delivery strategy for the urban poor in Kenya and India, and the South in general.

ITDG'S INTEGRATED APPROACH TO URBAN HOUSING DEVELOPMENT

The evolution of ITDG's integrated approach to urban housing development can be traced back to the experience gained through working with a housing cooperative in Chitungwiza Municipality in Zimbabwe in the 1990s.

Integrated Urban Development Project (IUDP)

Formed in 1988 by employees of the textiles factory from which it got its name, Cone Textiles Housing Co-operative (CTHC) first approached ITDG–Southern Africa (ITDG–SA) in 1989 for assistance to develop housing for its members. ITDG-SA subsequently worked with CTHC, strengthening its management capacity and lobbying for land for members to build their houses on, until 1995 when the factory closed down and 2000 workers were made redundant.

Recognizing that the immediate problem facing CTHC members was loss of incomes and not housing, employment creation and income generation were introduced alongside the housing development initiatives in 1997 under the Integrated Urban Development Project (IUDP). The IUDP sought to empower CTHC members to fulfil their aspirations through training and demonstration on how to use and manage appropriate technologies for housing and MSE development. The other principal project partners alongside CTHC and ITDG–SA were Chitungwiza Town Council and Civic Forum on Housing (CFH). The partnership was forged around the shared objectives of providing adequate housing and services for CTHC members by creating jobs and income, and promoting good urban governance (ITDG–SA, undated). The 'Action and Response Model' used in the IUDP is shown in Figure 9.1.

Integrated Urban Housing Development in Kenya and India Project (IUHP)

The underlying assumption in the Integrated Urban Housing Development in Kenya and India project (IUHP) was thus that an integrated approach to urban housing development would work better than a sectoral approach 'to increase the access of low-income households and the poor to adequate, safe and secure shelter' – the overall goal of the project. More specifically, the purpose of the IUHP was to 'to identify and promote a sustainable shelter-delivery strategy for the urban poor to be adopted by national and local government in Kenya and India'.

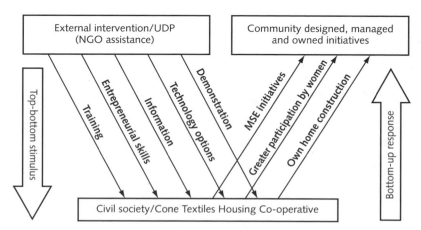

Figure 9.1   IUDP Action – Response Model
Source: ITDG–SA (nd)

Urbanization trends and urban poverty in Kenya and India

The share of urban population in Kenya has grown from 5.1 per cent in 1948 to 20.9 per cent at the last official census conducted in 1997. The poverty line is set at KSh1490 (US$19.60) per capita a month in urban areas, and 52 per cent of the total population is estimated to be living on less than a dollar a day (Gardner, 2003). Poor urban dwellers face manifold problems, among them unemployment, inadequate access to basic infrastructure and services, and inappropriate policy and regulatory frameworks governing land and housing supply resulting in insecure tenure and high cost of conventional building materials and housing. These problems have exacerbated the vulnerability of urban dwellers, a rapidly growing number of whom are living in poverty in health- and life-threatening conditions in overcrowded slums and informal settlements.

In India, 10.84 per cent of the population lived in urban centres in 1901, and the last census in 2001 puts this figure at 28.0 per cent. The current unofficial estimate is 32.0 per cent. Although the number of people living in poverty in urban areas has reportedly decreased by 12 per cent (Lall, 2002, undated), an estimated 24 per cent of the urban population, or about 67 million people, live below the poverty line (Gardner, 2003). Urban poverty is manifested in widespread inadequate housing, characterized by intermittent water supply from communal public taps, open drainage and sewage systems, indiscriminate defecation, high density/minimal per capita living space, poorly ventilated combined living/sleeping and cooking areas, and limited access to open spaces. A positive aspect of the housing situation of the urban poor in India though is secure title inherited from forebears (Lall and Lall, 2003).

Application of the sustainable livelihoods approach in the IUHP

The IUHP essentially set out to investigate whether improvements to shelter and related services can have a long-term pro-poor impact within the broader development agenda. However, recognizing that access to adequate shelter does not in itself reduce poverty, the project also investigated innovative initiatives that integrated improvements in housing conditions with enhanced income generation. The experience of the IUDP and other participatory action research projects conducted by ITDG had revealed the complexity and multidimensionality of urban poverty, and shown that single-sector interventions cannot sustainably improve the shelter conditions of urban poor households. Lessons learned included that improving shelter (physical capital) through the use of alternative building materials in urban areas involves building human capital through skills upgrading, strengthening community-based groups (social capital) and facilitating access to credit (financial capital), as well as reviewing regulatory frameworks.

The IUHP thus used DFID's Sustainable Livelihoods Framework (SLF) as a conceptual and analytical framework to test whether integrated interventions in the shelter and MSE sectors could have a long-term pro-poor impact on the livelihoods and overall quality of life of poor people living and working in informal settlements within the broader urban development agenda. The principal components of DFID's SLF are shown diagrammatically in Figure 9.2.

A livelihood *comprises the capabilities, assets (stores, resources, claims and access) and activities required for a means of living: a livelihood is* sustainable *which can cope with and recover from stress and shocks, maintain or enhance its capabilities and assets, and provide sustainable livelihood opportunities for the next generation; and which contributes net benefits to other livelihoods at the local and global levels and in the long and short term (Chambers and Conway, 1992: 7–8).*

Application of the SLF was intended to enhance understanding of the complex, multidimensional realities of people living in poverty in the urban South.[3] Schematic models of sustainable livelihoods (SL) approaches recognize that households develop their livelihoods on the basis of the assets to which they have access (Table 9.1) within a broader socio-economic and physical context (i.e. vulnerability context). Livelihood strategies are influenced by transforming structures and processes (i.e. the so-called PIPs box – policy, institutions and processes box), which in turn have a bearing on livelihood outcomes (i.e. the achievements or outputs of livelihood strategies). The main point of the asset pentagon in the SLF, as Carney (1998:7) underlines, is to compel users to 'think holistically rather than sectorally about the basis of livelihoods'.[4]

Table 9.1 Capital assets

Natural capital	The natural resource stocks from which resource flows useful for livelihoods are derived, e.g. land, water, biodiversity, environmental resources
Social capital	The social resources (relationships of trust, membership of groups, networks, access to wider institutions) upon which people draw in pursuit of livelihoods
Human capital	The knowledge, skills, ability to labour, information and good health important to the ability to pursue different livelihoods
Physical capital	The basic infrastructure (water, sanitation, energy, transport, communications), housing and the means and equipment of production
Financial capital	The financial resources which are available to people (savings, credit, regular remittances or pensions) and which provide them with different livelihood options

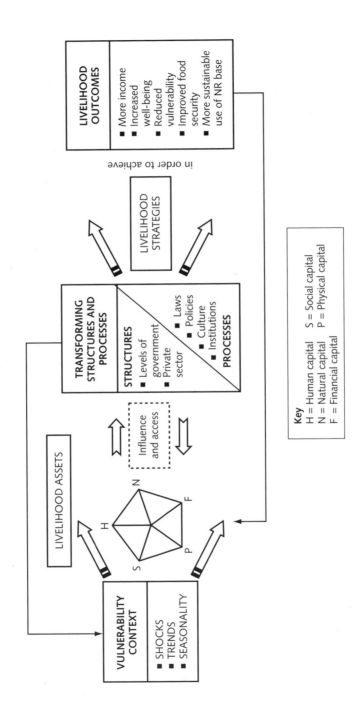

Figure 9.2 DFID's Sustainable Livelihoods Framework
Source: Ashley and Carney, 1999, p. 47

The integrated approach adopted in Kenya

Nakuru, the fourth largest town in Kenya, with a population of 289 988, has seen a rapid decline in its economy, a deterioration of urban services and a diminishing of employment opportunities – and it is the poor who have been most affected. The majority cannot afford to build or rent conventional housing because of its high cost and their low incomes. This has led to the uncontrolled development and expansion of informal settlements. Lowering the cost of building materials and construction and promoting income-generating activities (IGAs) through appropriate technological interventions were thus fundamental elements of the IUHP in Kenya. Recognizing the need to fully engage and build the capacities of poor communities so that they can effectively participate in housing and infrastructure development as well as IGAs, a process-oriented participatory approach that fostered partnerships among key stakeholders was adopted. A key project partner was the Municipal Council of Nakuru (MCN).[5] Following intense lobbying and advocacy by ITDG–EA, the Council designated seven informal settlements within its jurisdiction 'low-income settlements'. This enabled the application of the then recently promulgated revised building by-laws, popularly known as 'Code '95', in the settlements and more specifically permitted the use of alternative building materials.[6] The project worked with community-based organizations (CBOs) in three of the settlements: Bondeni, Kwa Rhonda and Lakeview.

In Nakuru, participatory appraisals and assessments were first conducted to determine the needs and aspirations of the target communities. The establishment of their shelter priorities was followed by gender-sensitive participatory design of house plans that conformed to Code '95. Community-based artisans were trained in the production, application and utilization of appropriate building materials and technologies to facilitate construction of affordable housing based on these designs. Potentials for increased income for small-scale landlords through better-quality rental accommodation, and for artisans through the establishment of small-scale material production units, were thus created. Efforts were thereafter concentrated on developing MSEs to increase the income-earning capacity of CBOs, especially women's groups. Skills and business training, and knowledge sharing and information exchange were other important project elements.[7] The conceptual model of the approach adopted by ITDG–EA in implementing the IUHP in Nakuru is shown in Figure 9.3.

The integrated approach adopted in India

A heritage town with a population of 260 000, Alwar has traditionally been the home of artisan communities engaged mostly in stone carving, weaving, pottery and leather embroidery. In earlier times, the communities

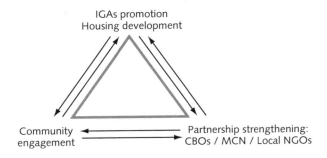

Figure 9.3   ITDG–EA Integrated Approach

prospered under a system of royal patronage. However, they became vulnerable to market mechanisms when it ended, and were unable to develop effective coping strategies to prevent them falling into poverty. Urban poverty reduction thus became a priority for the district administration, which entered into a partnership with SDS to support the IUHP in anticipation of a replicable housing development model as an outcome. Project activities in Alwar were implemented in old settlements characterized by inadequate basic services and rapidly deteriorating shelter conditions.

However, in the participatory surveys undertaken in the two project locations in Alwar to identify the problems, opportunities, goals and priorities of the residents, shelter upgrading was accorded a low ranking. On the basis of these results, the findings of an evaluation of a public sector low-income housing project in Alwar and SDS's long-standing experience, the initial emphasis in Alwar was consequently on IGAs with potential for substantial impact on the incomes of the project beneficiaries. Shelter improvement was expected to follow thereafter. This approach took full account of the need to promote home-based enterprises (HBEs) and MSE development, social development and environmental improvement in realizing the overall goal of the project. The SDS conceptual model is shown in Figure 9.4.

Key outputs of the IUHP

The goal of the IUHP was to 'to increase the access of low-income households and the poor to adequate, safe and secure shelter'. However, in adopting an SL approach, the project also sought to increase the overall robustness of households' asset portfolios in order to strengthen livelihood strategies and reduce vulnerability, assist in creating pro-poor outcomes, and increase positive linkages between the local authority and poor communities. The project further sought to increase the range of

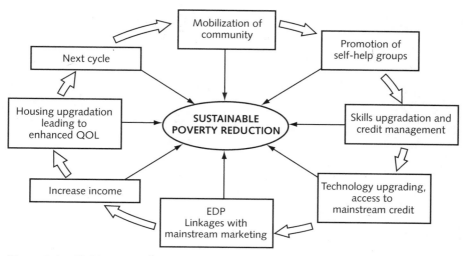

Figure 9.4   SDS Integrated Approach

livelihood options available to poor households and to build the capacity of community-based groups through networking and strengthening their knowledge and information systems.[8] In addition, the IUHP addressed the existing policy and regulatory frameworks for housing development in the two countries.

In trying to 'to identify and promote a sustainable shelter-delivery strategy for the urban poor to be adopted by national and local government in Kenya and India' (the project purpose), the IUHP tested whether poor people will invest in shelter development if their incomes increase. It was assumed that the strategy would be based on an integrated approach to urban housing development. The IUHP thus aimed to raise poor people's incomes (financial capital) and thereby increase their access to adequate shelter (physical capital) through group-based IGAs (strengthening social capital while increasing financial capital), skills upgrading and training (improving human capital), and access to productive assets, e.g. equipment/machines for MSEs (physical capital). Improved housing and sanitation conditions (physical capital) would have not only health benefits (human capital) but also impact positively on the environment (natural capital). But to achieve the desired livelihood outcomes the project had to address the policy and regulatory frameworks as well as existing institutions (at the community, local and national levels) and transforming structures and processes (the PIPs box). This approach is presented diagrammatically in Figure 9.5. The achievements of the project and outputs in each country are summarized below and in Table 9.2.

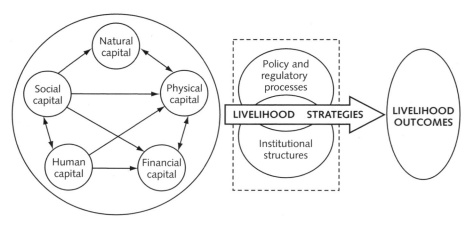

Figure 9.5   Sustainable Livelihoods Framework applied to the IUHP

Achievements of the IUHP in Nakuru, Kenya

The overall achievements of the IUHP in Nakuru can be summarized as follows.[9]

- *Group formation (social capital)*: 27 savings groups[10] and 16 IGA groups (with a total of between 200 and 300 members) have been established, and six of the IGA groups are actively operating. An apex body, the Nakuru Affordable Housing and Environmental Co-operative (NAHECO), formed to coordinate CBOs in the project settlements, is facilitating their developmental activities, networking, and also savings and access to credit. NAHECO has over 450 members, more than 50 per cent of whom are women.
- *Income generation (human/social/financial capital)*: technical training was imparted to 43 persons (28 women and 15 men) while 103 (44 women and 59 men) received business training. These trained beneficiaries have in turn trained others. MSE production machines granted to IGA groups through NAHECO are being used, and exposure visits were organized for IGA groups. A sample of 20 individuals in February 2003 showed that 68 per cent had an average increase in monthly income of 64 per cent; 55 per cent had taken on more employees; 75 per cent estimated that business volume had increased; and 85 per cent were maintaining savings.
- *Savings and credit (financial capital)*: NAHECO has been registered as a savings and credit organization (SACCO) and links for 27 savings groups made to finance institutions. The NAHECO revolving fund has disbursed 12 business loans and seven housing loans. And 20 loans

Table 9.2   Summary of project outputs

Proposed output	Actual output (May/June 2003)
Two integrated projects established and tested and four sectoral projects tested	Projects established in Alwar and Nakuru Working papers completed to study impacts of sectoral projects
100 persons in Kenya and 200 in India trained in marketable skills	143 persons in Kenya and 25 persons trained in India. Skills have increased income
3–5 viable firms established in Kenya, each employing an average of 10 trained people	6 IGA groups are operational with more than 10 members in each group (not quantified), 68% report increased incomes
200 people employed in profitable micro-enterprises or group enterprises in India	299 people engaged in micro-enterprises and show an overall increase in income
100 houses with access to water and sanitation built and occupied by project participants in Kenya	180 dwelling units built (51 projects), 33 with water and sanitation built by project-trained artisans for plot-owners, occupied by tenants
In India, 200 households assisted in building or improving shelters with access to economic and habitat services	Households assisted to improve home-based production, hygiene awareness. 42 households have toilets (17 individual, 1 4-latrine block for 25 households); 30 households have individual water connections; 30 households have gas connections
Housing strategy document	Working papers have explored integrated, multi-sectoral and single sector approaches to shelter delivery. Interim draft produced
Project results published and disseminated	Local dissemination of project activities and lessons One international workshop
Establishment of two Local Urban Observatories (additional output)	Two LUOs in preparation

Source: Gardner, 2003.

have been obtained from finance institutions independent of project support.

■ *Shelter (physical capital)*: five housing cooperatives have been formed, and one group of tenants has been able to purchase land on which they are planning to develop housing. Six individuals have obtained loans from NAHECO revolving fund, and two housing coop-eratives have secured loans from the National Co-operative Housing Union (NACHU). More affordable building materials and technolo-gies have been effectively demonstrated, and around 185 dwelling units (including 151 single rooms) have been constructed. Over 80 toilets have also been built, and hygiene awareness training con-ducted. Water and sanitation appraisals were carried out in collabora-tion with MCN, and three community-based water and sanitation committees established.

In addition, partnerships have been established with MCN and other agencies.

Achievements of the IUHP in Alwar, India

The achievements in Alwar can be summarized as follows.

- *Group formation (social capital)*: 23 groups (with a total of 299 mem-bers, 80 per cent of whom are women) have been formed. These include four weavers/embroidery groups and two potters groups in six settlements. Groups are cooperating in production and marketing activities.
- *Income generation (financial capital)*: significant improvements in productivity and marketability have been achieved. Weavers and embroiderers have reported increases in incomes from Rs30 (US$0.66) a day to Rs60–70 (US$1.32–1.54). Overall, income from project activities is reported to have increased by between 108 per cent and 212 per cent among the settlements to a maximum Rs2500 (US$54.91) per household per month.
- *Savings and credit (financial capital)*: groups in three settlements are saving Rs100 (US$2.20) each month, and in two settlements they are saving Rs50 (US$1.10) every month. There is group cooperation to build savings and agree individual loans: ten group bank loans have been acquired by four groups, one of which is for production; and 80 per cent of group members now have individual bank accounts for personal savings.
- *Shelter and sanitation (physical capital)*: with financial assistance from SDS/IUHP, a total of 17 individual toilets have been built in four settlements; one communal toilet block and one communal standpipe in one settlement; and 30 individual water connections installed in three settlements. Maintenance has been carried out on some houses, and 30 houses have been connected to a more environmentally friendly gas supply.

A key output of the IUHP was the establishment of a Local Urban Observa-tory (LUO) in both Alwar and Nakuru. Part of the Global Urban Observatory (GUO), established to monitor the implementation of the Habitat Agenda,

LUOs are a focal point for urban policy development and planning where collaboration among policy-makers, technical experts and partner groups is fostered.[11]

WHAT HAS BEEN LEARNED?

A number of lessons were learned through implementing the IUHP – indeed, SL principles underscore the importance of 'learning through implementation' (George, undated: 8). These were presented and deliberated upon at the end-of-project workshop.[12]

Meaning of integration

An integrated approach, as adopted in the IUHP, means taking into consideration physical, financial, human and social assets. The World Bank's Comprehensive Development Framework (CDF) similarly takes a holistic approach to development, seeking a better balance in policy-making by highlighting the interdependence of all elements of development – social, structural, human, governance, environmental, economic and financial. Partnerships between governments, donors, civil society, the private sector and other development actors are also underscored (Blake, undated).

From project experience, it is clear that integration should happen at both the level of activities and the level of partners (i.e. between actors at all levels, from local to national). However, whether integration could happen only at the settlement or neighbourhood level or whether it should extend to the town or city level is debatable. Indeed, in a study of NGOs working in urban settings, the difficulty they had in reconciling their concern for household and community poverty issues with city wide issues was evident (Sahley and Pratt, 2003).

With the increasing tendency for the poorest to be excluded from common development activities, integration should perhaps first be about social inclusion. The tenure status of many urban poor dwellers has precluded their involvement in urban governance, but changes in ethos and policy approaches have meant that residents in informal settlements are being increasingly integrated into systems of political decision-making (Meikle et al., 2001). The CDF alike seeks to give the poorest of the poor more of a voice in formulating their countries' development policies (Blake, undated), as does the poverty reduction strategy paper (PRSP) process. And while many countries are adopting poverty-reduction strategies, some cities are adopting innovative approaches for social inclusion through the improvement of living conditions of the urban poor (UN-HABITAT, 2002a).

All people need housing and all people need livelihoods: the two are interlinked, but more so for some than others. For people such as landlords, housing is their livelihood, but for others such as home-based entrepreneurs, housing is where they pursue their livelihood. However, the project found, and the end-of-project workshop agreed, that the relationship between income generation and the upgrading of shelter and related services is not as simple or straightforward as was originally assumed. Moreover, housing development from savings alone takes a very long time, and it may be unrealistic to expect to significantly improve access to shelter and infrastructure by the poor within a short time frame such as a four-year project cycle. Indeed, Majale (2003: 16) makes the point that '. . . it takes a middle-income family in the North several years to own a house through buying with a mortgage. [And] for a great many middle-income households in most cities and secondary towns in the South, home ownership will always remain out of reach.'

It may be also be necessary to abandon the concept of a self-contained house on its own plot if most people can afford no more than a single room, as is the case in cities and towns in Kenya. Multiform dwelling unit options should therefore be offered in an integrated approach to urban housing development targeted at the poor.

Practicalities

The IUHP underscored the importance of MSEs in poor people's lives, as others (Vanderschueren et al., 1996, cited in Albu and Scott, 2001: 5) have done:

> *Manufacturing and processing MSEs play an increasingly significant role in poor people's lives, and are one of the keys to lifting people out of poverty. Some have even described them as the backbone on which the urban economy (especially in secondary towns) survives in most countries in the South.*

However, before engaging community-based groups in particular MSEs, an analysis of the market and specific subsectors is needed to identify viable business opportunities.[13] Such an analysis may take considerable time, but as Albu and Scott (2001: 6) affirm: 'More than ever before, an effective analysis of market structures and market dynamics is essential to understanding the livelihood strategies and options of poor people who work in MSEs.'

Access to credit is crucial to the successful development of both MSEs and housing, as are training and skills upgrading. However, the emphasis should be not so much on 'technical know-how', but rather on 'practical how-to-do'.

Partnerships

Partnerships involving a range of stakeholders are vital to the effectuation of an integrated approach.[14] As Pieterse (undated) affirms, integrated development is only possible if there is a strong presence of multiple development institutions within poor communities and in civil society more broadly, to support and empower grassroots organizations and empowerment processes. A study of urban NGOs similarly found that a key factor of success appeared to be clarity of strategy over time and cognizance of the need to develop external relationships across a multiplicity of other actors. But, as was learned in implementing the project: 'Local partnerships challenge conventional ways of doing business, demanding the definition of new roles and responsibilities, new management techniques and capacities, and moreover a change of attitudes' (Materu et al., 2000: 6).

Partners need to have a common development vision; and effective partnerships can ensure that resources are maximized. The way partnerships work was summed up by the workshop as:

- vision: cognizance of the political system
- mission: a particular role being played by each partner (i.e. working with and building capacity of individual actors)
- ambition: empowerment of the poor.

Role of NGOs and authorities

The IUHP confirmed the important role that NGOs have to play in mobilizing communities, building capacity, forging partnerships, etc.[15] However, donor funding is tending to increasingly go to governments, which in turn are decentralizing some responsibilities and resources to local authorities.[16] Moreover, the profile and importance of cities and local authorities for sustainable development has been raised by the emergence of subsidiarity (UN-HABITAT, 2002b). In this regard, the World Bank's renewed strategy for urban and local government assistance similarly 'has achieved commitment . . . to work together in new ways in the urban arena and with newly energized local governments' (World Bank, 1999a). The comparative advantage of local governments in fostering democratic governance, and in designing, financing, managing, supervising and monitoring local development measures and initiatives aimed at reducing poverty is also emphasized by UNCDF[17] (Bonfiglioli, 2003). This could imply that, in future, local authorities may have to play an increased role in integrated development while that of NGOs decreases.

NGOs, along with CBOs and other civil society organizations, can nevertheless play a vital role in city governance in lobbying city government on behalf of the poor (Devas, 2002). Both city/municipal and central government need to be supportive of the integrated approach for it to work, but how best to engage the authorities may be open to question. The municipal authorities in both Nakuru and Alwar were supportive of the IUHP. However, as Bonfiglioli (2003:51) emphasizes, political will and commitment have to be based on a comprehensive understanding of the causal factors of poverty and translated into the development of 'integrated organizational structures that are empowered, through institutional capacity strengthening, to prepare for, and respond promptly and positively to the causes and effects of poverty.'

Community mobilization

A strong and viable civil society can bring real and sustainable benefits. This may explain why community projects in Latin America appear to be more successful than others elsewhere in the world.

Community organization is essential if the urban poor are to participate effectively in integrated development. The strengthening of communities' capacities to solve their own problems is one of the fundamentals of sustainable development. Moreover, strong CBOs can be effective and productive partners to NGOs, as found in implementing the IUHP as well as in the survey of urban NGOs reported by Sahley and Pratt (2003). In the Peruvian case presented at the end-of-project workshop, community mobilization came first, followed by networking and advocacy. Thereafter, a loosely integrated, but quite effective, project developed. The IUHP, on the other hand, started as a project that subsequently mobilized communities.

Lobbying and advocacy

The end-of-project workshop agreed that integrated projects should adopt a rights-based approach, e.g. to lobby for improved access to land, housing and services.[18] SL approaches and rights-based approaches are, in fact, complementary perspectives that seek to achieve many of the same goals (e.g. empowerment of the most vulnerable and strengthened capacity of the poor to achieve secure livelihoods). Most recent work, according to Toner and Howlett (2001: 9), suggests a fusion between the idea of rights and an SL approach to produce a 'livelihood rights approach'.

Integrated projects require strong policy and advocacy components – at local, national and global levels. In this respect, ITDG's policy advocacy efforts at all these levels have yielded unequivocal results, ranging from the promulgation of Code '95 and its adoption in informal settlements in Nakuru Municipality at the local level, to the successful book launch of *Double Standards, Single Purpose: Reforming Housing Regulations to Reduce Poverty* (Yahya et al., 2001) at the 25th meeting of the United Nations General Assembly in New York in 2001.

CONCLUSION

On the assumption that an integrated approach to urban housing development could be 'a sustainable shelter delivery strategy for the urban poor to be adopted by national and local government in Kenya and India', the IUHP worked with two main stakeholder groups: CBOs/MSE groups and plot-owners/landlords. Testing of the hypothesis of increased income leading to sustainable housing investment can therefore be said to have been in two parallel rather than integrated streams, i.e. MSE groups increasing incomes and plot-owners investing in appropriate building materials and technologies to improve their houses and rental accommodation. It is too early to ascertain whether increased incomes among the former group leads to investment in housing. However, the latter group have benefited by being able to improve their houses and, in many cases, charge higher rents, as have tenants who can afford the improved housing. But some renters will no doubt have been dislocated as a result of the increased cost of housing.

Still, implementation of the IUHP has provided varied opportunities to explore the inter-linkages between income and housing; the integration of processes and tools in project design and implementation; and the potentials of urban poor communities and municipal authorities in appropriate housing development for the urban poor. Using DFID's SLF provided a comprehensive understanding of the implications of project interventions which may not otherwise have been readily recognized.

The ability of the IUHP to mobilize and effectively employ the social capital of poor communities will itself help in sustaining community-led initiatives to improve access to adequate shelter. The opening up of channels for the community to work with other partners, in particular the local authority, also lays a firm foundation for sustainable urban housing development initiatives that use an integrated approach. This same social capital and the partnerships moreover have potential application in replication and upscaling.

The end-of-project evaluation (Gardner, 2003: 17) concluded that the IUHP has, in total:

> achieved a great deal in a short time. Working in two very different environments significant positive impacts have been made on the livelihoods of around 600 households, perhaps up to 4000 people.

The overall conclusion of the research teams and end-of-project workshop was that an integrated approach to urban housing development most certainly has significant potential – but it takes time for results to become evident.

CHAPTER TEN

Housing policy and economic reform: a comparative case of Argentina and Mexico

Cecilia Zanetta

INTRODUCTION

Like most countries in the region, Argentina and Mexico have undertaken economic liberalization reform programmes following the prescriptions of the so-called 'Washington Consensus.' As part of its Convertibility Plan, Argentine President Carlos S. Menem (1989–99) implemented a drastic set of reforms aimed at bringing inflation under control, reducing the role of the state in the economy, decreasing fiscal deficits and liberalizing the economy. In the case of Mexico, President Miguel de la Madrid (1982–8) took the first timid steps toward economic reform in the aftermath of the 1982 debt crisis. The reform process gained added momentum under his successor, Carlos Salinas de Gortiari (1988–94), who brought inflation under control, implemented an ambitious privatization programme and negotiated Mexico's entry into the North American Free Trade Agreement (NAFTA) between the US and Canada in 1994. The reforms continued under Ernesto Zedillo (1994–2000), who, after overcoming a serious financial crisis in December 1994, continued – and even deepened – the structural reforms initiated under the two previous administrations.

This chapter examines the housing policies implemented in Argentina and Mexico during the 1980s and 1990s to gain insights into the determinants of national sector policies in the context of economic reform programmes. Specifically, the housing policies implemented in these two countries are examined using two alternative criteria: technical soundness and political expediency. The technical assessment renders rather grim results, as we find that housing policies exhibited little rationality and that many of the lessons learned over three decades of sector work went largely ignored in both countries. Alternatively, an analysis of a more political nature provides a better understanding of the factors determining the housing policies implemented in Argentina and Mexico during the past two decades, showing how they have served to build the political support needed to sustain the economic reform programmes.

The chapter is organized in four sections. First, simulating a technocratic approach to policy-making, a set of broad policy guidelines is derived based on the characteristics of the housing deficits in each country and widely accepted technical principles. Second, the housing policies that were actually implemented in Argentina and Mexico during the 1980s and 1990s are contrasted against such technical policy guidelines, revealing that technical rationality was not the overarching criterion determining housing policies in these two countries. Third, an analysis of a more political nature, including political costs, bargaining and coalition building, is used to examine Argentina's and Mexico's housing policies, which explains more clearly the determinants of policy-making in the housing sector in the framework of economic reforms. The final section presents the main conclusions.

EXAMINING THE STRUCTURE OF HOUSING DEFICITS: A TECHNOCRATIC APPROACH TO POLICY-MAKING

The comparison of housing deficits in Argentina and Mexico reveals both significant differences and striking similarities. While housing needs are undoubtedly more pressing in Mexico due to faster population growth and an ongoing process of urbanization, housing deficits are significant in both countries, particularly among the poor. In both countries, the majority of the deficit can be addressed by improving and expanding the existing stock as opposed to building new, finished housing. Given the limited access to housing through formal channels, informal housing is becoming an increasingly vital force in the production of housing for lower-income sectors of the population.

Housing deficits in Argentina

A large proportion of Argentina's population faces serious housing deficiencies (see Table 10.1). It is estimated that over 3 million households – equivalent to 30 per cent of all Argentine families – have unsatisfied housing needs (Martínez de Jiménez, 2002). Almost 70 per cent of the deficit – the so-called 'relative deficit' – can be addressed by repairing, upgrading or expanding the existing stock. Alternatively, addressing the remaining 30 per cent of the deficit – the so-called 'absolute deficit' – would require the construction of additional housing to replace precarious structures and the relocation of households currently sharing their housing units with other households or those located in areas that are flood-prone or subject to endemic diseases (e.g. '*mal de Chagas*') (Ministerio de Economía, 2000; IADB, 2001).

Not surprisingly, the housing deficit is concentrated heavily among the poor. Low and low-middle income households accounted for 85 per cent of the overall deficit in 1991 – 39 per cent and 46 per cent, respectively (Martínez de Jiménez, 2002). With more than half the population living in poverty in the aftermath of the 2001–2 economic crisis, an even higher proportion of the housing deficit is expected to be currently concentrated among the poor.

Table 10.1 Housing indicators in Argentina and Mexico

	Argentina	Mexico
Housing deficit		
Overall housing deficit	30%	19.2% *
Relative deficit (Improvements and expansion)	70%	53.8%
Absolute deficit (New construction)	30%	46.2%
Housing deficits and poverty		
Housing deficit among the poor	85% of the overall deficit is concentrated among low- and low-middle income households	Over 40% of the demand for new homes and improvements is from households earning less than three minimum wages
Access to services	High disparities in coverage and level of service as a function of income and geographic location	High disparities in coverage and level of service as a function of income and geographic location
Informal housing		
% of new housing produced by informal sector	40%	53%
Irregular housing as % of existing stock	Relatively less significant Approximately 10% of population in Buenos Aires Metropolitan Area lives in irregular settlements	Very significant Approximately 40% of population in Mexico City lives in irregular settlements
Illegal tenure	17.9%	60%
Types of housing tenure		
Rental housing	13%	12.8%
Homeownership	65%	70%
Access to basic services		
Access to improved water source	79%	86%
Sewerage connection (network or septic tank)	72%	75%
Housing demand		
Total population growth rate	1.1% per year	1.8% per year
Urban population growth rate	1.2% per year	2.3% per year
New urban residents	350 000 per year	1.5 million per year

* It can be significantly higher according to non-official estimates.
Sources: Various sources as indicated in the text.

While there is little information on Argentina's informal housing stock, it is estimated that less than 10 per cent of the population in the Buenos Aires metropolitan area lives in irregular settlements, a proportion considerably smaller than in other Latin American cities (ECLAC, 2000). However, there is evidence of a substantial increase in illegal settlements during the past decade due to the widespread impoverishment of the population and the lack of effective public programmes. According to some estimates, up to 40 per cent of all new housing produced in 1999 was built informally (IADB, 2001).

Homeownership is the prevailing way of accessing to housing, with approximately 65 percent of all households being homeowners (Ministerio de Economía, 2000). Not all homeowners, however, hold legal tenure of their homes. It is estimated that approximately 1.7 million households – almost 18 per cent of all Argentine families – do not have legal tenure of their properties (IADB, 2001). In contrast, the supply of rental housing is limited, with only a small fraction of the population resorting to renting. The small share of rental housing is largely the result of over three decades of rent control legislation. While over 27 per cent of households resorted to renting in 1960, this percentage was reduced to 13 per cent by 2000, as rent control legislation consistently eroded investors' willingness to invest in rental housing. This, in turn, translated into the sustained decline in rental housing supply, in both absolute and relative numbers (Martínez de Jiménez, 2002).

Access to basic infrastructure in Argentina, safe water in particular, is lower than in other countries in the region. Approximately 79 per cent of Argentina's overall population has access to an improved water source compared to 85 per cent for Latin American countries as a whole (World Bank, 2001a). Moreover, there are marked differences in coverage and level of services by income. For example, 54.4 per cent of the poor lack running water in the house, compared to only 6.3 per cent for the non-poor. The same is true for sanitation, with 68 per cent of the poor lacking sanitation compared to 15.6 for the non-poor. In turn, poor access to water and sanitation translates into health problems, as water drawn from wells and other sources – and even piped water – is often contaminated by sewerage and chemical pollution (World Bank, 2000a).

Given Argentina's high level of urbanization, with 89 per cent of the overall population living in urban areas in 2001, most of the population growth occurs in cities (INDEC, 2001). However, given the country's relative slow population growth – which averaged 1.4 and 1.1 per cent per year during the 1980s and 1990s, respectively – cities are not under exceptional demographic pressure, with approximately 350 000 new resident per year during the 1990s (Zanetta, 2004). The lack of demographic pressure offered Argentine authorities the opportunity to approach the challenges in the housing sector with a medium and long-term perspectives conducive to the development of sustainable strategies.

Housing deficits in Mexico

The examination of Mexico's housing deficit shows a large proportion of the population facing serious housing deficiencies (see Table 10.1). Official estimates indicate that the housing deficit is over 19 per cent, with approximately 4.3 million Mexican families living in substandard housing or in overcrowded conditions. Mexico's housing deficit is heavily concentrated in the existing stock. Housing units in need of improvement, upgrading and expansion – e.g. relative deficit – account for over 58 per cent of the overall deficit. Alternatively, the absolute deficit accounts for 42 per cent of the overall deficit, calling for new units to house families currently living with other families and to replace precarious structures that cannot be recovered. These estimates, however, might be too conservative, as other sources suggest that up to 76 per cent of the 1990 housing stock might be in need of improvement (World Bank, 2002).

The housing deficit is concentrated largely among the poor. Households earning less than three minimum salaries represent more than 40 per cent of the demand for new housing and home improvement (World Bank, 2002). Many of the poor have resorted to the informal production of housing to solve their housing needs. Irregular settlements represent a high proportion of the overall housing stock. It is estimated that up to 40 per cent of the population of Mexico City lives in irregular settlements (ECLAC, 2000). The proportion of housing construction within the informal sector is estimated at 53 per cent (Herbert and Pickering, 1997).

The rate of homeownership is very high in Mexico, amounting to 80 per cent (Herbert and Pickering, 1997). The majority of households, though, have only *de facto* ownership of their homes, as it is estimated that approximately 60 per cent of all Mexican families lack full tenure (World Bank, 2002). The supply of rental housing is limited, as the result of decades of rent control legislation and ineffective public incentives programmes. Only 13 per cent of Mexican households resort to renting, a small percentage relative to the US, Canada and countries in Europe, where more than 30 per cent of households rent their housing (Herbert and Pickering, 1997).

Improving basic services can have a significant impact in improving housing deficits. Although 85 per cent of the population has access to an improved water source, there are marked differences in coverage and level of services both within and across cities as a function of income and geographic location (World Bank, 2002).

Although the process of urbanization has slowed significantly since its peak in the 1960s and 1970s, Mexican cities are still under considerable demographic pressure. Accounting for 75 per cent of the overall population, cities are growing twice as fast as Mexico's population. During the 1990–5 period, urban population growth was 4.2 per cent compared to 2.3 per cent for the total population. Consequently, Mexican authorities face the challenge of providing housing and infrastructure to approximately 1.5 million new urban residents per year (INEGI, 2001). Some Mexican cities, particularly those across the northern border with the US, are growing at a much faster rate, fuelled by the growth of export-oriented manufacturing sector, such as the *maquila* industries (Rodríguez, 1997). The high demographic pressure confronts Mexican authorities with the dual challenge of offering short-term solutions to the most pressing housing needs of the population while simultaneously developing strategies that are sustainable in the medium and long terms.

Technically grounded policy guidelines

Based on the structure and characteristics of housing deficits in Argentina and Mexico, some general policy directions can be outlined reflecting technical rationality and lessons learned in the past (see Table 10.2). In terms of poverty alleviation objectives, the sizeable housing deficit and its concentration among the poor, indicate that housing policies can play a central role in improving living conditions among the poor, effectively targeting those groups that are more likely to be negatively affected by actions taken as part of economic liberalization programmes.

The structure of the housing deficits in Argentina and Mexico indicates that the central focus of housing programmes has to be on improving and expanding the existing stock, as opposed to constructing new housing. Likewise, the concentration of the housing deficits among the poor makes highly relevant the lessons learned in the 1970s, including the importance of affordability, cost recovery and replicability (World Bank, 1974, 1975). Alternative housing solutions, such as site-and-services schemes, progressive housing and slum upgrading, can provide workable alternatives in addressing housing needs among the poor in both countries.

Informal housing processes, including illegal settlements, warrant special attention as well as the design of proactive strategies aimed at bringing informal housing production into formal channels. Land banks and technical assistance on construction techniques can have a strong impact in helping low-income households upgrade and expand their homes while, at the same time, promoting more rational urban growth patterns. Addressing widespread illegal land tenure should also be an important priority in both Argentina and Mexico. Likewise, the provision of basic services and neighbourhood improvements can effectively improve housing conditions for broad sectors of the population, which, in turn, calls attention to the need to coordinate efforts with municipal governments.

Drawing on the lessons learned during the 1980s, Argentine and Mexican authorities should ensure that their housing agencies have the institutional and technical capacity needed to formulate and implement systematic housing solutions. Similarly, effective and transparent subsidies are needed to maximize the impact of scarce public resources on the poor. Another important lesson learned during this period points to the importance of financial intermediation, which, coupled with sound criteria to allocate

Table 10.2   Technical policy guidelines

What does the structure of Argentina's and Mexico's housing deficits tells us?

■ **Housing deficits are significant, particularly among the poor** . . . therefore, housing policies can play a key role in poverty alleviation, ameliorating the negative impacts of structural adjustment and improving living conditions among the more vulnerable sectors of the population.

■ **The majority of the housing deficit is concentrated within the existing stock** . . . suggesting that the focus of housing policies has to be on upgrading and expansion. Small credits, construction materials banks and micro-credit initiatives can be effective in providing financial support for needed improvements and expansion.

■ **Given the widespread housing needs among the poor** . . . affordability has to be a key criterion informing the design of housing solutions, housing programmes and financial instruments. Non-traditional housing solutions, such as progressive housing, sites-and-services and basic modules, can be an effective way of increasing affordability.

■ **Since a significant proportion of new housing production is produced within the informal sector** . . . it is important to undertake proactive strategies, such as the development of land banks, to channel new growth into sound urban growth patterns. Likewise, upfront subdivisions with clear outlines for future streets and services can foster more orderly development patterns in irregular settlements.

■ **In Mexico, irregular settlements constitute a large proportion of existing the housing stock** . . . thus, a strong emphasis on slum upgrading is warranted.

■ **High levels of homeownership** . . . offer a good opportunity for collateralized lending.

■ **In view of the low proportion of rental housing** . . . there might be opportunities to improve the supply of affordable housing through the expansion of rental markets.

■ **The widespread lack of legal tenure, particularly in Mexico** . . . calls for aggressive land regularization efforts.

■ **Improving access to basic services** . . . can have a significant impact on improving housing conditions.

■ **Given high disparities, by both income and geographic region** . . . a decentralized approach might provide more flexibility in articulating appropriate responses. Likewise, a demand-based approach, as opposed to supply-based, might also result in more flexibility and a higher level of responsiveness. Community-based initiatives should be encouraged.

Other important lessons learned in the past

■ **Cost recovery** . . . is a fair, socially conscious practice that permits replicability.

■ **Effective targeting** . . . is another basic lesson that is often forgotten.

■ **Administrative reform** . . . of housing agencies, including streamlining excess bureaucracy, reducing recurrent costs and increasing transparency, can help ensure the effective use of financial resources.

■ **Financial intermediation** . . . can channel substantial resources into housing and municipal finances.

■ **Fostering private sector participation** . . . in housing finance, particularly to attend the needs of non-poor sectors of the population, permits the focus of scarce financial resources on those who are beyond the reach of the market.

■ **Adequate systems of incentives** . . . are key to induce desirable behaviour on the part of economic agents, institutional actors and individuals.

and more . . .

financing, can channel substantial resources into housing and municipal finance (World Bank, 1995).

The 1990s brought another set of valuable lessons, including the importance of having in place adequate systems of incentives to induce desirable behaviours among institutional actors. Likewise, there was renewed attention given to decentralization and its potential benefits, particularly in the face of a broad spectrum of local conditions. Another important contribution of the urban agenda of the 1990s points to the need to remove barriers artificially limiting private participation in the provision and financing of housing services. Likewise, it pointed out the potential impact of sound sector policies on poverty alleviation by removing barriers hampering the productivity of the poor (World Bank, 1993).

In summary, the technical analysis of the housing deficits in Argentina and Mexico, together with the rich knowledge base that has been developed over three decades of sector work, suggests a clear set of policy guidelines. With sophisticated policy-makers and well-developed institutions in both Argentina and Mexico, it could be expected that the housing policies implemented in these two countries would reflect technical rationality and the lessons learned in the past. However, a closer examination of the policies that were actually implemented in the framework of their economic reform programmes disproves such expectation.

THEORY VERSUS ACTUALITY: THE FAILURE OF THE TECHNICAL RATIONALITY

The examination of the housing policies implemented in Argentina and Mexico in the context of their respective reform programmes renders rather grim results. Argentina, widely praised for its reform efforts during the 1990s, exhibits an astounding conceptual poverty in its housing policies, as if untouched by the lessons learned over three decades of sector work elsewhere in the region and the world. In contrast, Mexico shows considerably more maturity in its housing policies, with a rich history of pro-poor housing strategies. However, despite their obvious superiority with respect to those of Argentina, Mexican housing policies also exhibit serious shortcomings, which were not tackled in the context of the reform programme.

Housing policies in Argentina

Argentina's housing policies had been traditionally ineffective, non-experimental and unresponsive to the needs of the poor. While other countries in Latin America were experimenting with innovative housing strategies, such as sites and services, slum upgrading and regularization of land tenure during the 1970s and 1980s, Argentina continued with the systematic eradication of slum areas. Curiously, the deep ideological differences between the various administrations, ranging from extreme-right military regimes to populist democratic governments, were not reflected in their low-income housing policies. In general, slum areas have been perceived as a negative phenomenon to be eliminated. Thus, policies toward irregular settlements have emphasized the elimination of slums and the relocation of displaced residents in either temporary or permanent housing units or, as under military rule in the late 1970s, simply offering them no alternative solutions (Zanetta, 2004). The narrow focus of housing policies in Argentina can be attributed to the smaller magnitude of irregular settlements relative to other Latin American countries, the military's distrust for social activism and the strong influence of economic groups benefiting from ongoing practices (Cuenya, 1997; Zanetta, 2004).

Argentina's primary housing institutions – the National Mortgage Bank (*Banco Hipotecario Nacional*; BHN) and the National Housing Fund (*Fondo Nacional de la Vivienda*; FONAVI) – have been characterized by their narrow focus on the production of costly finished housing and the Leviathan nature of their administrative structures. Created in 1860, the BHN was conceived as a source of financing for middle-income households that, with the help of long-term credit and low interest rates, had the savings capacity necessary to afford the full cost of housing. As originally conceived, the BHN served a financial intermediary, relying on publicly traded savings certificates to attract private investors. However, policies implemented at various periods, including the 1980s, had made the BHN largely dependent on central government transfers, transforming it in a mere channel of public subsidies (Buckley, 1991).

FONAVI was created in 1972 to attend to the housing needs of lower-income segments of the population. It was further consolidated and expanded under the military regime that took power in 1976. The institution was characterized by the typical shortcomings: high production costs and almost no cost recovery. It was estimated that only 2 to 5 cents for every dollar invested were recovered as the result of heavy indirect subsidies in the form of full financing of the units, payments only partially adjusted for inflation, long grace periods and poor foreclosure practices (Buckley, 1991). While FONAVI succeeded in reaching lower-income segments of the population that were previously excluded from BHN programmes, benefits were concentrated among just a few with respect to the latent demand (Aguilar and Sbrocco, 1997). During the period between 1976 and 1983, FONAVI produced an average of 23 320 housing units per year (Martínez de Jiménez, 2002), while there were still one million additional eligible poor households excluded from the system (Cuenya, 1997).

For the two decades following its creation, FONAVI continued to pursue the same narrow strategy, focusing solely on the production of new owner-occupied units financed with heavily subsidized loans. The emphasis on fully finished housing in large complexes benefited large, capital-intensive construction firms. Likewise, the use of a 'price adjustment' mechanism exempted firms from any long-term investment risks, providing them with extremely favourable conditions for investment (Yujnovsky, 1984). Over time, this strategy gave rise to a complex and stable political, financial and institutional web of special interests that fiercely resisted any attempts to change the system.

Interestingly, the wave of far-reaching reforms that was implemented as part of the Convertibility Plan of 1991 brought only superficial changes to public housing programmes and failed to introduce any substantial reforms. One notable outcome of the Menem administration was the privatization of the BHN, which has since then shifted its target population from medium- to higher-income customers. In addition, there was considerable progress made towards the development of mortgage-backed securities. While the new financial mechanisms can potentially have a significant impact by increasing the amount of private funds channelled into housing in the medium and long run, they are not expected to reach lower-income households. In addition, although legislation was approved providing the legal framework for regularization of illegal land tenure, the actual impact of land-regularization programmes was disappointing (Zanetta, 2004).

The lack of substantial changes in Argentina's public housing programme during the Menem administration is illustrated by its failure to reform FONAVI, which continued to control almost the totality of public resources allocated to housing and urban development – 97.5 per cent in 1999 (Ministerio de Economía, 2000). The national government took only two major actions with respect to FONAVI. First, it modified its funding formula, replacing employers' contribution – including those of the public sector – with a portion of the gasoline tax. Second, it decentralized FONAVI funds to provincial governments, virtually relinquishing its policy-making role in the housing sector. No incentives or enforcement mechanisms were introduced as part of the decentralization to ensure larger social coverage, a wider spectrum of housing solutions, and wider participation of economic and social agents in the production of housing (Cuenya, 1997). Moreover, the national government failed to enforce even the minimum performance requirements mandated in the FONAVI decentralization law (Zanetta, 2004).

Not surprisingly, FONAVI continues to be plagued with systemic inefficiencies (see Table 10.3). Although the majority of Argentina's current deficit is concentrated within the existing stock, FONAVI's historical bias toward new housing units persists. In 1999, 83 per cent of FONAVI's output corresponded to new units. Likewise, targeting of subsidies is still largely ineffective. While indirect subsidies amount to more than half of all FONAVI resources, only a third of all beneficiaries are among the poor. Similarly, unitary costs remain excessively high, well below the reach of low- and middle-income groups. In addition, cost recovery continues to be low, averaging 48.7 per cent in 1999. Moreover, administrative costs – such as personnel, fees and legal expenditures – have continued to climb steadily, reaching 22 per cent in 1999 (Ministerio de Economía, 2000).

Table 10.3   Performance of Argentina's and Mexico's main public housing institutions

Performance indicators	Argentina's FONAVI	Mexico's INFONAVIT
Market share		
% of public funds for housing at the federal level	97.3%	81%
% of total amount of formal housing finance	Approx. 33% before Dec 2001	82%
Programmatic effectiveness		
Finished units	83%	82.4%
Unitary costs	Very high US$26 000	High US$13 900
Subsidies		
Indirect subsidies	Very high 54% of all resources	Very high 51.4% of all resources
Overall targeting	Approx. 33% reaches the poor	38% for population income ≤ 3 minimum wages
Administrative performance		
Allocation criteria	Lack of transparency (Only 8 provinces have registers of beneficiaries)	n.a.
Cost recovery	Very low 48%	22.4% of portfolio in arrears in 2000 (compared to 46% in 1996)
Administrative costs	Very high 22.5%	Moderate 5.6%

Sources: Data for Argentina from Ministerio de Economía (2000); data from Mexico from World Bank (2002) and INFONAVIT (http://infonavit.gob.mx).

In summary, Argentina's housing policies reflect very little rationality, either before or after the implementation of the drastic reforms that swept across the public sector during the 1990s. Surprisingly, FONAVI remained untouched, despite widespread agreement over its main shortcomings and the potential impact it could have had on improving housing conditions of the poor.

Housing policies in Mexico

Mexican housing policies are consistent with many of the policy guidelines derived from the technical analysis of the country's housing deficit. This is not surprising, as Mexican authorities have traditionally assigned a high priority to housing policies, channelling substantial resources into a wide range of public housing programmes. Starting in the 1970s, housing policies have reflected an increasing understanding of the housing needs of the poor and of the intrinsic value of irregular housing processes, including irregular settlements and self-built housing. Similarly, public housing programmes have experimented with regularization of land tenure and upgrading schemes for several decades.

The preoccupation with the housing needs of the poor continued in the context of the economic liberalization programme implemented between 1982 and 2000, as reflected in the low-income housing initiatives implemented under President de la Madrid and the emphasis on community-based infrastructure investments as part of the President Salinas's anti-poverty programme, Solidarity. While housing and urban services subsequently lost some of their relative importance in the overall anti-poverty strategy vis-à-vis direct transfers, President Zedillo introduced additional housing programmes targeting the very poor (Zanetta, 2004). Overall, growth of the housing stock outpaced growth in population during the 1980–2000 period, increasing by 81 per cent relative to a 45.2 per cent increase in population (World Bank, 2002).

Despite these achievements, important shortcomings remain. In particular, Mexican authorities have failed to tackle the reform of INFONAVIT (*Instituto del Fondo Nacional de la Vivienda para los Trabajadores*) and FONHAPO (*Fondo Nacional de Habitaciones Populares*), two key public housing institutions. INFONAVIT, the single largest source of mortgage funds in the country, is undoubtedly Mexico's most important housing agency. Established in the late 1970s, INFONAVIT's central mission was to attend the housing needs of private-sector workers through a 5 per cent payroll tax paid by workers and employers (Ward, 1990). The new financing mechanism succeeded in boosting annual formal low-income housing production without imposing a major burden on fiscal finances. Consequently, INFONAVIT became a major player in the production of low-income housing, being responsible for more than half of all formal low-income housing units built during the 1971–82 period (Gilbert and Varley, 1991).

As reflected by its current share of the housing finance market – 82 per cent of the value of all new mortgage originations in 2000 – INFONAVIT continues to play a central role in Mexico's housing sector (see Table 10.3). Unfortunately, despite the obvious need to drastically reform this institution, only minor improvements have been achieved. There was some limited progress during the Salinas and Zedillo administrations, including limiting INFONAVIT's scope to financial activities and abandoning housing construction (World Bank, 2002). INFONAVIT's administrative performance has also exhibited some improvements, with administrative costs being reduced to less than 6 per cent and the percentage of the portfolio in arrears decreasing from 46 per cent in 1996 to 22.5 per cent in 2000 (INFONAVIT, 2000).

However, INFONAVIT is far from effectively utilizing the sizeable resources it receives through mandated pension fund contributions.

Instead, it continues to be highly inefficient, offering heavy indirect subsidies to middle-class households, about twice as large as those provided by other pubic agencies targeting similar groups (World Bank, 1999b). As a result, INFONAVIT introduces strong distortions in the housing finance sector, artificially limiting the participation of commercial lenders, which accounted for less than 6 per cent of all mortgage originations between 1995 and 2000 (Fox, 2002). At the same time, the huge subsidies going to middle-class workers take away resources that could alternatively be targeted toward lower-income groups (World Bank, 2002).

INFONAVIT also continues to focus primarily on new, fully finished housing, which accounted for over 82 per cent of its resources in 2000. Moreover, unitary costs remain high, with only 38 per cent of all loans going to beneficiaries earning three or fewer minimum wages (INFONAVIT, 2000). In summary, after almost two decades of reforms, Mexico's flagship housing agency continues to exhibit significant inefficiencies.

The reform of FONHAPO – Mexico's low-income housing agency – is also pending, despite estimates showing that more than 40 per cent of the current demand for housing corresponds to households earning less than three times the minimum salary. In this context, it is surprising that the government has not attempted to increase the effectiveness of FONHAPO. As part of two World Bank's low-income housing projects, considerable progress was made in expanding access to housing among low-income households through FONHAPO during the 1980s. However, these achievements were subsequently reversed, as the agency developed chronic poor collection rates and reverted its focus to finished housing instead of the alternative housing schemes, such as sites and services, starter homes and housing improvements, that had been promoted under the Bank's projects (World Bank, 2002).

In summary, despite the obvious superiority of Mexican housing policies, both in terms of levels of housing production and responsiveness towards the needs of the poor relative to those of Argentina, our analysis indicates that policy-makers in both countries seem to have avoided key actions. While there have been some programmes aimed at promoting non-traditional housing solutions, particularly in Mexico, there is still an overwhelming emphasis on the supply of costly, finished housing units. This is especially frustrating since housing deficits in both countries clearly point to the need to emphasize upgrading and expansion of existing units. There are large indirect subsidies in place that do not reach the poor, most of who are left to their own devices to solve their housing needs. Likewise, the main housing financial institutions – FONAVI in Argentina, and INFONAVIT and FONHAPO in Mexico – are still plagued with inefficiencies, as half-hearted reform attempts have largely failed. In synthesis, the first level of analysis using a technical lens points to the apparent failure of these two Latin American countries, with rather sophisticated policy-makers and well-developed institutions, to formulate technically sound housing policies.

STAKEHOLDER ANALYSIS: UNDERSTANDING POLICY THROUGH THE LENSES OF POLITICAL EXPEDIENCY

An analysis of a more political nature proves to be more apt in explaining key factors determining the housing policies adopted by Argentine and Mexican authorities as part of their respective economic reform programmes. In Argentina, housing policies received little attention in the context of the Convertibility Plan. Their potential impact on improving living conditions of the poor was overlooked given that poverty alleviation was not a central component of the reform agenda. Instead, housing policies were conditioned by the need to gain support for the reform programme among provincial governors, from whom depended the sustainability of the newly achieved macroeconomic stability. In Mexico, the erosion of the legitimacy of the PRI (*Partido Revolucionario Institucional*), the political party that had ruled Mexico unchallenged since its creation in 1929, was the key political issue facing Presidents de la Madrid, Salinas and Zedillo. Consequently, housing policies played a key role in their attempts to rebuild political support for the PRI.

Housing policies in the context of Argentina's Convertibility Plan

As noted by Stiglitz (2002), Argentina was the A+ student of the 1990s, fully embracing the free-market reforms advocated under the Washington Consensus. Unlike Mexico, where poverty alleviation was an important component of the reform programme, social considerations were not a central concern of the Menem administration. Ironically, Menem's Peronist background gave him the natural allegiance of labour unions and popular groups. Free from pressures from these groups, Menem's Convertibility Plan was implemented without giving much consideration to its social costs (Zanetta, 2004).

By the time Argentina began implementing its reform programme, there was much to be done to improve housing policies. Like other sector policies, however, housing policies did not become an integral part of the overall reform programme but rather evolved primarily from the need to reduce public spending and sustain political support for the reform programme (Gerchunoff and Torres, 1998). While considerable progress was achieved in increasing private sector participation, including the privatization of the BHN and some steps toward the development of secondary mortgage markets, the housing needs of the poor were largely ignored in the context of the Convertibility Plan (Zanetta, 2004).

The Menem administration subordinated actions affecting the housing sector to the primary objective of maintaining macroeconomic stability. First, the modification of FONAVI's funding formula resulted in significant savings for the national government, as it eliminated the payroll tax corresponding to public employees. Second, FONAVI funds were decentralized as part of the negotiation of the Fiscal Pact of 1992. As part of this agreement, provincial governors agreed to a 15 per cent reduction in revenue-sharing transfers in exchange for a minimum floor in revenue-sharing transfers and the transfer of FONAVI funds to provincial governments. In this way, the national government succeeded in reducing its automatic transfers to the provinces, a major step towards controlling fiscal deficits at the national level. In exchange, the transfer of FONAVI funds gave governors *de facto* control over this important mass of resources, with very little overseeing on the part of the national government (Zanetta, 2004).

In summary, the most notable characteristic of housing policies in Argentina during the 1990s was their absence. Housing policies evolved primarily from the need to reduce public spending, without considering their potential contribution in mitigating the negative impact of economic reforms on the poor by improving their access to shelter and basic services. Instead, they were used primarily to gain and maintain the support of the governors, using the transfer of FONAVI funds to the provinces as a bargaining chip in the negotiation of the 1992 Fiscal Pact.

Housing policies as a central component of Mexico's reform programme

The economic liberalization reforms implemented in Mexico between 1982 and 2000 clearly reflected the basic tenets of the Washington Consensus. At the same time, Mexico's reform programme exhibited distinctive characteristics, which reflected the country's political realities and its ideological heritage. One of these distinctive characteristics was the inclusion of poverty alleviation as a central component of the reform efforts, directly targeting the poor instead of relying on indirect targeting or the market to improve their living conditions.

As reflected in the 1917 constitution, the emphasis on balancing growth with social considerations has its roots in the Mexican revolution. While Mexico's social legacy is by no means one of equality, during most of the twentieth century the Mexican state largely succeeded in maintaining social stability by resolving tensions internally, diffusing conflicts between different sectors of society through assimilation and concessions. Therefore, the tendency of the Mexican authorities to try to balance economic growth with social considerations was natural, even under the new free-market model. Perhaps more important, addressing the needs of the poor was a matter of political survival for the PRI. As denoted by the results of the 1988 presidential election, the PRI was rapidly loosing its political support among the poor, who represent almost half of the Mexican population. Thus, it is not surprising that poverty alleviation occupied a prominent role as part of Mexico's reform programme (Zanetta, 2004).

Mexican authorities made housing policies an important element of the reform programme, using them to fuel economic growth, combat poverty and gain political support for the PRI. For example, President de la Madrid focused on housing construction to boost economic activity and generate employment opportunities during the economic recession that ensued after the 1982 debt crisis. He also relied on the low-income housing strategies implemented by FONHAPO to respond to the vocal demands of the popular urban movements that took momentum after the 1985 earthquake in Mexico City. Likewise, President Salinas focused on small community-based infrastructure investments as part of his Solidarity Programme to reach millions of poor households across the country, effectively regaining popular support for the PRI (Zanetta, 2004).

However, despite the strong importance given to housing policies in the context of the overall economic reform programme, it is clear the Mexican authorities backed away from those reforms generating strong opposition from powerful stakeholders, such as the reform of INFONAVIT and FONHAPO. Although the need to reform INFONAVIT had long been acknowledged, Mexican authorities consistently avoided such a challenge due to the high political cost it represented. INFONAVIT's board structure had equal representation from labour unions, the private sector and the federal government, giving the institution a degree of independence from government policies (World Bank, 1999a). Moreover, a powerful labour union had been in control of INFONAVIT since the late 1970s, using it to benefit its own members (Ward, 1990). Thus, the lack of political will on the part of the government to take on this challenge can be explained in terms of political expedience, suggesting an implicit alliance between the government and labour unions by which unions continued to benefit from large housing subsidies in exchange for their support of the overall reform programme (Trejo and Jones 1998). In other words, subsidies in consumer goods, including housing, were used to compensate labour unions for other losses resulting from over two decades of reforms. Clearly, maintaining the support of labour unions proved more important to Mexican authorities than reforming INFONAVIT.

Similarly, the persistent bias towards finished housing can be explained by the significant control that private developers have in determining the use of funds under INFONAVIT and other housing programmes. This monopolistic power has allowed developers to bias housing solutions to their advantage, as beneficiaries must accept the product offered – in this case, finished housing units – in order to receive the subsidy. They have also succeeded in absorbing a substantial part of the subsidy – up to half of the total subsidy according to some estimates (World Bank, 2002). Although Mexican authorities have begun experimenting with providing up-front subsidies to final beneficiaries in an attempt to shift the influence towards the demand side, the magnitude of these programmes is still negligible, leaving the undue dominance of private developers largely intact (Zanetta, 2004).

Finally, urban popular movements have also been effective in blocking the reform of FONHAPO, Mexico's low-income housing agency, thus retaining considerable influence over its operation. Community groups affiliated with both the PRI and the opposition became very skilful in using their political influence to their advantage, effectively opposing efforts to improve repayment of FONHAPO loans. This, in turn, translated into chronically poor collection rates for FONHAPO. In addition, private developers were able to influence the agency, pressuring it to provide loans for finished housing instead of the alternative housing strategies that had been promoted under the bank's projects. Although some improvements have been introduced aimed at increasing the transparency and fairness in the selection of final beneficiaries, FONHAPO continues to respond to the demands of private developers and urban popular movements (Trejo and Jones, 1998).

In summary, none of the three Mexican presidents leading the country's economic liberalization reforms between 1982 and 2000 confronted the difficult challenges posed by the housing sector. Clearly, maintaining the political support of labour unions, private developers and urban popular movements was a more important determinant of the housing policies implemented as part of Mexico's economic reform than the desire to implement technically sound policies.

MAIN CONCLUSIONS AND POLICY IMPLICATIONS

The examination of the housing policies implemented in Argentina and Mexico as part of their economic reform programmes renders important insights into the factors determining these policies. In particular, the analysis indicates that housing policies in both countries were not dictated by technical rationality or the desire to enhance their overall effectiveness. Instead, they responded mainly to political considerations.

In the case of Argentina, housing policies were clearly subordinate to the need to maintain macroeconomic stability, the primary objective of the Convertibility Plan. This, in turn, depended largely on gaining and maintaining the support of provincial governors, who are powerful powerbrokers given the country's large degree of fiscal federalism and provincial autonomy. Consequently, the policies toward the housing sector clearly responded to the demands made by the governors, who called for the unqualified decentralization of FONAVI. In turn, the decentralization of FONAVI funds to the provinces was not opposed by private developers, particularly local ones, as it left intact – or even enhanced – their ability to influence the adoption of favourable housing strategies. Alternatively, other constituencies, such as labour unions, popular urban movements and the poor in general, did not command enough political leverage to warrant them any special concessions or prerogatives as part of the housing policies implemented in the context of the reform programme.

Mexican authorities faced a more complex challenge in ensuring political support for their economic reform programme. While the traditionally strong powers of the presidency ensured them the allegiance of state governors, Mexican presidents had to respond to the demands of a broad spectrum of political actors, including labour unions, popular groups and the construction industry. To counteract the eroding legitimacy of the PRI and the negative impacts of the reform programme on individual groups, Mexican authorities tailored their housing policies to help distribute benefits among labour unions, private developers and popular urban groups as a way of ensuring the support of these key constituencies.

The housing policies implemented in Argentina and Mexico during the 1980s and 1990s illustrate the strategies used by national authorities to sustain the coalitions of support for their reform programmes. As Bruhn (1996) rightly observes, sustaining free-market policies requires not only significant economic growth but also flexibility and compromise on the part of policy-makers. The findings also suggest that, as the International Monetary Fund and the other Washington institutions focused most of their attention on policies affecting macroeconomic stability, particularly fiscal performance, national politicians may have resorted to sector policies, including housing policies, to help gain and maintain support for the economic liberalization reforms among key constituencies.

CHAPTER ELEVEN

Land for housing the poor in African cities: are neo-customary processes an effective alternative to formal systems?[1]

Alain Durand-Lasserve

INTRODUCTION: REGIONAL CONTEXT AND TRENDS

According to recent UN estimates, Africa has the world's highest rapid urbanization growth in the world, with an annual average of 4.0 per cent. Thirty-seven per cent of the total population of Africa currently live in urban areas and by 2030 the urban population is expected to account for more than half of the total population.

Over the next two decades, nearly 90 per cent of the population growth in Africa will take place in urban areas (Lopez-Moreno, 2003).

A high rate of urbanization combined, in most countries, with a consistent economic decline over the past two decades has resulted in a rapid increase in the number of urban poor: in sub-Saharan African countries, it is estimated that more than 40 per cent of urban residents are living in poverty. In the vast majority of sub-Saharan African cities, the urban poor as well as large segments of low- and middle-income groups do not have access to land provided by the public and the formal private sectors.

In all countries covered by the research project, except in South Africa, *public provision of serviced land and housing* is steadily declining. There are many reasons for this:

- the scale of the problem
- lack of resources
- lack of political will, widespread corruption and illicit practices
- administrative and technical bottlenecks, especially in the identification of land rights
- a failure to reach targeted low-income groups.

As for the *formal private sector*, it does not contribute to the provision of land and housing, unless heavily subsidized. The private sector is usually deterred from investment in low-cost housing development schemes because of political risks, the chronic weakness of housing finance systems, a lack of reliable land information and registration systems, and low profit margins.

The failure of government urban land and housing policies and the inability of the formal private sector to provide land for housing the poor have strengthened the attractiveness of informal land markets. The African continent has today the largest proportion of urban population living in *informal settlements* with no proper access or no access at all to basic urban services and less security of tenure than in formal settlements.

Depending on the city, access to land through informal processes covers a wide range of situations, from squatting to various forms of informal/illegal commercial land subdivision. At the periphery of sub-Saharan African cities, informal land delivery processes are strongly influenced – and occasionally even dominated – by actors who refer to *customary legitimacy.*

Emerging forms of customary land delivery in urban areas

During the past two decades, *customary land management practices* have undergone various adjustments (Toulmin and Quan, 2000). In most countries, they have proved to have a surprising capacity to adapt to the new economic and social context introduced by the globalization of national economies and to the rapid spatial expansion of urban areas.

Customary land 'ownership' refers to the communal possession of rights to use and allocate agricultural and grazing land by a group sharing the same cultural identity. A single person usually administers on behalf of the group. Decisions – made on a consensual basis – must comply with the cultural tradition of the community concerned. The extent of the rights to use the land depends on the agreement passed between the customary community and the person receiving the rights. Within the group, social institutions defend or protect these rights against other claims regarding the land.

However, in urban areas, customary land delivery in the strict sense of the term does not operate according to this model. It still survives at the periphery of most African cities, but it has been progressively eroded during the colonial and post-colonial period. Recent empirical observations suggest that it is being replaced by what we can call *neo-customary practices*: a combination of *reinterpreted customary practices with other informal and formal practices.* As highlighted in the case of South Africa, the definition of neo-customary tenure includes urban and peri-urban areas where land rights were initially delivered by customary systems, and where practices that have been part of a customary system are currently being used. The current land and housing situation in African cities cannot be explained without reference to neo-customary practices.

Neo-customary land delivery systems include all the stakeholders and all the practices that claim to be rooted directly or indirectly in the custom. They work *through individuals* who sell as market commodities more rights than they have received through a customary system. Alternatively, these systems may operate *through groups* that replicate familiar elements of customary systems and thus inspire confidence among those obtaining land. Group practices derived from customary practices deliver land rights to their members.

Neo-customary systems are *based on trust* that assumes that others will support an individual's claim. This trust arises from a confidence in the customary social relationships that are embedded in the land delivery process, because the land rights were first obtained directly from a customary delivery system or because they came through a system that used customary practices or both. These systems provide cheap and fast access to land, and often provide better security of tenure than other informal land delivery systems.

Neo-customary practices *involve social institutions*, including central and local government institutions, but the basis of these neo-customary social institutions remains the group. Neo-customary actors play an important political and social role at settlement level, and are often able to position themselves as necessary intermediaries between the communities and the administration, even in cities and countries (such as Senegal or Cameroon) where they are not officially recognized. In countries where they are formally recognized, such as parts of Ghana, neo-customary actors are closely associated in the decision-making process at the lowest levels of local governance.

All case studies confirm that commodification is the most important factor to transform customary into neo-customary land delivery systems. *The neo-customary sector deals with land rights that have been commodified.* As noted in the case of Senegal, as soon as customary land is subject to a monetary transaction, it enters within the neo-customary sphere.

Points of difference between neo-customary and other informal land delivery systems are not always easy to establish. Neo-customary land delivery systems are considered as one category of informal land delivery systems. The main distinction between neo-customary and informal land delivery systems is the status of the primary tenure right of the land. The Cotonou case study, Benin, underlines that the entire land delivery process (from land subdivision and the sale of individual plots by customary owners to the delivery of a housing permit by government institutions following the land readjustment and redevelopment scheme – *operation de lotissement-remembrement*) clearly follows a neo-customary logic. Being recognized by the administration, owners of building plots are incorporated within the sphere of the modern law (the Civil Code) and they have no more links with custom. In fact, in the absence of formal title registration, the land remains under the customary regime.

Another approach is put forward by the Kenyan case study. It stresses that the distinction is provided by *a belief* that a group in a social institution will defend claims to the land. This belief is probably created with reference to customary social practices, in the form of the seller's claim that he/she received rights from a customary land delivery system *or* in the form of a practice that imitates a familiar customary practice. This is the case in

Nairobi, where group ownership of a formal claim (which has not been delivered by a customary system) is managed by the group and informal rights are divided among the members.

In the case of Tanzania, a distinction is made between *customary tenure* (where land is alienable, or can be transferred only after very wide-ranging consultation with, and consensus of, clan members) and *quasi customary tenure*, where land is alienable. The right to sell involves customary requirements, but lies mainly in the hands of the individual landowners. *Informal land delivery* refers to cases where transaction in land no longer involves customary requirements such as the consent of the extended family or 'elderly indigenous inhabitants', but could be between anyone seeking land, and anyone who purports to own the land. Areas covered by quasi-customary (or neo-customary) tenure and informal tenure coincide with what is generally referred to as 'unplanned settlements'.

What is the scale of the population in the city area that relies on these practices for access to land for housing?

According to all empirical observations, a significant proportion of the urban population relies on neo-customary practices. However, especially in those countries where customary practices are not recognized, and which accordingly do make any distinction between various forms of informality, it is difficult to provide accurate figures regarding the numbers who have relied on neo-customary systems for access to land for housing. In Ghana, most peri-urban land in the country is held under customary law. In Yaounde, Cameroon, more than 70 per cent of the population of suburban settlements live on customary lands. In Tanzania, it is generally officially stated that some 70 per cent of Dar es Salaam's residents live with informal tenure in unplanned areas, with traces of customary or quasi-customary tenure. In Dakar, Senegal, between 1982 and 1987, 91 per cent of housing production was considered as informal. It can be assumed that most of it has taken place on customary lands. In Cotonou and Porto Novo, Benin, it can be estimated that about 80 per cent of land development in the past two decades has taken place on land provided by the neo-customary system. Most of the land in Kampala City, in Uganda, is managed and delivered according to neo-customary practices by the Buganda Land Board. More than 56 per cent of the population of Nairobi, Kenya, is living in informal settlements.

It is estimated that only 9 per cent of all households in South Africa live under traditional, informal, inferior and/or officially unrecognized forms of tenure, primarily in rural areas (Royston, 2002). The informal allocation of land by traditional authorities is observable in towns that are close to former homeland boundaries (Cross, 2002). With time, the urbanization of urban areas such as Durban, which are surrounded by land under tribal authority, will depend on adjustments to traditional land allocation.

CURRENT CHANGES AND TRENDS REGARDING NEO-CUSTOMARY LAND DELIVERY PRACTICES IN URBAN AND SUBURBAN AREAS

Depending on the country, there are three main types of situations regarding customary rights.

■ *Customary land management is formally recognized by governments* (by law and in the Constitutions). However, recognition is usually limited to particular types of lands and/or to particular areas/regions. This is the case in Ghana, especially in Kumasi region, and in South Africa, where the Communal Land Rights Bill, voted in February 2004 (Republic of South Africa, 2003) has formally considerably extended the land management prerogatives of traditional leaders. In the Kampala area, Uganda, the Buganda Land Board acts on behalf of the Kabaka, who is the traditional leader of the Buganda people. The rights held by the Kabaka to extensive lands surrounding earlier boundaries of the Municipality of Kampala have been transferred to users by the Board.

■ *Formal recognition of the customary system is limited to rural areas, but customary land management practices and transactions by neo-customary actors are tolerated in suburban areas* under certain circumstances, depending on the local political context. Neo-customary land subdivisions are usually recognized by government administrations, although they are not legal in the strict sense of the term (Benin, Cameroon, Namibia).

■ *Customary land management is not recognized or is limited strictly to rural areas* (Tanzania, Senegal). This does not mean that customary actors cannot operate. Usually they can, but at their own risk, given the discretionary power of central government regarding land administration. In former French colonies this situation is clearly linked with the conception of freehold as defined in the Napoleonic Code, and along the lines of the French centralist political model. It is characterized by: (i) a state monopoly on land, and state control over land markets and centralized land management systems; and (ii) access to land mainly through conditional and revocable administrative permits to occupy and/or housing permits delivered by government administrations.

Over the past decade, trends towards *de facto* recognition of customary rights and practices can be observed in several countries studied, including those that used to have repressive attitudes regarding neo-customary land management. This shift is linked with land administration reforms: in Senegal in 1970, where some neo-customary land developments have been recognized by government administrations; in Tanzania in the 1980s and 1990s, where judiciary decisions showed some recognition for customary tenure in urban areas (Kironde, 2000); and in Cameroon in the 1990s.

The case of Kenya, where there is no significant customary land management (the customary land is held in trust by the government and not managed by customary actors at all), does not fit into any of these three categories.

Converging trends in the provision of land for housing in sub-Saharan African cities

In all the countries studied, except in South Africa, converging trends can be identified in the provision of land for housing.

In a first phase, from political independence to the early 1990s, newly independent governments took over the land management responsibilities of the colonial powers, in a context of rapid population increase in all cities of the region. The formal private sector had limited capacities to respond to the housing needs of urban middle-income groups because of the combined effect of weak housing finance mortgage systems, legal dualism regarding tenure, centralized and over-complicated procedures for obtaining administrative approvals, corruption and illicit practices. Public provision of land (more rarely of housing) at subsidized prices, using public land reserves, was mainly targeted towards emerging low-middle and middle-income groups, especially government officials and employees/state clienteles. Pressure of the demand for land for housing from the urban poor continued to increase. However, depending on the cities, the urban poor had a limited number of housing options.

- They could settle as squatters, usually on public land.
- They could become tenants in formal and informal low-income settlements on the periphery of the cities or in overcrowded and usually dilapidated areas in city centres.
- They could apply for a temporary permit to occupy on public-owned land on the periphery of cities (in most Francophone West African cities).
- They could settle on a plot of land bought from customary owners on the city peripheries. Depending on government policies, some of them were entitled to apply later for a permit to occupy or a leasehold.

In a second phase, from the early 1990s onwards, most countries are confronted with state disengagement from the urban land and housing sector, in relation to the economic crisis, the role of international finance institutions and structural adjustment plans, and the limited achievement or failure of most public land and housing policies. In all cities public urban land reserves are drying up, following massive allocation of land for housing to government clientele. The state can hardly cope with the demand from the emerging urban middle classes. In the meantime, demand for urban land is boosted by the speculative behaviour of middle and high-income groups: in contexts where investment opportunities in the productive sectors are limited for holders of monetary assets, investing in urban land is seen as an inflation-proof investment. In all countries studied, lack of social protection systems for the majority of the urban population is further encouraging micro-speculation behaviour, ownership of urban plots of land being seen as a long-term security. One can also observe the re-emergence of customary claims in most Francophone West African countries (including Cameroon and Senegal) where customary law and practices had been abolished: public land reserves are frequently claimed back by customary communities. In most countries this claim results in a greater tolerance regarding customary practices on the part of the states and, accordingly, in improved security of tenure for buyers of plots of land. Better security of tenure tends to increase demand from middle-income groups, thus raising the market price of land and resulting in a scarcity of customary land in the nearer urban fringe areas. In this context, access to neo-customary land delivery systems by the urban poor is increasingly difficult in suburban areas. The only option for the urban poor is to settle on customary land far from the city boundaries or in suburban areas unsuitable for urbanization, to be a tenant in the substandard rental sector or to settle as a squatter, usually on public land (Durand-Lasserve and Royston, 2002).

Although the situation is different in South Africa, where tenure systems, land administration and the government's attitude regarding customary practices have been strongly influenced by the legacy of apartheid, one can observe some similarities with other sub-Saharan African countries. Recognition of traditional or customary rights and practices, especially in the former homelands, and increased scarcity of land for housing in the urban fringe of cities have generated a high demand for customary land from low- and low-middle-income groups (Mogale et al., 2003).

As emphasized in the South African case study of Mandela Village, neo-customary land delivery systems have emerged in peri-urban settlements incorporated within metropolitan and urban areas where customary control and land administration are being challenged and eroded, due to large numbers of people seeking access to residential land who lack the social relations characteristic of the rural based customary system. However, they want to retain the advantages of the customary system of land delivery, i.e. cheap and fast access to bigger plots, a grassroots land management body that can mediate and arbitrate land disputes and make requests for services and development to public authorities. This land delivery is usually followed by a phenomenon of self-initiated and self-funded house construction and upgrade which produces a feeling of tenure security.

Given the current pressure of demand for land for housing in rural areas within commuting distance of urban centres, the Communal Land Rights Bill (passed by the National Assembly in February 2004), which gives traditional leaders power over rural land, is going to have a major impact on the revival of customary land management practices and the supply of land for the low- and low-middle-income groups. As observed in other

countries in the region, access of the poorest segment of the urban population to land through neo-customary land delivery systems is progressively
declining, especially in rural-urban fringe areas located near densely
urbanized areas. Given the current pressure of market forces on land,
many observers consider that the adoption of the new Land Rights Bill
may further erode the existing rights of the poorest and most powerless
sector of society.

In all sub-Saharan African countries, two converging dynamics that
narrow the gap between formal practices and informal/neo customary
practices can be observed.

Dynamics of government institutions

Given the limits and failures of public and private formal land delivery systems, the *contribution of neo-customary actors in the provision of land for
housing is progressively acknowledged* in an increasing number of sub-
Saharan African countries (Payne, 2002). This shift may be the result of
political pressure exerted by customary/traditional leaders on the state, as
in South Africa; or it may be linked with the emerging role of civil society
organizations, democratization processes, and the acknowledgement by
governments of the limitations of public land and housing delivery systems
(Kombe and Kreibich, 1999).

Ongoing *decentralization processes*, and pressure from municipalities on
central governments to put an end to the state monopoly on land, facilitate
the involvement of local councillors together with customary actors in the
land delivery process, as observed in Dakar and Ouagadougou from the
mid-1990s onwards (Durand-Lasserve, 2002; UNCHS, 1999). As a result,
neo-customary actors are now providing land with fairly sound *de facto*
security of tenure.

More flexible government policies regarding existing informal settlements, a corresponding sharp decrease in the number of forced evictions
during the past five years and renewed government interest in *tenure regularization or on-site upgrading programmes* generate a sense of tenure
security in those who have access to land through neo-customary land
delivery (Yahya, 2003).

In all countries, the poor people using neo-customary land delivery systems have problems with conventional registration and titling processes
(Deininger, 2003). For this reason, many countries have started land law
reforms or have initiated pilot projects to provide *new forms of evidence
and approaches regarding customary land rights*. Systematic titling is not
considered as the only option (Augustinus, 2003b; Christiensen et al.,
1999).

In some countries (e.g. Uganda, Ghana and South Africa) *new types of
tenure are being introduced under new land law codes*: they include occupancy rights, anti-eviction rights, communal rights and family or group
rights (Augustinus, 2003a).

Dynamics of neo-customary actors and communities living on land delivered by neo-customary systems

These communities are increasingly agreeing to comply with a minimum set of rules and formal procedures, especially regarding registration of land rights and transactions, planning rules and delivery of some basic services.

Land transactions in the neo-customary sector are being progressively formalized: in most cities, the use of witnesses to land transactions is being institutionalized, and transactions are frequently authenticated by local and sometimes central government administrations. Although land purchasers are rarely given any formal title deed, they can usually provide a paper of some sort (usually a deed of sale countersigned by local government officials, or a certificate delivered by administrations in charge) that protects them against eviction attempts. Furthermore, keeping records of informal land transfers and transactions at local level helps solve one of the main problems experienced by neo-customary land delivery: the multiple allocation of the same plot of land to different buyers. This is a common practice, observed in all case studies, with the collusion of customary and local authorities. It also provides improved security of tenure: to defend their rights, people will refer to both the paper and to customary evidence.

Neo-customary systems are beginning to incorporate elements of planning: new concerns to comply with *planning rules* (especially layout plans) are being observed, such as those seen in Uganda and Kenya, but especially in Francophone African countries, where professional surveyors involved in neo-customary land delivery play an important role (Cameroon).

Limitations of these converging dynamics

On the one hand, for government institutions' integration of neo-customary practices is made difficult by the land management and planning reference models from the colonial period and by centralist administrative traditions, especially in relation to land management and administration, and a resistance to decentralization from central government administrations. The situation is further compounded by a lack of human and financial resources and inadequate administrative capacities at local authority level. Widespread corruption and illicit practices surrounding land allocation are hindering the capacity of government institutions to streamline and integrate informal land delivery processes. A further handicap is the low level of registration of titles and deeds and a lack of appropriate land information systems and cadastres: conventional land registration and titling systems are too complicated and too expensive, especially for the poor. Organization at community level is usually weak, and further complicated by political problems, with customary leaders and democratically elected representatives competing over legitimacy.

On the other hand, the neo-customary system is being eroded. Although considerable customary land reserves are available in rural areas far from city centres, customary land reserves are drying up in the inner city fringes. Access to customary land is now possible only in areas far from city centres. In addition, neo-customary owners are being marginalized by intermediaries and brokers, including land surveyors, who are playing an increasingly important role between buyers, customary owners and government administrations. A lack of resources, technical culture, skills and know-how on the part of neo-customary developers is creating a series of additional planning and environmental problems.

ARE CUSTOMARY LAND DELIVERY SYSTEMS A VIABLE ALTERNATIVE TO FORMAL SYSTEMS IN PROVIDING ACCESS TO URBAN LAND FOR THE POOR?

Given the weakness of public and formal private land and housing delivery systems, neo-customary systems are strong enough and effective enough in terms of quantity delivered to be an alternative to formal systems. They are less bureaucratic and more flexible: delivery time is short, transaction costs are lower and they provide enough security of tenure to encourage investment in housing. As suggested by the Kenyan case study, neo-customary land delivery systems can thrive even when they use land that has not been provided by a customary system. However, their effectiveness in reaching the poorest segments of the urban population as well as their long-term sustainability and accessibility must be questioned, especially in the absence of appropriate public policies.

Viability of neo-customary land delivery systems and practices can be questioned on the following points.

Supply of land

On the periphery of most cities, the supply of customary land at reasonable commuting distance from cities is drying up. In the inner part of the urban fringe, it has already been alienated through the sale of small plots of land, or large tracts of customary land to informal developers. However, it should be noted that in cities such as Nairobi, neo-customary land delivery systems can operate without using land that was once delivered by a customary system (Kiamba, 1999).

In most cities studied, customary land reserves still available for urban development are now further and further from city boundaries. Distance from places of employment as well as the lack of public transport severely limits the capacity of the neo-customary sector to respond to the demand for land for housing.

However, more often than not, the scarcity of land and marginaliztion of neo-customary owners by intermediaries does not put an end to neo-customary practices. The Kenya case study illustrates how, even without land reserves, neo-customary leaders can intervene, especially in resolving land disputes, in community organization, and in mediation between residents and public authorities.

Security of tenure

Populations living in irregular urban settlements are all confronted with tenure problems (Augustinus, 2003b; Baharoglu, 2002). However, it must be stressed that informality does not necessarily mean insecurity of tenure. Empirical observations show that residential tenure arrangements, which prevail in neo-customary land delivery systems, can guarantee a reasonably good level of security, even when this is not formally recognized by the state.

Recognition by the community itself and by the neighbourhood is often considered more important than recognition by public authorities for ensuring secure tenure. However, this arrangement may deteriorate under some circumstances:

- when the customary system is in crisis
- when leadership conflicts arise within the group of customary owners, especially between those who allocate the land and other members of the group
- when multiple allocations of the same plot generate a series of conflicts within the community (this may be the result of illicit land sales by unauthorized persons, a common phenomenon in the absence of any land information and record systems)
- when a major conflict arises between customary owners and public authorities about the ownership and use of the land or about the legitimacy of the customary claim. In such cases, alliances often develop between customary owners and the community against the public authorities.

Provision of basic services

It becomes more difficult to implement policies to plan land development and install service facilities because of all of the neo-customary land delivery systems that we have studied, although some of these systems are moving toward more cooperation.

One of the greatest shortcomings of the neo-customary system is its inability to provide land with adequate services. However, official recognition of neo-customary tenure claims and authority improves land management and housing and infrastructure provision, since this increases the confidence that landowners have in their land. Officials can then give these systems advice, legal powers and technical assistance to proceed, and they can also assist them in securing internal or external support.

It seems that neo-customary developments located near cities boundaries and usually targeted at low-middle and middle-income groups are likely to make the necessary land reservations for the future provision of urban services. However, neo-customary actors do not have the required financial resources or guarantees (in terms of security of tenure) to provide basic urban services. If they did, this would inevitably impact on the selling price of land. Provision of services is usually left to local authorities and residents, to be provided at a later stage, once the self-initiated house construction is well advanced.

Conversely, in areas far from city centres, and/or in local contexts where neo-customary land developments are not likely to be integrated into the city web in the near future, neo-customary developers will not make the necessary provisions for the delivery of basic urban services, but prefer to keep the cost of land development as low as possible and proceed as rapidly as possible.

Planning impact

Neo-customary actors do impose on public authority land use and spatial growth patterns in a way that is not usually compatible with long-term planning objectives. Unplanned settlements and inappropriate layouts have created spatial planning and environmental problems in urban areas and have had serious implications for housing development and infrastructure provision, both at settlement and city levels. Urban houses are constructed in areas without adequate infrastructure and are allowed to stand vacant while their owners wait for infrastructure to be provided. Even in cases like Kumasi, Ghana, where the customary system operates within a legal framework, the planning authorities are unable to expedite action on planning applications from developers. This leads many people to carry out their developments without permission. However, it is worth noting, as emphasized in the Benin case study, that future recognition and integration of neo-customary land developments will be facilitated if the development conforms to a minimum set of rules regarding road accessibility, charges, layout and land reservations for public spaces and services.

Urban sprawl

In most cases studied, *uncontrolled urban sprawl* is clearly associated with neo-customary land developments. A steady increase in the price of urban land close to cities, along with the absence of constraining regulations in areas not within municipal administrative boundaries, encourages the spatial expansion of cities, especially in countries where neo-customary institutions and community organization are not in a position to limit land speculation processes at settlement level. In the long term, the cost of urban sprawl borne by public authorities (provision of infrastructure and services) and by the population concerned (higher costs for basic services and for transport) will be considerable.

In the context of South Africa, current development in neo-customary land delivery in the Gauteng and North West provinces is clearly linked with massive subsidies for the provision of basic services in these settlements. The ongoing decentralization process and cost recovery for service delivery is likely to impact on the long-term sustainability of neo-customary settlements.

Accessibility of the urban poor

Diagnosis in all countries suggests that neo-customary land delivery will continue to operate as long as formal land markets remain unresponsive to the needs of the majority of urban dwellers. However, except for Kenya and Namibia, all case studies confirm that neo-customary land delivery systems are responding increasingly to the demand from middle- and low-middle-income groups who have no access to public land and housing development projects. They are less and less effective in reaching poor people in urban areas, either in contexts where neo-customary practices are recognized (Ghana and Uganda), or where they are tolerated and streamlined by inclusive administrative practices (Benin) or are not formally recognized at all (Cameroon, Senegal).

In such contexts, the urban poor have to rely on squatting (in the strict sense of the term) and on the substandard rental sector (in squatter settlements, informal land subdivisions, backyard shacks and dilapidated buildings in city centres).

Alternatively, the poor will settle on customary claimed land in areas unsuitable for urbanization near cities, or in neo-customary development located in the outer peripheries, thus accelerating urban sprawl.

Current trends observed suggest that accessibility of the poor to housing is decreasing rapidly in most cities. However, neo-customary land delivery seems to have a positive impact on the economic situation of low-middle-income groups to which it remains accessible (South Africa, Gauteng Province case study).

The basic contradiction inherent in all policies aiming to improve the performance of neo-customary land delivery systems can be summarized as follows. If neo-customary land delivery practices are formally recognized, and not merely tolerated, they will probably lose their main advantages for low-income populations (fast, simple and cheap delivery); if this is not recognized, public authorities will be denying themselves the possibility of having any influence on neo-customary practices and dynamics, and on some of their major shortcomings.

Dealing with neo-customary land delivery systems: current shifts in public policies

Current neo-customary land delivery processes at the periphery of sub-Saharan African cities have and will have major policy implications in the forthcoming years, and require appropriate public policies. Responses cannot be formulated in strictly technical terms.

From a legal point of view, inclusive administrative practices are more important than formal legal recognition of neo-customary land delivery practices. Benin is a good example of such an approach: although not formally recognized by law, neo-customary practices are accepted, regulated and streamlined by government administrations, through land readjustment and redevelopment processes. This gives households living in land sold out by neo-customary owners a sound security of tenure. In return, the households concerned comply with administrative requirements.

Another limitation of purely technical approaches can be illustrated by the current debate on *land records and registration issues* (Augustinus, 2003a). Conventional land registration systems are not adapted to neo-cus-tomary land delivery, especially in the absence of land-related information systems such as cadastres. Although *de facto* security of tenure is usually provided to households who settle in neo-customary developments, the lack of formal registration or local records of land transfers may generate a series of conflicts (multiple allocation of land). For households living in such settlements, this situation can impact on their access to credit, for public authorities it can affect taxation, and for providers of urban services it affects cost recovery. However, it can be argued that credit may be given without formal land title, taxes can be charged without formal ownership registers, and some services can even be paid for without them. To a large extent, these limitations exist mainly because the formal sector views of neo-customary land delivery systems do not provide a basis for overcoming these obstacles. As noted by Burns et al. (2003: 22):

> 'In many instances customary tenure or informal land administration systems are sufficiently secure in themselves to make large-scale titling programmes unnecessary. Indeed, the formal land registration system in most countries is often not neutral and where titling is implemented, customary tenure people may in fact lose their rights. Women and overlapping rights holders are very vulnerable in these circumstances.'

Analysis of current trends and shifts regarding access of the poor to urban land in sub-Saharan African cities suggests that *ad hoc institutions or administrative procedures* must be set up, especially at local/municipal levels, to ensure compatibility and adequate articulation between the formal and the neo-customary land management procedures and prac-tices (UN-Habitat, 2003c). The main objective is to limit the impact of neo-customary land delivery shortcomings on planning, environment and service provision (advisory planning, conflict resolution, incremental service delivery). The South Africa, Ghana and Benin case studies provide good examples of this.

In this perspective, the role of community-based organizations (CBOs) seems to be essential. *Population participation* improves transparency in land management and does allow a better integration of neo-customary practices into formal processes. In all the cases studied, co-operation between CBOs and public authorities and other stakeholders has resulted in improvements to the settlements concerned, increased access to services and income-earning opportunities, increased community cohesion and improved local governance, and improved environmental conditions.

CHAPTER TWELVE

Street trade in Kenya: the contribution of research in policy dialogue and response[1]

Winnie V. Mitullah

INTRODUCTION TO MICRO AND SMALL ENTERPRISES

Street traders are a subsector of the micro and small enterprises (MSEs) that dominate the Kenyan economy. On average, Kenyan MSEs employs 1.8 employees. The majority of MSEs are micro enterprises with fewer than 10 employees, while 70 per cent of them are one person, own account workers. This infers that the majority of MSE entrepreneurs are operating at the bottom of the economy, with a significant percentage falling among the 53 per cent of Kenyans living below the poverty line of US$1 per day. The latter are largely for subsistence and engage in economically uncompetitive activities both in the urban and rural areas.

The 1999 Baseline Survey (CBS, ACEG & K-REP, 1999) indicated that there were 1.3 million MSEs which contribute 18 per cent of Kenya's gross domestic product (GDP). The survey stated that about 64 per cent of the MSEs are in trade, under which street vendors fall. This subsector is engaged in the buying and selling of goods. Income from the trade subsector is ranked lowest among the MSE sector, but their income is vital to the livelihoods of many urban and rural poor. Micro trade activities are sometimes referred to as 'survivalist' enterprises – they allow entrepreneurs to survive with hardly any savings.

Most of these enterprises operate within the informal economy, referred to in Kenya as *Jua Kali*. The Kenya Labour Force Survey Report of 1998/99 indicates that this informal sector covers all semi-organized and unregulated activities that are small scale in terms of employment. The report notes that the activities are largely undertaken by self-employed persons or employees with few workers in the open markets, in market stalls, in both developed and undeveloped premises, in residential houses or on street pavements (ROK, Labour Force Survey, 2003b).

In Kenya, the concepts of informal economy, MSEs and *Jua Kali* are often used interchangeably. The sector is a major source of employment and income and about 48 per cent of MSE operators are women. By the end of the year 2001, informal employment was estimated at 4.6 million, accounting for 72 per cent of total wage employment and 81 per cent of private sector employment. The contribution of MSEs is more than double that of the medium and large manufacturing sector that stands at 7 per cent of the GDP (ROK, 2003a). Overall, the MSEs employ 2.4 million people and create 75 per cent of all new jobs. Estimates based on the 1999 Baseline Survey of MSEs show that in the year 2002 alone, the MSE sector employed about 5 086 400 people up from 4 624 400 in 2001. This was an increase of 462 000 persons and consisted of 74.2 per cent of total national employment (CBS, ACEG, K-REP, 1999).

Policies for MSEs

The MSE operations cut across almost all sectors of the economy, and sustain a high percentage of households in Kenya. In the 2003 national budget speech, the Minister for Finance noted that the MSE activities form a breeding ground for businesses and employees, and provide one of the most prolific sources of employment. Their operations are more labour intensive than the larger manufacturers. At the same time, they are the suppliers of low-cost products and services in the domestic market.

Dating back to the 1972 International Labour Organization (ILO) study on incomes and employment, the Kenya Government has recognized the role of the informal economy in several policy documents (ROK, 1986, 1992, 2002, 2003a,b). The current Development Plan points out that various rules and regulations that affect the operation and growth of the sector have been reviewed. Other policy responses have included:

- elimination of trade licensing at central government level
- harmonizing, rationalization and implementation of Single Business Permit (SBP)
- ongoing review of labour laws; relaxing business regulations
- broadening access to finance
- proposed enactment of MSE Act
- measures aimed at ensuring control and regulation of hawking within the Central Business District (ROK, 2002).

The Economic Strategy for Wealth and Employment Creation (ROK, 2003a) points out that according to government, employment creation is the most effective strategy for reducing poverty. The government, through this strategy, will address factors responsible for the poor performance of productive sectors, which include:

- high cost of engaging in productive activities
- high cost of capital, particularly for MSEs
- lack of supportive services and weak institutions.

The goal is to remove the kind of regulatory controls that increase the cost of doing business.

In spite of the subsector being a major source of livelihood for a large majority, especially those living below the poverty line, the government has not managed to implement major policy provisions geared for the development of the subsector. During the past three decades, there has been an emphasis on the private formal sector as opposed to the private informal sector. The National Rainbow Coalition (NARC) government intends to change this trend as highlighted in the Economic Strategy Paper. The paper states that the formal and informal sectors are basically the same. The key difference is in access to services and infrastructure and in payment of taxes. The Economic Strategy Paper will eliminate this dichotomy by providing infrastructure and services, particularly financial, to MSEs and by ensuring that they pay taxes.

In the past, the emphasis on the formal private sector has exposed the private informal sector to the vagaries of bad governance, dominated by inefficient and rent-seeking bureaucrats and policy-makers. Such officers have been more concerned with rent seeking than ensuring the formulation of adequate policies and efficient implementation of policy provisions. The policy concern therefore has been how to provide equal opportunities to both the informal and formal sectors of the economy. The NARC government's policy objective is to promote the growth and competitiveness of employment in MSEs by reducing the cost of doing business and generally creating an enabling environment for economic activity.[2]

Creating an enabling environment requires the joint effort of all stakeholders. Under the concept of an enabling environment, a wide range of approaches are taken, by governments, civil society, MSE representative organizations and international donor agencies. An enabling environment includes the social and cultural context, the political systems, including the influence of governance, and the economic systems and policies. Each of these variables affects the markets in which the private sector operates. In turn, they influence the growth and competitiveness of businesses. They should be addressed if MSEs are to thrive.

The government plays a crucial role in MSE development, as displayed by activities performed by different arms of government. The key organs of government such as Parliament and related policy-making institutions such as local authorities (LAs) have to grasp the role of government in MSE development, and be more aware of the impact of new policies and laws on the operations of small enterprises. In this process, the government has to set the institutional framework for business and the rules of the game, and ensure that enterprises receive appropriate incentives to facilitate efficient performance. Such interventions have potential for mainstreaming the informal economy alongside larger formal enterprises.

The dichotomous policy perception of formal and informal has contributed to ineffective policies on the informal economy. It was not until the beginning of 2003 that government debate on the need to integrate the two sectors began. The debate and examination of the sector revealed that the development of both the informal and formal sector and their integration as one vibrant economy has been constrained by regulatory requirements. Most of these requirements date back to the colonial period and have no relevance in independent Kenya. While this has been an obvious fact, the government did not address the issue until the dawn of Structural Adjustment Programmes, and related reform programmes.

In the area of street trade, the Kenya Local Government Reform Programme (KLGRP) has been particularly relevant. The reforms in Kenya began in 1999 with a key policy and programme priority of focusing on reduction of poverty and unemployment, coupled with spurring the economy into higher rates of growth. The reforms had three components:

- improving local service delivery
- enhancing economic governance
- alleviating poverty.

These objectives were to be achieved through increasing efficiency, accountability, transparency and citizen ownership.

The KLGRP is specifically structured as a policy instrument designed to achieve the above goals. Its immediate policy focus has been the removal of unnecessary regulatory barriers and the reduction of costs of doing business. In particular, the government initiated two nationwide reform efforts, namely: the Single Business Permit (SBP) and the Local Authority Transfer Fund (LATF) The SBP in relation to small businesses is a response to business licensing problems faced by SMEs. Business licensing was aimed at protecting consumers from exploitation, health and safety hazards, and control of business activities.

Business licensing imposes costs on businesses that are often out of proportion to the benefits delivered. Further, in practice, the regulatory provisions are abused and have become merely income-earning opportunities for those charged with enforcing the regulations (Devas and Kelly, 2001). While the move to have an SBP is appreciated, it has largely benefited the small and medium firms and not micro firms where the street traders fall. The micro firms have had ad hoc policy responses from both the central and local government levels. These responses have included relocation of street traders and affirming government commitment to the sector, as discussed in the section dealing with policy dialogue.

RESEARCH PROCESS

The overall objective of the research was to generate information and document the level of organization of women street vendors, policies and regulations affecting their operations, and how they respond to such policies and interact among themselves and with policy-makers, planners, administrators and other stakeholders.

Methodology

A total of six research issues[3] were investigated using survey method, focus group discussions (FGDs), key informant interviews, and local and national policy dialogue workshops. The research covered four urban areas (Nairobi, Kisumu, Migori and Machakos). Nairobi, which is the capital city and the largest town covered in the study, had 99 respondents, Kisumu had 84 respondents, Machakos 60 and Migori 58. In total, 301 respondents were interviewed in the four towns. Key informant interviews covering those who deal with street vendors in the areas of policy, planning, enforcement, health requirement, credit, training and general management were also conducted. Information gathering was followed up with local workshops aimed at disseminating the preliminary research findings to the stakeholder groups, discussing findings, and proposing and making recommendations on the way forward for street vending in each of the four urban councils.

The research process culminated in a national workshop aimed at bringing together the four urban councils, government departments, street vendors' associations and other agencies who support street vendors, to discuss pertinent issues regarding the findings. This workshop provided a forum for street traders to interact and lobby urban authorities and other agencies that support small-scale economic activities.

During the first phase of the project, contacts were established in the sampled urban centres. This was followed by identification of existing street vendors' associations. There was, however, no reliable documented information on street vendors' associations per se, mainly because most groups were registered as women's or self-help groups. To overcome this bottleneck, civil society organizations that support street vendors and relevant government offices were consulted. This was followed by basic fact finding, involving walking and talking to both existing street vendors' associations and street vendors themselves. Through this approach, a number of Revolving and Savings Credit Associations (ROSCAs) were identified. In addition, a 1998 Baseline Survey on street vendors was used to back up information gathered from this process.

The preliminary phase of the project showed that existing street vendors' associations were few, with many being ROSCAs. Only a total of five street vendors' associations (three in Kisumu, and one each in Nairobi and Migori) that focus on street vending issues and advocacy were found in the four towns. In total, 28 associations were covered in Nairobi, 23 in Kisumu, 16 in Machakos and 15 in Migori.

Information gathering and further identification of additional street vendors' associations was done during the data collection phase. Interviews were conducted with representatives (leaders and/or spokesperson) of street vendors associations/ROSCAs in the four towns. Using a questionnaire, information on the nature and form of existing associations, membership, purpose and objectives, form of governance, and the links with LAs and other organizations was obtained.

FGDs with representatives of street vendors' associations/ROSCAs were held in each of the four towns. Once the questionnaires had been administered, key informants interviewed, and FGDs conducted and analysed, local dialogues bringing stakeholders together were held in each of the four urban centres.

Local dialogues were followed by a national dialogue bringing together the four urban councils, government and United Nations agencies, street vendors; associations and other agencies who support street vendors. This was aimed at discussing the pertinent issues regarding overall findings on the sector at the national level. The national workshop also provided a forum for the urban councils to interact with each other, and with those who support SMEs. Further, it offered a good opportunity to forge partnerships, notably for possible funding of programmes for street vending within respective urban councils.

Summary of findings

On the issue of policies and regulations, the research found that most urban authorities in Kenya were operating on colonial by-laws that had yet to be reviewed. The policies were deficient and the urban authorities had not only failed to enforce them, but in reality given their form and coverage, they were not possible to enforce. The research further revealed that licensing, which had originally been intended to enable entrepreneurs to conduct their businesses productively and profitably, had become a stumbling block.

In spite of the number of people who can be licensed being limited, once the licence is given, it is shrouded with many other outdated restrictive requirements relating to public health, building requirements and other regulations outlined in the Local Government Act. This had resulted in most traders evading licences, and therefore flouting most regulations laid down by authorities. At the same time, prohibited commodities such as cooked food originating from unknown sources were being sold to the public.

The study concluded that there was need for LAs to put in place relevant policy frameworks and reviews of the existing by-laws if they have to conform with government policy of enhancing the performance of MSEs. During the research, only one of the sample urban councils had reviewed by-laws relating to street trade. The other three councils continued to put emphasis on enforcement without clarity on policies and regulations. The councils had not hit a balance between order, and promoting the activities and performance of informal sector operators such as street traders. Three of the councils were merely handling street traders as a temporary problem, bound to disappear, although experience had shown the contrary.

The study revealed that the inability to address the issues was intensified by lack of effective organization among street traders, especially in the area of representation and advocacy on issues affecting them. At the conclusion of the research, a summary of action areas was made with the aim of reaching bureaucrats and policy makers at the LA and central government level. A number of action areas were used in sensitizing street traders, urban authorities and other stakeholders as discussed in the section below.

POLICY RESPONSES ON MSE DEVELOPMENT

Kenya has made a number of policy responses targeting MSEs since the research on street vending began in 1999. Apart from the research, the policy responses owe their origin to the Structural Adjustment Programmes (SAPs), especially the LGRP, pressure from civil society organizations, and the stakeholders participatory approach adopted by the research and in policy development.

In spite of the government having recognized the potential of MSEs way back in 1972, there were very few programmes targeting MSEs before the SAPs. The first major step taken by the government was the establishment of the Department of Micro and Small Enterprise Development within the Ministry of Labour and Human Resource Development. The Department is charged with the coordination of all issues, programmes and projects relating to the development of MSEs.

The Deregulation Project that was part of the Department of MSE Development, and a collaborator in the Institute for Development Studies (IDS) research, examined laws and regulations that impede on the growth and development of MSEs. Their work revealed that 'the licensing laws and by-laws which are set up to control, prohibit or regulate various business activities were the single, greatest deterrent to entry into, and growth of businesses in the private sector, including street vending in Kenya'. This was highlighted by two studies; one examined the non-compliance cost of doing business (Kobonyo et al., 1999), while the other examined the situation of street vending (Alila and Mitullah, 2000).

The two key research outputs and work by the Deregulation Project resulted in the government addressing the regulatory problems facing MSEs. A number of regulations and licensing requirements that retard businesses were recommended for removal. Of particular note is the implementation of the SBP by LAs that began in 1999, with mandatory implementation by all LAs effected in January 2000.

The efforts to support MSE development have been intensified by the NARC government since it came into power after winning the 2002 national elections. A number of Ministries support the MSEs, and the Ministry of Labour and Human Resource Development is the lead Ministry. The Ministry has finalized a draft sessional paper on the 'Development of Micro and Small Enterprises for Employment Creation and Poverty Reduction'. The draft sessional paper highlights a number of issues relating to legal and regulatory frameworks, markets and marketing, credit and finance, physical infrastructure, entrepreneurship, business development services, gender, environment, information, management and institutional frameworks for MSE sector coordination.

The Ministry of Labour and Human Resource Development constituted a task force in May 2003 to look into issues affecting MSE performance and growth. The task force had a number of tasks including review of policies, MSE programmes, concerns of MSEs, strengths and weaknesses of MSE umbrella associations, governance and institutional capacity of MSEs for job creation and economic growth. A key output of the task force has been the observation that associations are important for ensuring the efficient operation of MSEs.

The themes of the draft sessional paper and the task force paper are in line with the NARC Government's national policy on economic development, highlighted in the paper on Economic Strategy for Wealth and Employment Creation and the current Development Plan (2002–2008). The economic development paper emphasizes the need to integrate the formal and informal sectors of the economy. For three decades, these sectors were viewed as separate, and with different potential. The increasing poverty and concentration of the population on the informal economy has justified the policy focus on MSE development.

Street trade

Most national programmes geared for MSEs have focused on the small-scale manufacturing enterprises, as opposed to micro trade enterprises where the street traders fall. Until the beginning of 2003, when relocation of street traders began, the latter were exposed to harassment, insecurity, and lack of infrastructure and services. Over the years, this has been justified by the fact that the street traders are not licensed, and are therefore operating illegally. Business licensing has been used by LAs as a control, with negative effect on MSE performance and growth.

While a number of policy responses on MSEs began during the year 2000, those directly affecting street traders began in 2002. The 2002–2008 Kenya Development Plan indicates that measures aimed at ensuring control and regulation of hawking within the Central Business District (CBD) would be taken. Most major urban LAs have begun implementing this policy with a number of problems, the major problem being the reluctance of policy-makers and administrators to allow street traders to trade within the inner circle of the CBD, and the lack of adequate space for all street vendors within the CBD.

For instance in the case of the CBD of the capital city of Nairobi, where over 50 000 street traders operate, the city has only managed to set aside sites that can accommodate about 7000 traders. This move is positive, although the tenure remains unclear, with the urban authorities viewing the sites as temporary while the vendors view them as permanent. Although the urban authority had a plan to charge some fees, this has not been possible due to a mix-up in allocation. There were cases of double allocations, infiltration by those not allocated sites and hostility directed at the City Council authorities. This has resulted in a stand-off situation that can only be solved through dialogue and negotiation.

Most of these sites lack infrastructure and services, and are congested. The congestion is due in part to infiltration by vendors not allocated sites, and also by vendors allocated unfavourable sites where there is insecurity and fewer customers. These are aspects that should have been taken into consideration before relocation. Past experience of ad hoc street traders' relocation indicate that without critical consideration of access to customers and security, relocation efforts have been resisted and fruitless.

In the relocation process, associations have not been used effectively, partly due to their fragmentation and weakness. The city authorities opted to use representatives of street traders drawn from different areas of the CBD. The role of these representatives was largely to listen to the packages being offered by the authorities, as opposed to negotiation and dialogue. Their 'listening' role and failure to negotiate for appropriate relocation sites and an efficient allocation process made most street traders feel betrayed.

The relocation policy would have been more successful if the street traders had a unifying body advocating and negotiating on their behalf. Ensuring a dynamic MSE sector requires functioning associations that support entrepreneurs, lobby and hold dialogue with authorities for enabling MSE policies and programmes. Associations are useful for purchasing raw materials, marketing, bulk transport, sharing tools and equipment, guaranteeing loans, providing market information, and linking up with training and business service providers.

The IDS research identified a number of issues for dialogue and negotiation between the street traders and other stakeholders, especially urban authorities. In relation to sites of operation, the research noted that availability of an acceptable site of operation is a pre-condition for compliance with various statutes relating to business operation.

Respective urban authorities are charged with the responsibility of setting aside vending sites. However, most urban authorities, as demonstrated in the case of Nairobi, are reluctant to allocate vending sites within the CBD, and allocate sites outside the CBD which vendors often decline to move to. The research concluded that there was a need to allocate safe and accessible sites for vending activities and identified points for policy dialogue and negotiation as follows.

- Urban authorities in collaboration with stakeholder groups need to come up with appropriate long-term vending sites, which are recognized and planned.
- In cases where long-term vending sites cannot be designated, temporary sites with specified hours and days of operation must be designated.

- The conflict between vendors operating around established formal markets and those operating within the markets needs to be resolved through collaboration of stakeholder groups and efficient planning, which allows co-existence.
- Urban authorities in collaboration with vendors and other stakeholder groups are to provide basic services (toilets, water and storage facilities) in areas designated for vending.
- Urban authorities in collaboration with stakeholder groups are to design an appropriate mobile vending rack and/or structure for vending operations.
- Urban authorities and other stakeholder groups are to enable street vendors to take responsibility and ensure that their operations do not contravene the agreed policies and regulations.
- Once allocated sites (preferably communal), the vendors must ensure that they do not trade in prohibited or restricted areas, do not turn the sites into accommodation, and that they respect and observe the rights of other users of space and all other citizens affected by their activities.
- Urban authorities are to consider establishing pilot vending sites within the CBD, to allow review of street vendors organizational capacity and further integration of their activities within the CBD.

The above points were raised and discussed with LAs at the local and national level. However, few of these issues have been given critical policy consideration. In particular, meaningful engagement of stakeholder groups has only been initiated with pressure from fragmented street traders' associations. In order to have effective policy dialogue and negotiation there is a need for joint action both at the local and national level by the various street traders' associations, urban authorities and other stakeholders.

Associations and policy development

The IDS research revealed that the existing street traders' associations were weak and required capacity building to enable effective participation in policy development and implementation. The draft sessional policy paper on MSE development indicates that the government will provide an enabling policy environment, including investment in human resource development and basic welfare.

The need to build capacity of associations of street traders resulted in the development of a second research proposal by IDS in collaboration with StreetNet, a global organization that supports street traders. The proposal was on 'Facilitation of Street Traders Organization in Kenya'. The research covers seven urban authorities in Kenya and has eight objectives.

- Exposing and sensitizing street vendors to the benefits of forming local and national alliances of street vendors.

- Facilitating regular policy dialogue between street vendors and local authorities.
- Facilitating holding regular follow-up meetings with street vendors' associations.
- Providing a link between street vendors and other authorities.
- Packaging relevant information on street vendors and their activities.
- Collecting and documenting relevant information on street vendors.
- Supporting street vendors' local travel and communication.
- Extending coverage to areas not covered by the IDS study.

The facilitation has enabled the fragmented street traders' associations to begin coming together in policy advocacy and negotiation. Kisumu City Council provides a good example of organizing for policy dialogue. When the IDS conducted research on policies, regulations and organization of street traders in 1999, Kisumu had fragmented street vendors' associations that had no knowledge of each other and were not making any joint effort in addressing issues affecting their enterprises. The relations between the Kisumu City Council and the street traders was poor and a 1958 by-law was the operating point of reference for enforcing regulations.

The research brought the different street traders' associations together in FGDs and in policy dialogue forums with the city authorities. These two activities became 'eye-openers' for both the street traders and the urban authority. The two parties realized that a number of problems, including strained relationships can be solved through dialogue. This could not be successfully achieved by fragmented street vendors' associations. The associations had therefore to identify issues that cut across the board and create an institution that could pursue the issues with policy-makers.

The process of establishing a joint street vendors' and informal traders' association began in 2001. It culminated in 2002 with the establishment and registration of Kisumu Alliance of Street and Informal Traders (KASVIT). The alliance has a number of objectives, including: bringing together different associations of street vendors, mediating between local authority and street vendors, improving socio-economic status of members, encouraging and enlightening women to assume leadership positions in organizations popularizing street vending locally and internationally, and advocating for the rights of vendors among others.

In the area of policy dialogue, the alliance has identified issues of engagement. However, the city authority continues to deal with the street traders in an inconsistent manner, which diverts the dialogue and negotiation process. A recent case is reflected in how the planned relocation of street traders in Kisumu has been handled. While the alliance has been ready to negotiate, the urban authority to some extent is still pursuing autocratic approaches of management. A case in point was a notice from the City Council of Kisumu dated 21 September giving notice for the relocation of street traders on Ojino Okew street. KASVIT responded to the council in a letter dated 23 October (ses Box 12.1).

Box 12.1   Letter from KASVIT to the town clerk, Kisumu Municipality

We are aggrieved and sad after receiving the notice from your office because we agreed that we should be holding dialogue to discuss such matters. We also see ill motive since the notice was issued last month (21 September 2003) and we only received it on 22 October (a month later), yet it was supposed to be a 14 days notice.

We got the notice at the time we were preparing to attend the national workshop of street vendors (26 to 28 October) in Nairobi. The notice is also against the Ministerial statement that stopped such actions, which we welcomed.

The said hawkers have been hawking at the site for the past ten years and paying levies to the council and they are often harassed without a solution. They are also members of Kenya Women Finance Trust and are paying loans. We therefore request to have an audience with you on Friday 31 October 2003, when we come back from the workshop in your office at 2pm to discuss the issue.

We are hoping for positive response.

Source: KASVIT File (2003)

This letter by KASVIT would not have been written before the exposure through the research process. The street vendors have become aware that policy positions should not be accepted without participation and dialogue.

LESSONS ON POLICY DIALOGUE AND DEVELOPMENT

Positive policy responses depend on efficient engagement of stakeholders in dialogue and policy development, and efficient storage of information and institutional memory. In order for this to happen, stakeholders have to have the capacity to engage in policy development, access and store information. On the part of the government, an inclusive approach that integrates the stakeholders in the policy process has to be adopted. In Kenya, as in many other developing countries, there has been a tendency for policy-makers to respond to external pressures, as opposed to local internal dynamics.

While it is appropriate to argue that the external pressures are triggered by the prevailing internal conditions, the exclusion of key stakeholders in determining policy directions cannot be justified. The lack of involvement of stakeholders partly owes its origin to the dictatorial regimes that prevailed in Africa prior to the adoption of participatory approaches that accompanied SAPs.

The reform programmes lay emphasis on participatory policy development, planning and implementation of programmes. This approach has largely benefited organized stakeholders who understand the dynamics of policy development. At the beginning of the IDS research, the street traders could not conceptualize the possibility of contributing to the policy processes. In one of the policy dialogue forums, a woman street vendor had to quietly ask one of the researchers whether it was appropriate for her to contribute to the debate on trade licensing and enforcement of by-laws in the presence of chief officers of the Municipal Council. She further wanted to know from the researchers whether a negative comment on the council would result in future victimization. The researchers shared her fear, which was representative of other street traders, with the chief officers during the forum. The officers assured the representatives of street vendors and other stakeholders that there would be no victimization, and that the forum was aimed at soliciting ideas for improving MSE operations and general governance within the council.

Another lesson is the relevance of adequate information relating to policy processes and appropriate storage of information and institutional memory. The IDS research findings showed the LAs have poor information systems and loss of institutional memory due to rapid transfers of chief officer. During our research and facilitation of street traders' organizations, it was revealed that information relevant for follow-up and management of policy processes is hardly available. In some cases, the information could only be accessed by locating the individual officer who dealt with an issue. In some cases the information was available but storage and classification was poor and could not be accessed easily.

The research further noted that there was a need for LAs to create a communication forum with street traders either through their associations or through a standing committee. Associations such as KASVIT are currently serving such roles, and have managed to engage their LAs on issues relating to street trade. Communication needs to go hand in hand with information dissemination, including making policies and regulations easy to read and understand. The MSE task force report has suggested the establishment of a *Jua Kali* Authority comprising of Government Ministries and a cross-section of stakeholders. The authority will drive the implementation of MSE policy, as well as coordination of the sector. The establishment of this authority has potential to improve the performance of MSEs.

The answers we need now to prepare for our urban futures

Shlomo Angel

We conclude this volume on our urban futures with a list of questions, questions that now need urgent answers, answers that can prepare us all for managing our urban futures in a more efficient, equitable and sustainable manner. A cursory glimpse of this long list should convince the reader that – while the questions may sound familiar – the answers to most of them are not at all obvious, let alone convincing. Were we in possession of better answers to these questions, our actions would be better informed, our efforts more likely to yield fruitful results and our limited resources more likely to be put to better use. Yes, we know a lot more about developing country cities than we did 30 years ago. Yes, we know a lot more about interventions that do not work, and a little more about interventions that do. But, on the whole, our knowledge is still sketchy and much of it is fast becoming outdated. We now know how to phrase many questions, but we are short on reliable answers, and we have spent precious time acting out of wishful thinking.

The following questions are presented here in the hope that they can stimulate a resurgence of useful research and debate on cities in the developing countries. Useful in the sense of informing future urban policies, plans, programmes and projects; useful not only for national governments and international agencies, but to all urban stakeholders, be they public authorities, private corporations, civic organizations, communities or individual families. Such research and debate is not likely to be undertaken unless able and creative researchers see its potential value and move to pursue it, and unless those who will need to fund it appreciate its potential usefulness.

The questions that follow have been grouped into ten categories:

1. the process of urbanization
2. cities and development
3. land use, development and tenure
4. urban poverty
5. urban governance
6. urban and housing finance
7. urban subsidies, taxes and transfers
8. houses and communities
9. urban infrastructure
10. urban research.

THE PROCESS OF URBANIZATION

- Can much-needed rural development efforts slow down the rates of rural–urban migration? Is there reliable evidence to demonstrate that successful rural development keeps people on the farm?
- How widespread is the realization that the process of urbanization in the developing countries is so powerful, that – short of forcefully restricting the freedom of movement – little can be done to slow it down, reverse it or channel it?
- Are there any examples of public policies and programmes that have successfully diverted migrating rural populations from the primate city to secondary cities, or from developed regions to developing regions?
- Can cities ever become more productive and more livable without attracting more people into them?
- Is there any convincing evidence to support the contention that actively preparing for the absorption of new rural or international migrants into cities accelerates in-migration?
- What are the relative costs and benefits of investing or not investing in making active preparations for urban expansion to absorb the projected urban population growth in the developing countries?

CITIES AND DEVELOPMENT

- Is there reliable evidence that cities produce a greater share of the gross national product (GNP) than their share of the population?
- Are larger cities more productive than smaller ones? Why are some cities in similar circumstances more productive than others?
- Are cities with dispersed employment opportunities more productive that cities with concentrated employment opportunities? Are low-density cities more productive than high-density ones?
- Why are some cities growing faster than others? Are the faster-growing cities in any given country the more productive?
- How much of rural development can be attributed to remittances and income transfers from urban areas? To what extent is the rural economy integrated with the urban economy?
- To what extent is globalization making cities more similar? What do cities do to preserve their individual identities and exploit their unique advantages?
- Should countries concentrate their resources in a few of their cities to compete more effectively in global and regional markets?

LAND USE, DEVELOPMENT AND TENURE

- Is squatting – the illegal occupation of land – in developing country cities on the decrease?
- Is land hoarding and land speculation on the urban fringe on the increase?
- Who will be helped from better urban land title registers – the urban poor or those who amass land for purposes of speculation?
- In which developing country cities have programmes that issue land titles to squatters on public and private lands been successful and why? Are title documents of more value to women-headed households?
- On the whole, are poorer cities denser than richer ones? If so, is land consumption per capita likely to increase as economic conditions in cities improve?
- Are the mixed land-use patterns in developing country cities more efficient and equitable than the single-use zoning patterns in industrialized countries?

URBAN POVERTY

- Are the income distributions within cities more or less equal than the income distributions in entire countries?
- To what extent are rural migrants better or worse off than they were before migrating to the city? Are the urban poor better off than the rural poor?
- Why is there so little homelessness in developing countries? Is the absence of homelessness likely to persist?
- To want extent do rural and urban areas provide cushions for each other in times of crisis? To what extent is it still possible for people to move back and forth between the two?
- Do the poor gain more political power by moving to the cities? Under what conditions are they able to exercise this power to improve their lot? Are cities more democratic than rural areas?
- What is the present value of the illegal – or informal – housing assets of the urban poor? Has the urban distribution of urban wealth become less skewed over time?

URBAN GOVERNANCE

- To what extent are standards, norms and values from industrialized countries still being applied uncritically in developing countries?
- In which cities have measures to introduce appropriate and affordable land subdivision standards and building codes been successful?

- To what extent is the informal sector – whether in transport, business or housing – gradually becoming formal over time?
- Is legal activism – both on the national and international front – a promising approach to managing urban challenges in developing countries? Is strengthening the rule of law working to the benefit of the urban poor seeking housing and work?
- Is decentralization an unmitigated good, or has it – in some cases – gone too far? Is the governance of developing country metropolitan areas improving over time? To what extent does the existence of metropolis-wide authorities affect their performance?
- To what extent are developing country cities vulnerable to terror, and how can they be made less vulnerable? To what extent are ungovernable informal settlements a threat to national and international security?
- When are public, private or civic organizations most effective in urban service delivery? When are partnerships among them most effective in urban service delivery?

URBAN AND HOUSING FINANCE

- Have long-term mortgages in developing country cities become more widespread and affordable? Are mortgage markets too volatile and too risky for lower-income families?
- Are developing country municipalities becoming better able to attract and manage long-term credit for public works projects by themselves?
- Can micro-credits and small subsidies be applied on a broad scale to increase economic activities within homes? Can they be applied on a broad scale to reduce overcrowding?
- Are developing countries succeeding in creating secondary mortgage markets? Are they succeeding in selling mortgage instruments in their own – or in global – capital markets?
- Are loans by multilateral organizations for urban projects yielding their expected benefits? What needs to be done so that adequate resources are allocated for the proper and timely evaluation of such projects?
- How can more long-term investments be directed towards meeting future – rather than present – needs, so that there is a better balance between absorbing new urban growth and meeting current needs?

URBAN SUBSIDIES, TAXES AND TRANSFERS

- To what extent do urban plans, policies, programmes and projects in developing countries pay adequate attention to the availability of resources to implement them at the required scale?
- Do developing country metropolitan areas pay their share of government revenues, or do they subsidize the rest of the country?
- Is the share of public revenues collected directly by municipalities on the increase or on the decrease?
- Are housing subsidies on the decrease? Is the share of direct demand-side housing subsidies – to assist families in buying, improving or renting a home – on the increase?
- Is rent control on the decrease? Are rents requiring a larger share of household incomes?
- What are the most effective means for the public to share in the increase of land values brought about by public actions? In which developing country cities have measures to recover the costs of extending infrastructure services been successful and why?

HOUSES AND COMMUNITIES

- With the number of urban homes being built frequently exceeding the rate of household formation, why is there still talk of the 'housing deficit'?
- On the whole, is the urban housing stock improving or getting worse? Where, and under what conditions, is it getting worse? On the whole, are urban evictions on the increase or on the decrease?
- What percentages of homes in developing country cities are constructed illegally, in illegal subdivisions, or on illegally occupied land? Are these percentages on the increase?
- Has housing in developing country cities become more or less affordable? Have the developers of formal-sector housing been coming down market, producing cheaper and more affordable housing?
- How do remittances of international migrants affect the quality and prices of residential real estate in their home countries?
- Is crime in the settlements of the poor on the increase or on the decrease? To what extent do crime levels in informal settlements affect land and house values?
- How can the dilapidated historical centers in developing country cities be effectively preserved without displacing their poor occupants?
- Is home ownership in developing country cities on the increase or on the decrease? What accounts for variations in home ownership rates among developing country cities? Is home ownership an unmitigated good, or is there more to be done to promote rental housing?

URBAN INFRASTRUCTURE

- Should metropolitan authorities assemble land now – for transport rights of way and open space preservation – in advance of the coming doubling-up of the size of cities in developing countries?
- For cities scheduled to double in size in the next 20 years, is there new room for grand visions of broad avenues, public parks and civic architecture in the City Beautiful tradition?
- Are urban upgrading programmes becoming more expensive and more limited in scope, rather than more extensive and national in scope? To what extent do urban upgrading projects increase land and house values? To what extent do they lead to gentrification?
- Is the privatization of urban services yielding its promised benefits? Is the contracting of urban services to international corporations yielding its promised benefits?
- Are water and sewerage service and quality levels on the increase or on the decrease?
- In which developing country cities have measures to make public transport serve a growing share of commuters been successful and why?

URBAN RESEARCH

- Why are there so few high-quality research papers published on developing country urban themes? To what extent are research results from industrialized countries applied uncritically in developing countries?
- Can intelligent global conversations on developing country cities be carried out on the Internet by creating global forums and allowing users to rate each other's comments?
- What kind of comparative research will most likely generate the 'norms' that decision-makers need to plan for and measure performance? To what extents are such norms likely to be regional, rather than global?
- How do urban development 'fashions' – such as 'sites and services', 'title regularization', 'urban upgrading' or 'direct demand-side subsidies' – take off, become the norm and then subside?
- Can we ensure that 'best practices' – with a potentially global application – are evaluated objectively in a timely manner, possibly by employing highly critical 'pro' and 'con' evaluators sharing the same data?
- Can cross-sectional data for a relatively small, global sample of cities be collected in a cumulative fashion over time, so as to make the testing of important hypotheses in a rigorous manner possible and affordable?

Our understanding of key urban phenomena in the developing countries can only be deepened by undertaking and funding systematic and rigorous research. For too many years already, urban investments have been undertaken and urban policies implemented on the basis of an impressionistic understanding of the problems at hand, of the complex conditions underlying them, and of the limited human and institutional resources available to manage them properly. With the prospect of the doubling of the urban population in the developing countries in the next 30 years – and the possibility that the built-up areas of these cities will more than double – we have been given yet another chance to get it right, so to speak.

We are now facing an historical moment that will not occur again – a moment when developing country cities are moving to basically complete their process of urbanization. We now have a singular opportunity to apply the lessons we learned during the first wave of rapid urbanization in the second half of the last century, to answer the questions we could formulate given these lessons, and to move ahead more intelligently to transform developing country cities into cities that are more efficient and productive, more equitable and caring, and more livable and sustainable than the cities we have created to date. It is now more apparent than ever that the public resources available for guiding, facilitating and supporting the coming wave of urbanization are indeed limited, especially given the dire conditions and critical shortages already facing existing urban populations.

We can only hope that an adequate share of these public resources – national as well as global – will be directed towards the accumulation of our understanding of urban processes and policies. And that committed urban researchers, for their part, using research tools that have only recently become available (such as low-cost satellite imagery and low-cost global communications through the Internet) will develop new, low-cost data collection and analysis methods that can provide reliable answers to many of the questions listed above, within the severe budget constraints they will face.

Notes on authors

Shlomo Angel received his degree in architecture at the College of Environmental Design, University of California, Berkeley, in 1967, and his PhD in city and regional planning at the same college in 1972. In 1987, he worked as an international consultant to the UN Development Programme and to the World Bank drafting the UN's Global Strategy for Shelter for the Year 2000 in 1988. Recently, he has worked as a consultant to the World Bank and the Inter-American Development Bank, preparing and conducting numerous housing sector assessments in Latin America. In 2000, he published *Housing Policy Matters: A Global Analysis*, a comparative study of housing conditions and housing policies in 53 countries, based on data collected in the Housing Indicators Programme. He has combined his research and consultancy work with teaching urban planning and housing policy. He currently teaches at the Robert F. Wagner Graduate School of Public Service at New York University, and at the Woodrow Wilson School of Public and International Affairs at Princeton University. He is presently working on a comparative study of global urban expansion supported by the World Bank, entitled *The Urban Growth Management Initiative: Confronting the Expected Doubling of the Size of Cities in the Developing Countries in the Next Thirty Years*.

Yves Cabannes is a senior research affiliate at the Center for Urban Development Studies at the Harvard Design School. Until December 2003 he was the regional coordinator of the UNCHS/UNDP Urban Management Programme (UMP) for Latin America and the Caribbean based in Quito, Ecuador. Prior to joining the UMP in 1997, he worked in Brazil, with the NGO Cearah-Periferia and GRET in Fortaleza from 1990, whose main activities involved working with extremely poor communities (housing, income-generating activities), local government and social movements. Yves is an economist, planner and urban specialist, having completed doctoral-level studies in Paris. He has worked in several Asian, Arab and African countries, as well as in Latin America and the Caribbean, and has particular experience and interest in public policy, low-cost housing, appropriate technology, credit community development and local empowerment. He has been and continues to be a consultant to the United Nations, European Union and other international organizations, visiting post-graduate lecturer in various European, American and Latin American universities, and researcher in habitat-related issues.

Alain Durand-Lasserve is a senior researcher at the Centre National de la Recherche Scientifique (CNRS), France. He is currently attached to the SEDET Research Centre, University Denis Diderot, Paris. During the past few years he has been involved in a series of research studies on urban land tenure policies and the regularization of informal settlements in developing countries for bilateral and multilateral aid agencies in African, Asian and Latin American countries.

Steven Friedman is a senior research fellow at the Centre for Policy Studies, an independent research institute in Johannesburg, South Africa. He has edited two books on South Africa's negotiated transition and is the author of a study the South African labour movement. He has acted as a consultant on urban politics and has written journal articles, book chapters and monographs on this politics in the cities. He is currently studying the relationship between inequality and politics, primarily in new democracies. *Kenny Hlela* and *Paul Thulare* are researchers at the Centre, currently engaged in a study of associational life and citizenship among people living and working in informal settings.

Nabeel Hamdi qualified as an architect at the Architectural Association in London in 1968. He worked for the Greater London Council between 1969 and 1978, where his award-winning housing projects (PSSHAK) established his reputation in participatory design and planning. From 1981 to 1990, he was Associate Professor of Housing at the Massachusetts Institute of Technology (MIT), where he was later awarded the Ford International Career Development Chair. Hamdi won the Habitat Scroll of Honour in 1997 for his work on community action planning. He has consulted to all the major international development agencies, to charities and NGOs worldwide, on participatory action planning and the upgrading of slums in cities. He has authored one book (*Housing Without Houses*), co-authored two (*Making Micro Plans* and *Action Planning for Cities*) and edited one (*Educating for Real*). His forthcoming book (*Small Change: The Art of Practice and the Limits of Planning in Cities*) will be published by EarthScan in autumn 2004.

Jane Handal is an architect and an urban designer. She received her BSc in architecture from Birzeit University, Palestine, and her MA and PhD in urban design from Oxford Brookes University. She worked as an architect in two offices in Palestine and as an urban designer/planner for the Ministry of Planning and International Co-operation (under Norwegian and Palestinian Management) between 1995 and 1999 – an era in which the rebuilding of Palestine presented tremendous opportunities and challenges. During her PhD ('Rebuilding the Identity of the City in History') she also gained work experience in academia and in the development and investment world by spending six months in the World Bank, Washington, DC, working on urban and social development in North Africa. Her PhD research explored the relationship between urban design and development, and places special emphasis on reconstructing identity in post-conflict settings. She carried out the field work for her doctoral studies in Palestine.

Trudy Harpham, PhD is Professor of Urban Development and Policy at London South Bank University. An urban geographer by PhD, she has worked in international public health for the past 20 years and is a co-principal investigator on the Young Lives project – an international study of child poverty. She has produced major texts on urban health in developing countries and has a particular interest in social capital and mental health. She teaches research methods and uses both quantitative and qualitative methods in her research projects. She was a member of the US National Academy of Science's expert panel on urban population dynamics, 1999–2003.

Sunil Kumar has a PhD in development planning form the Development Planning Unit, University College London. He currently lectures on social policy and planning in developing countries, and international housing and social change at the Department of Social Policy, London School of Economics and Political Science. He works on urban issues in cites in developing countries and his specific research interests are housing, housing tenure, poverty, livelihoods, informal institutions and local politics. In 1987, he was the Asian Regional Coordinator for a programme on non-governmental organizations and human settlements as part of the International Year of Shelter organized by the United Nations Centre for Human Settlements (UNCHS Habitat). He has undertaken consultancies and conducted research for the UK Department for International Development (DFID). His latest major publication is entitled *Social Relations, Rental Housing Markets and the Poor in Urban India, 2001*.

Michael Majale was, until August 2003, an international projects manager with the Intermediate Technology Development Group. Now a lecturer in Overseas Development at the University of Newcastle upon Tyne, his research interests focus on urbanization and urban development in the South, and improving the lives and livelihoods of poor people living and working in informal settlements.

Winnie V. Mitullah is a researcher and a lecturer at the Institute for Development Studies (IDS), University of Nairobi. She holds a PhD in political science and public administration. Her PhD thesis was on urban housing, with a major focus on policies relating to low-income housing. Over the years, she has researched, written and consulted in the area of urban development, with a focus on housing, informal urban economy, politics, institutions, governance and the role of stakeholders in development. Recently completed works include a contribution to the *Global Report on Human Settlements 2003*, case study of Nairobi; contribution to the forthcoming *World Development Report on Investment Climate and Informal Enterprises*, a case study of street trade in Africa; a study commissioned by the International Labour Organization on the *Informal Labour in the Construction Industry in Kenya: A Case Study of Nairobi* and a book chapter on 'Gender inclusion in transition politics: a review and critique of women's engagement'.

Caroline Moser is currently Senior Research Associate, Overseas Development Institute (ODI), and Adjunct Professor, New School, New York. From 1990 to 2000 she worked at the World Bank, first in the Urban Development Division, and then as Lead Specialist Social Development in the Latin American Department. Previously she was a lecturer at the London School of Economics, and before that at the Development Planning Unit, University College London. Recent research includes participatory urban appraisals of urban violence and exclusion in Colombia, Guatemala and Jamaica, and research on urban poverty in the context of adjustment in Ecuador, Zambia, Philippines and Hungary. She received a PhD in social anthropology from Sussex University, a postgraduate diploma from Manchester University and a BA from Durham University. Among her numerous publications are: *Gender Planning and Development: Theory, Practice and Training* (1993); *Confronting Crisis: A Comparative Study of Household Responses to Poverty and Vulnerability in Four Poor Urban Communities* (1996); co-author of *Violence in a Post-Conflict Context: Urban Poor Perceptions from Guatemala* (2000) and *Urban Poor Perceptions of Violence and Exclusion in Colombia* (2001); co-editor of *Gender, Armed Conflict and Political Violence* (2001) and *Women, Human Settlement and Housing* (1987).

Mary Racelis is a research scientist of the Institute of Philippine Culture, Ateneo de Manila University, and its former director. A sociologist, she has published extensively on poverty and well-being, urbanization, community organizing, people's empowerment, civil society, gender, children and socio-cultural change. Her development experience includes having been Regional Director, UNICEF Eastern and Southern Africa, Nairobi, Kenya; Country Representative, Ford Foundation, Manila; and a member of several NGO national and international boards. These board memberships represent her professional and personal commitment to improving the lives of poor people through the Community Organization of the Philippines, Community Organizers Multiversity, Freedom to Build, International Institute of Rural Reconstruction, Oxfam America, Solidarity Group of Marginalized Urban Poor and Urban Poor Associates. She has acted as a consultant to the Government of the Philippines as well as to the

Asian Development Bank, AusAID, the Rockefeller Foundation, UNICEF, United Nations Development Programme and the World Bank. Her most recent set of activities relates to her appointment in 2003 by United Nations Secretary General Kofi Annan to serve on the High Level Panel of Eminent Persons on United Nations Relations with Civil Society.

David Satterthwaite is a senior fellow at the International Institute for Environment and Development (IIED) and also on the teaching staff of the London School of Economics and of University College London. He has been editor of the international journal *Environment and Urbanization* from its inception in 1989. He is also a member of the Millennium Taskforce on Improving the Lives of Slum Dwellers and served on the US National Academy of Sciences Panel on Urban Population Dynamics (2001–3) and on the Inter-Governmental Panel on Climate Change (2001–3). He has written or edited various books, including *Squatter Citizen* (with Jorge E. Hardoy), *The Earthscan Reader on Sustainable Cities, Environmental Problems in an Urbanizing World* (with Jorge E. Hardoy and Diana Mitlin) and *Empowering Squatter Citizen; Local Government, Civil Society and Urban Poverty Reduction* (with Diana Mitlin), which are all published by Earthscan, London.

Mona Serageldin is Adjunct Professor of Urban Planning at the Harvard University Graduate School of Design, where she has been a member of the faculty since 1985. She is also the Associate Director of the Center for Urban Development Studies. She has over 30 years of professional and academic experience and has worked in Eastern Europe, the Middle East and North Africa, sub-Saharan Africa, Central Asia, Latin America and the Caribbean on projects sponsored by the World Bank, the Inter-American Development Bank, UNDP, UNCHS/HABITAT, USAID, and various foundations and governments. She has worked on: decentralization, participatory processes in urban planning and management, land tenure, infrastructure services, microcredit for housing and infrastructure, community-based development and revitalization of the historic urban fabric. Her more recent work focuses on issues of local development and emphasizes strategic planning, social inclusion, policy evaluation, programme performance assessment, financing capital improvements and building the capacity of local stakeholders. She leads the Center's involvement in UNCHS/Habitat Best Practices and Local Leadership Programmes, the Microcredit Summit, and the Cultural Heritage and Development Networks and its participation in the coalition for sustainable urbanization.

Anshu Sharma trained as an urban planner and presently holds the position of Programme Director in the Sustainable Environment and Ecological Development Society (SEEDS), a voluntary organization working in the areas of planning and development in India. He started his career working in the field of environmental impact assessment and environmental management planning. He is currently involved in disaster management research and community-based disaster mitigation programmes, including an initiative on reducing risk in vulnerable urban communities through participatory planning.

Elda Solloso Rodríguez received a Master's in urban planning from the Harvard Design School in 2003 and a BA in sociology from the University Complutense of Madrid in 2000. From 1998 to 2000 she studied regional planning in the University of Paris X-Nanterre (France). She interned in the agency in charge of the Casal Ventoso revitalization in Lisbon, a project financed through a European Union–URBAN grant targeting troubled urban districts and promoting sustainable development. Since June 2003, she has worked as research fellow at the Center for Urban Development Studies. As part of the UN Millennium Project, she worked with Mona Serageldin to prepare the background paper for Task Force 8 on 'Improving the Lives of 100 Million Slum Dwellers by 2020'. Her primary interests are strategic and regional planning and social inclusion.

Leo Thomas is a social development consultant with ongoing professional interests in the relationship between poverty, inequality, violence and informal governance systems in urban areas. Previously, he has worked with the Department for International Development (DFID) as an urban poverty advisor in Jamaica and as a senior researcher with the International NGO Training and Research Centre in Oxford analysing the performance of urban NGOs in Dhaka, Ahmedabad, Johannesburg and Addis Ababa.

Luis Valenzuela is an architect and was awarded a Master's in architecture by the Universidad Católica de Chile in 1999. He has taken graduate courses in the School of Architecture at the University of Wisconsin, Milwaukee, and is a professor in the same university. He was the Academic Secretariat there from 1997 to 2002. He has developed several professional works and competitions which have been published in Chile. In 2002, his team won the second prize in the Bicentennial of Santiago for the urban design of Portal Cerrillos. Currently, he is a doctorate candidate at Harvard University Graduate School of Design. His thesis research is on the 'The Changing Face of Home: Affordable Housing Capabilities in Santiago of Chile 1906–2000'.

Cecilia Zanetta is an assistant professor in the Department of Urban and Regional Planning at the University of Tennessee. She has a degree in architecture from the National University of Buenos Aires and a Master's and PhD in urban and regional planning from the Ohio State University, where she attended as a Fulbright grantee. Her main areas of interest include public policy in developing countries, with a focus on the urban and housing sectors and public sector modernization among subnational governments. During the past ten years, she has worked as a consultant to the World Bank and other international financial institutions in several countries in Latin and Central America, including Argentina, Brazil, Chile, Ecuador, El Salvador, Honduras and Peru. Her academic research, which is firmly grounded on her professional work, is aimed at building a bridge between practice and the world of ideas to ultimately improve living conditions in developing countries.

Notes

CHAPTER 1

1. This is a shorter and updated version of Satterthwaite (2002). Unless otherwise stated, global and regional urban statistics are drawn from United Nations (2002). Most national statistics are drawn from censuses (the author has reviewed inter-census changes in the population of individual urban centres drawing from over 200 different censuses). Historical data are also drawn from Chandler (1987) and Bairoch (1988).
2. This figure of 50 000 urban centres in the world is a rough estimate, based on an extrapolation from many censuses reviewed that gave the total number of urban centres in that particular country.
3. Urban statistics from United Nations 2002; for the size of nations' economies, World Bank 2001b (with the size of national economies calculated using figures adjusted for ppp).
4. Based on analyses of censuses held in the past 15 years where data were available on the population of all urban centres.

CHAPTER 2

1. This paper first appeared in the proceedings of a Workshop on Urban Longitudinal Research Methodology which was held at the Development Planning Unit on 28–29 May 2003. It was organized under the joint auspices and support of the Development Planning Unit (DPU), the Overseas Development Institute (ODI), the UK Department for International Development (DFID) and the World Bank. Co-organizers were Caroline Moser (ODI) and Michael Safier (DPU), with assistance from Deepa Narayan (IBRD). The workshop provided an opportunity to review both qualitative and quantitative methodological approaches used in longitudinal studies, identifying the advantages and limitations of each for future research projects. This linked the interests of researchers at ODI and DPU currently designing new phases of longitudinal research projects, the World Bank, which is developing a 23- to 40-country study on 'Pathways out of Poverty: freedom from the bottom up', and DFID supported researchers who have recently undertaken new longitudinal research. Workshop researchers who have already undertaken urban research utilizing longitudinal methodologies came from universities in the UK, including the LSE, University of Sussex, University of Westminster and Oxford University, as well as University of Illinois and Trinity College in the United States, and the University of Natal, South Africa, and the Catholic University of Lima, Peru. Among the participants in the process of developing longitudinal research projects, in particular, were DPU-linked research institutions in the Netherlands, India, Zambia and Nigeria. Finally, other participants were researchers with a broad

knowledge of urban poverty research relevant to the workshop, including UK-based urban researchers with an interest in this research area.
2. Comments made by the various speakers at the workshop (see note 1).

CHAPTER 3

1. The first phase of Young Lives was funded by the UK Department for International Development (DFID) and is implemented by a consortium of: Reading University, London School of Hygiene and Tropical Medicine, London South Bank University, Institute of Development Studies, South African Medical Research Council, UK Save the Children Fund and numerous institutions in the four partner developing countries.

    This paper draws on: Harpham, T., Huttly, S., Wilson, I. and De Wet, T. (2003) Linking public issues with private troubles: panel studies in developing countries, *Journal of International Development*, 15: 353–363, and is used here with permission of John Wiley and Sons Ltd.

CHAPTER 4

1. There are arguments to suggest that violence itself reduces the state's ability to promote greater social inclusion and economic equity.
2. See the international crime statistics produced by Interpol as well as Moser and Winton (2002).
3. Burgess (1998) argues that in many cities these racial, ethnic and religious conflicts are the dominant form of urban violence, fuelled at a more fundamental level by issues of increasing inequality coinciding with vertical social categories. He cites Algiers, Durban, Karachi, Mumbai and Jakarta as examples.
4. See also Fraser et al. (2003) and Moser and McIlwaine (1999) for general participatory approaches to researching urban violence.

CHAPTER 5

1. In the last budget year, the Minister of Finance requested parliamentary approval for R2.2 billion in 'roll overs' (a process in which money is carried forward to the next budget year) for unspent money (Manuel, 2001).
2. See for example the request by local councillors to a training institution that they be trained in how to deliver services, not in how to represent voters, in Kabemba and Friedman (2001).
3. For a defence of this view, which originated in the Johannesburg branch of the governing party see iGoli Online, Introduction – 1.2 *Why the City Needs Change*. For a critique, see Kihato (1997).
4. Local Government: Municipal Structures Act No. 117 of 1998 clauses 72–77.
5. Local Government: Municipal Systems Act No. 32 of 2000, Chapter 4, clauses 16, 17.
6. Municipal Systems Act, Chapter 5.
7. Briefing, senior city manager, August 1999.
8. In 2000, the percentage poll in Johannesburg was 39% compared to 48% for the country. See IEC, 2000.

9. The council originally proclaimed a desire to become a 'world-class city'. The adjective 'African' was added later.
10. I am grateful to Caroline Kihato for this observation.
11. www.joburg.org.za/2003/budget
12. As implied above, the phenomena described here are more complex than the term 'informality' suggests. It includes dispersed and casual work, which is not necessarily informal, and unemployment. It is used as shorthand, therefore, to denote economically active people who are not working in formal workplaces.
13. Municipal Systems Act, Chapter 4, Clause 21.

CHAPTER 7

1. Mona Serageldin, Associate Director, Center for Urban Development Studies, and Yves Cabannes, Regional Coordinator, UMP-LAC (UN-Habitat Urban Management Program), are jointly undertaking a study to document and analyse the impacts of migratory flows in Cuenca, Ecuador and Maracaibo, Venezuela. This study is sponsored in part by the David Rockefeller Center for Latin American Studies at Harvard University. We wish to acknowledge the information and documentation received from the Mayor of Cuenca, Mr Fernando Cordero Cueva, who gave generously of his time, the department heads and their staff. Their inputs were instrumental in the successful completion of the field mission. We also wish to acknowledge the information received from Mr Bolivar Saquipay and Luis Quinde, presidents of the Tarqui and the Turi Parishioner Committees, respectively; Mr Humberto Cordero, President of the Construction Chamber; Ms Marcela Cassaro, President of the Association of Peruvians in Cuenca; Mr Franklin Ortiz, Director of the Social Pastoral; and Mr Raffael Estrella and Mr Pedro Andrade, Director of Photography and Director of Ojo Rojo Produccion, respectively, all of whom gave important insights on the range of issues raised by this challenging research effort.
2. Quoted in *Social Development*. IADB, August 2003. http://www.iadb.org/sds/soc
3. *Sending Money Home: An International Comparison of Remittance Markets*. Multilateral Investment Fund of the Inter-American Development Bank, February 2003.
4. *Remittance Senders and Receivers: Tracking the Transnational Channels*, p. 7. The Pew Hispanic Center, Fondo Multilateral de Inversiones, Banco Inter-Americano de Desarrollo, Washington, D.C., 24 November 2003.
5. *Sending Money Home: An International Comparison of Remittance Markets*. Multilateral Investment Fund of the Inter-American Development Bank, February 2003.
6. Quoted in: Orozco (2001).
7. *Remittances to Latin America and the Caribbean*, Multilateral Investment Fund and Inter-American Development Bank, February 2002.
8. 'Causas del reciente proceso emigratorio ecuatoriano', p. 3. In *Cartillas sobre la Migración, Plan Binacional Ecuador-España 'Migración, Comunicación Desarrollo'*, Enero 2003, N.3, ILDIS-FES, Quito.
9. 'Las remesas de los emigrantes y sus efectos en la economía Ecuatoriana', p. 3. In: *Cartillas sobre la Migración, Plan Binacional Ecuador-España 'Migración, Comunicación Desarrollo'*, Mayo 2002, N.1, ILDIS-FES, Quito.
10. *Las remesas de emigrantes entre España y Latinoamérica*. Report financed by the IDB, November 2002.
11. *Receptores de Remesas en Ecuador. Una Investigación del Mercado*, p. 4. The Pew Hispanic Center, Fondo Multilateral de Inversiones, Banco Inter-Americano de Desarrollo, Quito, Ecuador, Mayo 2003.

12. *Receptores de Remesas en Ecuador. Una Investigación del Mercado*, p. 4. The Pew Hispanic Center, Fondo Multilateral de Inversiones, Banco Inter-Americano de Desarrollo, Quito, Ecuador, Mayo 2003.
13. *Receptores de Remesas en Ecuador. Una Investigación del Mercado*, p. 8. The Pew Hispanic Center, Fondo Multilateral de Inversiones, Banco Inter-Americano de Desarrollo, Quito, Ecuador, Mayo 2003.
14. Cities Alliance, PGU, Alcaldía Municipal de Cuenca y ACUDIR, *Plan Estratégico de Inversiones para el Desarrollo Local de la Ciudad de Cuenca*, Julio 2001.

CHAPTER 8

1. This chapter is based on a research project entitled 'Integrating Rental Housing Supply Mechanisms into Housing Policy, India' (R6856) conducted for the Infrastructure and Urban Development Department, Department for International Development, UK government. It was presented at the Second Urban Research Symposium, 15–17 December 2003, World Bank, Washington, D.C. The full report can be accessed at http://www.worldbank.org/urban/poverty/docs/social-relation-kumar.pdf
2. The four main tenures are owners, landlords (who let rooms or full housing units), tenants (who rent rooms or houses on payment of rent) and sharers (who do not pay any rent). In this chapter, housing tenure refers to tenure in relation to housing and is different from land tenure, which refers to the tenure status of land.
3. The term 'housing' encompasses the elements that combine to produce the dwelling (land, finance, building materials and labour for construction) and the physical (water, sanitation, drainage, electricity, roads) and social (health, education, parks, police etc) infrastructure. 'Housing policy' refers to the frameworks (put into place by national or bi- and multilateral development agencies) that seek to address issues of access to housing. Housing policy thus includes a number of housing strategies (for example, sites-and-services and upgrading), institutional initiatives (such as reform of housing finance, the building materials and construction industry) and mechanisms for delivery (for example through NGOs or public–private partnerships).
4. The few attempts to encourage rental housing have been indirect. For example, in the 1970s and 1980s, the World Bank and USAID funded sites-and-services projects in Asian and African cities encouraged allottees to build rooms for rent to ease the burden of loan repayments.
5. See, for example, the collection of papers in *Environment and Urbanisation*, 1997, 9(2) on the theme – 'Tenants: addressing needs, increasing options'.
6. There are problems in English usage of the terms 'landlord' and 'tenant' where gender issues are concerned. The *Oxford Encyclopaedic English Dictionary* (1991) defines a *landlord* as 'a **man** who lets land, a building, part of a building, etc., to a tenant'. A *landlady* is defined in a similar manner with the word 'man' being replaced by the word **woman**. This chapter uses the word *landlord* to mean a **person** who lets accommodation. Specific reference to sex will be made only when gender issues are relevant (as in the relationship between women and men as landlords or tenants).
7. The city of Bangalore (Municipal limits) comprises of 100 census wards which are the same as the election ward, each having one elected councillor. However, the situation in Surat is very different. The city comprises of 66 census wards but 33 election wards. In many cases the boundaries of these ward categories are different, making comparison difficult. In addition, a socio-economic survey of the city's slum population (Das, 1994) uses completely different boundaries.

8. Women-managed households are those households where the male is present but does not contribute to household income due to ill health, personal injury or forms of addiction (alcoholism being the main form of addiction in Indian cities). Women-headed households are those households where the male is absent as a result of death, divorce or desertion.
9. 74th Constitutional Amendment that attempts to accord a greater participatory decision making role for local representatives.
10. In Surat, for example, 98 of the 99 councillors belonged to the same political party governing the state of Gujarat. In such a situation, it is comparatively easier for policy dialogue to take place as a result of which neither the state government or the Surat Municipal Corporation is likely to raise the issue of changes to the policy role of the Municipality. Bangalore, in contrast, has councillors from a range of political parties and, from a different standpoint – one of conflict – they are unlikely to bring about changes in the policy-making role of the Bangalore City Corporation.

CHAPTER 9

1. The term 'South' is used to refer collectively to the countries of the developing world, while the term 'North' refers to highly developed/industrialized countries.
2. Adequate shelter, as defined by UNCHS (1997: 35) means 'more than a roof over one's head. It also means adequate privacy; adequate space; physical accessibility; adequate security; security of tenure; structural stability and durability; adequate lighting, heating and ventilation; adequate basic infrastructure, such as water supply, sanitation and waste management facilities; suitable environmental quality and health-related factors; and adequate and accessible location with regard to work and basic facilities: all of which should be available at an affordable cost.'
3. DFID's SLF was also used to evaluate two housing projects targeted at low-income and poor households in Nairobi. The findings are reported in two of the project working papers: *NACHU Housing Credit Scheme: Huruma Informal Settlement, Working Paper 3* (Mwaura, 2000) and *Assessment of the Mathare 4A Development Programme against the Sustainable Livelihoods Approach, Working Paper 4* (Kamau and Ngari, 2002).
4. For a better understanding of the SL approach, see the DFID Sustainable Livelihoods Guidance Sheets (http://www.livelihoods.org/info/info_guidancesheets. html).
5. Ng'ayu (2003), however, observes that MCN involvement was more through Council staff as individuals rather than at the institutional level. Still, a crucial communication channel was opened through which the Council's objectives and policies were imparted to the local communities, and dialogue on other matters of more general local concern enabled.
6. The existing by-laws, inherited from the British colonial authorities, were material-specific, stipulating the use of conventional building materials that were unaffordable by the urban poor majority. Code '95 is performance-oriented and allows the use of alternative materials such as stabilized soil blocks (SSBs) and micro-concrete roofing (MCR) tiles.
7. Many poor households lack access to information, broader overviews and a knowledge of prior experiences outside their own local area. They may consequently adopt livelihood strategies that are inappropriate at best or doomed to failure at worst (Meikle et al., 2001).

8. Access to pertinent knowledge and information can be crucial in enabling people living in poverty to make the most effective use of limited livelihood assets, as affirmed by Schilderman (2002).
9. The achievements are based largely on the findings of the end-of-project evaluation (Gardner, 2003).
10. These include 'daily savings groups' and 'merry-go-rounds', a form of rotating savings and credit association (ROSCA).
11. The Global Urban Observatory (GUO) addresses the urgent need to improve the worldwide base of urban knowledge by helping governments, local authorities and civil society organizations to develop and apply policy-oriented urban indicators, statistics and other urban information. SDS is one of three training partner institutions contracted by the Urban Indicators Programme (UIP) to implement capacity-building projects with interested cities and countries by conducting regional and national training for establishing local and national urban observatories. See http://www.unhabitat.org/programmes/guo/ for more information.
12. See *Report on the International Workshop on Integrated Urban Housing Development,* 17–18 March 2003, held at the Schumacher Centre for Technology and Development, Bourton Hall, Bourton-on-Dunsmore, Rugby, United Kingdom. http://itdg.org/docs/shelter/iuhd_workshop_ report_2003.pdf
13. A study of the roofing subsector in Nakuru conducted in the course of project implementation (Majale and Albu, 2001) underscores the need for market analyses.
14. Sahley and Pratt (2003) observe that the word and concept 'partnership' means different things to different actors. With respect to NGO–municipal partnerships, many NGOs report some aspects of joint initiatives or collaboration with local authorities but are less comfortable describing these as partnerships. They thus propose a continuum from intolerance and rejection through to partnerships through mutual gain (see Sahley and Pratt, 2003: 100).
15. The activities of NGOs usually fall into one of the following: capacity building in the form of information; dissemination and training; rights-based and interest group advocacy; support and facilitation of infrastructure and social service delivery, and direct delivery; policy dialogue support and facilitation; and public policy research (Pieterse, undated).
16. Satterthwaite (undated) makes the point that most recipient governments in the South seek to limit the amount of funding that multilateral and bilateral agencies are able to channel directly to local NGOs, as well as organizations of the urban poor. See also Satterthwaite (2001).
17. United Nations Capital Development Fund is a member of the United Nations Development Programme (UNDP) group, established in 1966 as a special purpose fund primarily for small-scale investment in the poorest countries. UNCDF presently works to help eradicate poverty through local development programmes and microfinance operations.
18. As Kothari (2001) observes, housing has been repeatedly recognized as a fundamental human right in the Istanbul Declaration and the Habitat Agenda, with states reaffirming 'our commitment to the full and progressive realization of the right to adequate housing, as provided for in the international instruments'. Nevertheless, the right to adequate housing remains unrealized for the vast majority of poor and vulnerable households the world over.

CHAPTER 11

1. This chapter refers to some of the preliminary findings of an ongoing French–British research project on current changes in customary land delivery systems in sub-Saharan African cities. It is coordinated by Alain Durand-Lasserve (CNRS, France) and Michael Mattingly (DPU-UCL, UK), with the assistance of Rasmus Precht, University of Paris VII. It is jointly supported by the Programme de Recherche Urbaine pour le Développement (PRUD), Ministry of Foreign Affairs, France, and the Department for International Cooperation (DFID) UK. This project covers nine sub-Saharan countries. In each of them, case studies on 'Current changes in customary/traditional land delivery systems' have been carried out in 2002–3 in a selected number of cities, following the same terms of reference and set of questions.

   - Country report on Benin: case study of Cotonou and Porto Novo, by Rasmus Precht.
   - Country report on Cameroon: case study on Cotonou and Porto Novo, by Athanase Bopda and Benoit Mougoue.
   - Country report on Ghana: case study on Kumasi, by Seth Opuni Asiama.
   - Country report on Kenya: case study on Cotonou and Porto Novo, by Njambi Kinyungu and Luke Obala.
   - Country report on Namibia: case study on Oshakati, by Joas Santos.
   - Country report on Senegal: case study on Dakar, by Rasmus Precht.
   - Country report on South Africa: case study on Gauteng and North West Province, by Beno"t Allanic.
   - Country report on Tanzania: case study on Dar es Salaam, by Lusugga Kironde.
   - Country report on Uganda: case study on Kampala, by Y. Okulo-Epak.

CHAPTER 12

1. The research was conducted by the Institute for Development Studies (IDS) University of Nairobi, with the support from the Canadian International Development Research Centre (IDRC) and the British Department for International Development (DFID), with input from Women in Informal Employment Globalising and Organising (WIEGO). The research was conducted by a team of two principal researchers (Professor Patrick Alila and Dr. Winnie Mitullah), and a project assistant, Anne Kamau.
2. Business environment relates to those features found outside the enterprise itself. This includes an array of influence ranging from economic, social and cultural systems, to policies, laws and other kinds of rules, to public and private institutions and the effect of other enterprises. MSEs can face greater disadvantages or biases in the business environment than do larger enterprises.
3. The six research issues included: policies and regulations; site of operation and planning regulations; licensing/daily fees; enforcement of policies and regulations; communication between street traders and other stakeholders; and organizational capacity of street vendors.

References

Aguilar, M. and Sbrocco, M. (1997) Salta frente al POSFONAVI ¿Una historia circular?, in: Cuenya, B. and Falú, A. (eds), *Reestructuración del Estado y Política de Vivienda en Argentina*, Centro de Estudios Avanzados, Universidad de Buenos Aires, Buenos Aires.

Aina, T.A. (1990) Petty landlords and poor tenants in a low-income settlement in metropolitan Lagos, Nigeria, in: Amis, P. and Lloyd, P. (eds) *Housing Africa's Urban Poor*, Manchester University Press, Manchester, pp. 87–101.

Albu, M. and Scott, A. (2001) *Understanding Livelihoods that Involve Micro-Enterprise: Markets and Techological Capabilities in the SL Framework* (http://www.livelihoodtechnology.org/ocs/man2Intro/FINAL%20ANALY-SIS%20PAPER.PDF).

Alila, P.O. and Mitullah, W.V. (2000) *Enhancing Lobbying Capacity of Women Street Vendors: The Challenges in the Kenya Policy Environment*, University of Nairobi, Institute for Development Studies, Nairobi, and IDRC Centre File, 98–8556/55399.

Amis, P. (1984) Squatters or tenants – the commercialization of unauthorized housing in Nairobi, *World Development*, 12(1): 87–96.

Anderson, J. (2003) Accumulating advantage and disadvantage: urban poverty dynamics in Peru, in: Moser, C. (2003) *Urban Longitudinal Research Methodology: Objectives, Contents and Summary of Raised at the Joint DPU-ODI-World Bank-DFID Workshop*, Working Paper No. 124, The Development Planning Unit, University College London, London, pp. 41–47.

Angel, S. and Amtapunth, P. (1989) The low-cost rental housing market in Bangkok, 1987, *Habitat International*, 13(3): 173–185.

Angeles, J.G.V. (1997) *The Role of the Naga City Urban Poor Federation in the Passage of Pro-Poor Ordinances and Policies, Relations State Civil Society, in Policy Making*, Wui, M.A. and Lopez, M.G.S. (eds), Diliman, University of the Philippine Third World Center, pp. 97–112

Angeles, J.G.V. (2000) 'The Naga City urban poor sector organizing experiences from 1986 to 2000'. Paper presented at the Workshop on Human Security and Regional Development, 5–8 December 2000, Nagoya, United Nations Center for Regional Development.

Ashley, C. and Carney, D. (1999) *Sustainable Livelihoods: Lessons from Early Experience*, Department for International Development, London.

Augustinus, C. (2003a) Comparative analysis of land administration systems: African review, with special reference to Mozambique, Uganda, Namibia, Ghana, South Africa. Work undertaken by the World Bank, funded by DFID.

Augustinus, C. (2003b) 'Surveying and land information for secure land tenure'. Paper presented at the USK/CASLE/UN-Habitat Regional Seminar on Security of Land Tenure, 12 June 2003, Nairobi, Kenya.

Baharoglu, D. (2002) *World Bank Experience in Land Management and the Debate on Tenure Security*, Background Series No. 16, Housing and Land. Urban and Local Government, The World Bank.

Bairoch, P. (1988) *Cities and Economic Development: From the Dawn of History to the Present*, Mansell, London.

Banco Central del Ecuador (2001) No. 130 Cuaderno de Trabajo: 'Las remesas de ecuatorianos en el exterior', Dirección General de Estudios, Cuenca.

Baulch, B. (2003) Assessing poverty dynamics: lessons from panel household surveys for urban longitudinal studies, in: Moser, C. (2003) *Urban Longitudinal Research Methodology: Objectives, Contents and Summary of Raised at the Joint DPU-ODI-World Bank-DFID Workshop*, Working Paper No. 124, The Development Planning Unit, University College London, London, pp. 28–33.

Bayat, A. and Denis, E. (2000) Who is afraid of Ashwaiyyat: urban change and politics in Egypt, *Environment and Urbanization*, 12(2): 185–199.

Beall, J. (2002) *Social Capital, Social Exclusion and Rights: Opportunities and Constraints in Pro-Poor Urban Governance* (www.worldbank.org/urban/symposium2002/docs/pres-paper/pres-pdf/beall.pdf).

Bennett, M. (2003) *Organising in the Informal Economy: A Case Study of the Clothing Industry in South Africa*, SEED Working Paper No. 37, International Labour Organisation, Geneva.

Bhorat, H. (2003) *The Post-Apartheid Challenge: Labour Demand Trends in the South African Labour Market, 1995–1999*, Working Paper 03/82, Development Policy Research Unit, University of Cape Town, Cape Town.

Black-Michaud, J. (1975) *Feuding Societies*, Basil Blackwell, Oxford.

Blake, R.C. (undated) *The World Bank's Draft Comprehensive Development Framework and the Micro-Paradigm of Law and Development* (http://www.yale.edu/yhrdlj/vol03/blake.htm).

Bocquier, P. (2004) Analyzing urbanization in sub-Saharan Africa, in: Champion, T. and Gugo, G. (eds) *New Forms of Urbanization; Beyond the Urban-Rural Dichotomy*, Ashgate, Aldershot, UK, pp. 133–150.

Bonfiglioli, A. (2003) *Empowering the Poor: Local Governance for Poverty Reduction*, United Nations Capital Development Fund, New York.

Bruhn, K. (1996) Social spending and political support: the 'lessons' of the national solidarity in Mexico, *Comparative Politics*, 28(2): 151–177.

Bryant, J.J. (1989) The acceptable face of self-help housing: Subletting in Fiji squatter settlements – exploitation or survival strategy, in: Drakakis-Smith, D. (ed.) *Economic Growth and Urbanisation in Developing Areas*, Routledge, London, pp. 171–195.

Buckley, R. (1991) The measurement and targeting of housing finance subsidies: the case of Argentina, *Public Finance*, 31: 355–372.

Burgess, R. (1998) Urban violence: the next agenda? *CENDEP Newsletter Autumn 1998*, Centre for Development and Emergency Practice, Oxford Brookes University.

Burns, T., Grant, C., Brits, A.M., Nettle, K. (2003) *Comparative Study of Land Administration Systems. Critical Issues and Future Challenges*, report prepared for the World Bank by Land Equity International.

Cain, A., Daly, M. and Robson, P. (2002) *Basic Service Provision for the Urban Poor; The Experience of Development Workshop in Angola*, IIED Working Paper 8 on Poverty Reduction in Urban Areas.

Carney, D. (ed.) (1998) *Sustainable Rural Livelihoods: What contribution can we make?* DFID, London.

Castells, M. and Hall, P. (1994) *Technopoles of the World: The Making of 21st Century Industrial Complexes*, Routledge, London and New York.

Census of India (1998) *State Profile 1991: India*, Controller of Publications, New Delhi.

Center for Asia Pacific and Women in Politics (CAPWIP) (2003) *From Shanties to Empowered Communities: The ZOTO Experience*, Writeshop on the Conceptual Framework of Building Transformative Communities, Metro Manila.

Central Bureau of Statistics (CBS) African Centre for Economic Growth (ACEG) and K-REP Holdings (1999) *National Micro and Small Enterprises Baseline Survey*, CBS, Nairobi.

Centre for Policy Studies (2002) *Civil Society and Poverty Reduction in Southern Africa*, CPS, Johannesburg, mimeo.

Chambers, R. and Conway, G. (1992) *Sustainable Rural Livelihoods: Practical Concepts for the 21ˢᵗ Century*, IDS Discussion Paper No. 296, IDS, Brighton.

Champion, T. and Hugo, G. (eds) (2003) *New Forms of Urbanization; Beyond the Urban-Rural Dichotomy*, Ashgage, Aldershot, UK.

Chandler, T. (1987) *Four Thousand Years of Urban Growth: An Historical Census*, Edwin Mellen Press, Lampeter, UK.

Chevanne, S.B. (2002) *Learning to be a Man: Culture, Socialization and Gender Identity in Some Caribbean Countries*, University of the West Indies Press, Mona, Jamaica.

Christiensen, S.F., Hoejgaard, P.D. and Werner, W. (1999) *Innovative Land Surveying and Land Registration in Namibia*, Working Paper No. 93, DPU-UCL, May 1999.

Commission on Human Security (2003) *Human Security Now; Protecting and Empowering People*, Commission on Human Security, New York.

Cornish, W. and Clark, G. (1989) *Law and Society in England, 1750–1950*, Sweet and Maxwell, London.

Coulomb, R. (1989) Rental housing and the dynamics of urban growth in Mexico City, in: Gilbert, A. (ed.) *Housing and Land in Urban Mexico*, Monograph Series 31, Centre for US-Mexican Studies, University of California, San Diego, pp. 39–50.

Cross, C. (2002) Why the urban poor cannot secure tenure: South African tenure policy under pressure, in: Durand-Lasserve, A. and Royston L. (eds) *Holding their Ground. Secure Land Tenure for the Urban Poor in Developing Countries*, Earthscan Publications, London. pp. 195–208.

Cuenya, B. (1997) Descentralización y política de vivienda en Argentina, in: Cuenya, B. and Falú, A. (eds) *Reestructuración del Estado y Política de Vivienda en Argentina*, Centro de Estudios Avanzados, Universidad de Buenos Aires, Buenos Aires.

Dale, A. and Davies, R. (1994) *Analysing Social and Political Change: A Casebook of Methods*, Sage, London.

Das, B. (1994) *Socio-Economic Study of Slums in Surat City. Surat: Centre for Social Studies*, South Gujarat University Campus, Surat.

Datta, K. (1995) Strategies for urban survival? Women landlords in Gaborone, Botswana, *Habitat International*, 19(1): 1–12.

de Swaan, A. (1988) *In Care of the State*, Cambridge University Press, Cambridge.

de Swaan, A., Manor, J., Oyen, E. and Reis, E.P. (2000) Elite perceptions of the poor: reflections for a comparative research project, *Current Sociology*, 48(1): 43–54.

Deininger, K. (2003) *Land Policies for Growth and Poverty Reduction*, World Bank Policy Research Report, The World Bank, Oxford University Press, Oxford.

Dercon, S. (2001) *Assessing Vulnerability*, Economics Department, Oxford University, Oxford.

Desai, A. (2002) *We Are the Poors: Community Struggles in Post-apartheid South Africa*, Monthly Review Press, New York.

Devas, N. and Kelly, R. (2001) Regulation or revenues? An analysis of local business licences, with a case study of Single Business Permit reform in Kenya, *Journal of Public Administration and Development*, 21: 381–391.

Devas, N. (2002) Urban livelihoods – issues for urban governance and management, in: Rakodi, C. and Lloyd-Jones, T. (eds) *Urban Livelihoods: A People-Centred Approach to Reducing Poverty*, Earthscan, London.

Duffield, M. (1999) *Internal Conflict: Adaption and Reaction to Globalisation*, The Corner House Briefing No.12, The Corner House, Sturminster Newton, UK.

Durand-Lasserve, A. (2002) Innovative approaches to tenure for the urban poor. Current changes and trends in sub-Saharan Francophone African countries: Benin, Burkina Faso and Senegal, in: Payne, G. (ed.) *Land, Rights and Innovation,* Intermediate Technology Publiactions, London, pp. 114–134.

Durand-Lasserve, A. and Royston, C. (eds) (2002) *Holding their Ground: Secure Land Tenure for the Urban Poor in Developing Countries,* Earthscan Publications, London.

Economic Commission for Latin America and the Caribbean (ECLAC) (2000) *From Rapid Urbanization to the Consolidation of Human Settlements in LAC: A Territorial Perspective* (http://www.eclac.cl).

Edwards, M. (1982) Cities of tenants: Renting among the urban poor in Latin America, in: Gilbert, A., Hardoy, J.E. and Ramirez, R. (eds) *Urbanisation in Contemporary Latin America,* John Wiley & Sons, London, pp. 129–158.

Edwards, M. (1983) Residential mobility in a changing housing market: the case of Bucaramanga, Colombia, *Urban Studies,* 20: 131–145.

Edwards, M. (1990) Rental housing and the urban poor: Africa and Latin America compared, in: Amis, P. and Lloyd, P. (eds) *Housing Africa's Urban Poor,* Manchester University Press, Manchester, pp. 253–272.

Edwards, M. and Hulme, D. (2000) Scaling up NGO impact on development: learning from experience, in: Eade, D. (ed.) *Development, NGOs and Civil Society,* Oxfam GB, Oxford.

Esping-Andersen, G. (1990) *The Three Worlds of Welfare Capitalism,* Princeton University Press, Princeton, NJ.

Esping-Andersen, G. (1996) (ed.) *Welfare States in Transition: National States in Global Economics,* Sage, London.

Fay, M. and Opal, C. (2000) *Urbanization Without Growth: A Not So Uncommon Phenomenon,* World Bank, Washington, D.C.

Feenan, D. (2002) Researching paramilitary violence in Northern Ireland, *International Journal of Social Research Methodology,* 5(2): 26–43.

Fernandes, E. and Varley, A. (eds) (1998) *Illegal Cities: Law and Urban Change in Developing Countries,* Zed Books, London.

Fowler, A. (1997) *Striking a Balance; A Guide to Enhancing the Effectiveness of Non-governmental Organizations in International Development,* Earthscan, London.

Fox, V. (2002) *Segundo Informe de Gobierno, Anexo Estadístico, Desarrollo Humano y Social,* Distrito Federal, Mexico.

Fraser, E., Thirkell, A. and McKay, A. (2003) *Tapping into Existing Social Capital: Rich Networks, Poor Connections,* Department for International Development, London.

Friedman, S. (2001) *Free But Unequal: Democracy, Inequality and the State in Latin America and Africa,* Research Report, Centre for Policy Studies, Johannesburg.

Friedman, S. (2002) A quest for control: high modernism and its discontents in Johannesburg, South Africa, in: Ruble, B.A., Stren, R.E., Tulchin, J.S. with Varat, D.H. (eds) *Urban Governance Around the World,* Woodrow Wilson Center for International Scholars, Washington, D.C.

Friedmann, J. (1993) 'Where we stand: a decade of world city research'. Paper prepared for the Conference of World Cities in a World System, April, Center for Innovative Technology.

Gallin, D. (2001) *Propositions on Trade Unions and Informal Employment in Times of Globalisation,* Antipode, Global Labour Institute, Geneva, pp. 531–549.

Gardner, J. (2003) 'Report of the Evaluation of the Integrated Urban Housing Development Project in Kenya and India', unpublished report.

Gasper (1999) Violence and suffering, responsibility and choice, *European Journal of Development Research,* 11(2): 1–22.

George, C. (undated) *Enterprise Development and Sustainable Livelihoods* (http://www.enterprise-impact.org.uk/word-files/EDandSustainableLivelihoods.doc).

Gerchunoff, P. and Torres, J.C. (1998) Argentina: the politics of economic liberalization, in: Vellinga, M. (ed.) *The Changing Role of the State in Latin America*, Westview Press, Boulder, CO.

Gilbert, A. (1983) The tenants of self-help housing: choice and constraint in the housing markets of less developed countries, *Development and Change*, 14 (3): 449–477.

Gilbert, A. (1987) Latin America's urban poor: shanty dwellers or renters of rooms? *Cities*, 4(1): 43–51.

Gilbert, A. (1991) Renting and the transition to owner occupation in Latin American cities, *Habitat International*, 15(1/2): 87–99.

Gilbert, A. and Varley, A. (1989a) From renting to self-help ownership? Residential tenure in urban Mexico since 1940, in: Gilbert, A. (ed.) *Housing and Land in Urban Mexico*, Monograph Series 31, Centre for US-Mexican Studies, University of California, San Diego, pp. 13–37.

Gilbert, A. and Varley, A. (1989b) *The Mexican Landlord: Rental Housing in Guadalajara and Puebla*, Institute of Latin American Studies, London.

Gilbert, A. and Varley, A. (1990) Renting a home in a third world city: Choice or constraint?, *International Journal of Urban and Regional Research*, 14 (1): 89–108.

Gilbert, A. and Varley, A. (1991) *Landlord and Tenant: Housing the Poor in Urban Mexico*, Routledge, New York.

Gilbert, A. and Ward, P.M. (1982) Residential movement among the poor: the constraints on housing choice in Latin American cities, *Transactions of the Institute of British Geographers*, NS 7: 129–149.

Gilbert, A., in association with Camacho, O.O., Coulomb, R. and Necochea, A. (1993) *In Search of a Home: Rental and Shared Housing in Latin America*, UCL Press, London.

Gilbert, A., Mabin, A., McCarthy, M. and Watson, V. (1997) Low-income rental housing: are South African cities different?, *Environment and Urbanization*, 9(1): 133–147.

Giliomee, H. and Schlemmer, L. (1989) *From Apartheid to Nation-Building*, Oxford University Press, Cape Town.

Gizewski and Homer-Dixon (1995) *Urban Growth and Violence*, Occasional Paper, Peace and Conflict Studies Program, University of Toronto, Toronto.

Götz, G. and White, G. (1997) *Family Therapy? Rethinking Intergovernmental Relations.* Policy: Issues and Actors, Centre for Policy Studies, Johannesburg.

Graham, C. (2003) Happiness and hardship: lessons from panel data on mobility and subjective well being in Peru and Russia, in: Moser, C. (ed.) *Urban Longitudinal Research Methodology: Objectives, Contents and Summary of Raised at the Joint DPU-ODI-World Bank-DFID Workshop*, Working Paper No. 124, The Development Planning Unit, University College London, London, pp. 17–27.

Grant, M. (1996) Vulnerability and privilege: transitions in the supply pattern of rental shelter in a mid-sized Zimbabwean city, *Geoforum*, 27(2): 247–260.

Greater Johannesburg Metropolitan Council (GJMC) (2002) iGoli Online.

Greater Johannesburg Metropolitan Council (GJMC) (2003) *Integrated Development Plan 2003/4* (www.joburg.org.za/2003/budget/idp/).

Green, G. (1988) The quest for tranquilidad: paths to home ownership in Santa Cruz, Bolivia, *Bulletin of Latin American Research*, 7(1): 1–15.

Hardoy, J.E. and Satterthwaite, D. (1989) *Squatter Citizen: Life in the Urban Third World*, Earthscan Publications, London.

Hardoy, J.E., Mitlin, D. and Satterthwaite, D. (2001) *Environmental Problems in an Urbanizing World: Finding Solutions for Cities in Africa, Asia and Latin America*, Earthscan Publications, London.

Harpham, T. (2003) Young Lives: An International Longitudinal Study of Child Poverty, in: Moser, C. (2003) *Urban Longitudinal Research Methodology: Objectives, Contents and Summary of Raised at the Joint DPU-ODI-World Bank-DFID Workshop*, Working Paper No. 124, The Development Planning Unit, University College London, London, pp. 34–40.

Harpham, T., Huong, N., Long, T. and Tuan, T. (2004) Participatory child poverty assessment in rural Vietnam, *Children and Society*, 18: 1–15.

Harriss, J. (2002) *Depoliticising Development: The World Bank and Social Capital*, Anthem Press, London.

Harriss, J., Kannan, K.P. and Rodgers, G. (1990) *Urban Labour Market Structure and Job Access in India: A Study of Coimbatore*, International Institute for Labour Studies, Geneva.

Harriss-White, B. (2003) A town in South India: two decades of revisits, in: Moser, C. (2003) *Urban Longitudinal Research Methodology: Objectives, Contents and Summary of Raised at the Joint DPU-ODI-World Bank-DFID Workshop*, Working Paper No. 124, The Development Planning Unit, University College London, London, pp. 68–77.

Hasan, A. (2004) *Urban Change in Pakistan*.

Herbert, C. and Pickering, N. (1997) *The State of Mexico's Housing*, Joint Center for Housing Studies of Harvard University, Cambridge, MA.

Hill, Z. (2002) Reducing attrition in panel studies in developing countries, *Young Lives*, Working Paper Series No.5, London.

Hinojosa Ojeda, R. (2003) The *Theory and Practice of Regional Integration: Trans-Atlantic Lessons for the New World*, Inter-American Development Bank, Washington, DC.

Hoffman, M.L., Walker, C., Struyk, R.J. and Nelson, K. (1991) Rental housing in urban Indonesia, *Habitat International*, 15: 181–206.

Holland, J. (2003) Discussant's comments on Caroline Moser's paper, in: Moser, C. (2003) *Urban Longitudinal Research Methodology: Objectives, Contents and Summary of Raised at the Joint DPU-ODI-World Bank-DFID Workshop*, Working Paper No. 124, The Development Planning Unit, University College London, London, pp. 93–95.

Ikejiofor, U. (1997) The private sector and urban housing production in Nigeria: a study of small scale landlords in Abuja, *Habitat International*, 21(4): 409–425.

Independent Electoral Commission (IEC) (2000) *Local Elections 2000 Voter Turnout Report* (http://www.elections.org.za).

Institute for Democracy in South Africa (Idasa) (1998) *Public Evaluations of and Demands on Local Government*, Idasa, Cape Town, February.

Institute for Social and Economic Research (2000) *The Future of UK Longitudinal Studies*, ISER, Colchester, UK.

Instituto del Fondo Nacional de la Vivienda para los Trabajadores (INFONAVIT) (2000) *Informe Annual de Actvidades 2000* (http://infonavit.gob.mx).

Instituto Nacional de Estadística, Geografía e Informática (INEGI) (2001) *XII Censo General de Población y Vivienda*, INEGI, México City.

Instituto Nacional de Estadísticas y Censos (INDEC) (2001) *Censo Nacional de Población*, Ministerio de Economía, Buenos Aires.

Inter-American Development Bank (IADB) (2001) *Argentina: Programa Nacional de Vivienda*, Perfil I, Proyecto No. AR–0274, Washington, D.C.

International Federation of Red Cross and Red Crescent Societies (2001) *World Disasters Report: Focus on Recovery*, Kumarian Press, Bloomfield.

International Labour Organization (ILO) (1972) *Employment, Incomes and Equality*, ILO, Geneva.

IPCC (2001) *Climate Change 2001; Impacts, Adaptation, and Vulnerability, Contribution of Working Group II to the Third Assessment Report of the*

Intergovernmental Panel on Climate Change, Cambridge University Press, Cambridge.

ITDG-SA (Intermediate Technology Development Group–Eastern Africa) (undated) 'An Integrated Approach to Urban Poverty Alleviation Among Economically Displaced Groups: A Case Study of Chitungwiza's Cone Textiles Housing Co-operative', unpublished report.

Kabemba, C. and Friedman, S. (2001) *Partnership and its Problems: The Institute for Democracy in South Africa, Democratisation Strategy and Foreign Aid*, Research Report, Centre for Policy Studies, Johannesburg.

KALAHI-CIDSS-KKB (2003) NGO External Monitoring Groups for the KALAHI-CIDSS-KKB: Interim Report, Quezon City, quoting *Enhancing Ownership and Sustainability: A Resource Book on Participation* (undated, no publisher details).

Kamau, H.W. and Ngari, J. (2002) *Assessment of the Mathare 4A Development Programme against the Sustainable Livelihoods Approach*, Working Paper 4 (http://itdg .org/ docs/shelter/iuhd_wp4_mathare_4a_assessment.pdf).

Karaos, A.M.A. (2003) 'Populist Mobilization and Manila's Urban Poor: The Case of SANAPA in the NGC East Side'. Research submitted to the Institute of Popular Democracy.

Keen (1997) *The Economic Function of Violence in Civil Wars*, Adelphi Paper 320, Oxford University Press, Oxford.

Kiamba, C.M. (1999) 'Tradition versus realism. The emerging forms of land tenure arrangements in the urban areas of Kenya'. Paper presented at Tenure Security Policies in South African, Brazilian, Indian and Sub-Saharan African Cities: A Comparative Analysis, 27–28 July, Centre of Applied Legal Studies, Johannesburg.

Kihato, C. (1997) *'Megacity' Model is Not the Route Greater Johannesburg Should Adopt*, Synopsis 1.4, Centre for Policy Studies, Johannesburg.

Kironde, J.M.L. (2000) Understanding land markets in African urban areas: the case of Dar es salaam, Tanzania, *Habitat International*, 24: 150–165.

Kobonyo, P., Mitullah, W.V., Ikiara, G., Ongile, G., Abuodha, C. and McCormick, D. (1999) *Complying with Business Regulations in Kenya: A Benchmark Study of the Trade Licensing and Registration of Business Acts, 1997–1998*, Discussion Paper No. 63, University of Nairobi, Institute for Development Studies (IDS), Nairobi.

Kombe, W.J. and Kreibich, V. (1999) 'Reconciling informal and formal land management: an agenda for improving tenure security and urban governance in poor countries'. Paper presented at the International Conference on the Interaction between Formal and Informal Urban Land Management in Africa, 25–27 December, Dar es Salaam.

Kothari, M. (2001) *The Right to Adequate Housing is a Human Right*, United Nations Chronicle Online Edition, XXXVIII(1) (http://www.un.org/Pubs/chronicle/2001/issue1/0101p36.htm).

Kumar, S. (1996a) Landlordism in Third World urban low-income settlements: a case for further research, *Urban Studies*, 33(4/5): 753–782.

Kumar, S. (1996b) Subsistence and petty capitalist landlords: a theoretical framework for the analysis of landlordism in Third World low income settlements, *International Journal of Urban and Regional Research*, 20(2): 317–329.

Kumar, S. (1996c) 'Subsistence and Petty-capitalist Landlords: An Inquiry into the Petty Commodity Production of Rental Housing in Low-income Settlements in Madras', unpublished PhD thesis, Development Planning Unit, University College London.

Kumar, S. (2001) *Social Relations, Rental Housing Markets and the Poor in Urban India*, Department of Social Policy, London School of Economics, London.

Kumar, S. (2002) Round pegs and square holes: mismatches between poverty and housing policy in urban India, in: Townsend, P. and Gordon, D. (eds) *World*

Poverty: New Policies to Defeat an Old Enemy, The Policy Press, London, pp. 271–295.

Lall, S. (2002) *Housing for the Poor and Urban Development – The Indian Dynamics*, Working Paper 5, Society for Development Studies (http://itdg.org/docs/shelter/ iuhd_wp5_housing_for_the_poor.pdf).

Lall, S. (undated) *Employment Strategies for the Poor in India: Search for Sustainability*, Working Paper 7, Society for Development Studies (http://www.itdg.org/docs/shelter/iuhd_wp7_employment_strategies_for_the_ poor_in_india.pdf).

Lall, S. and Lall, V. (2003) 'Integrated urban housing strategy. experiences of a secondary town – Alwar'. Paper presented at the International Workshop on Integrated Urban Housing Development, 17–18 March, Rugby, UK.

Lanjouw, P. and Stern, N. (eds) (1998) *Economic Development in Palanpur over Five Decades*, Clarendon Press, Oxford.

Laurie, H., and Sullivan, O. (1991) Combining qualitative and quantitative data in the longitudinal study of household allocations, *Sociological Review* 39(1): 113–130.

Lederman, D. and Loayza, N. (1999) *What causes crime and violence, in Latin America and Caribbean Region Sustainable Development*, Working Paper No. 5, World Bank, Washington, D.C.

Lemer, A.C. (1987) *The Role of Rental Housing in Developing Countries: A Need for Balance*, The World Bank, Washington, D.C.

Lopez Moreno, E. (2003) *Slums in the World: the Face of Urban Poverty in the New Millennium*. Monitoring the Millennium Development Goals, Target 11, Worldwide Slum Dwellers Estimations, UN-Habitat, The Global Urban Observatory.

Lund, F. (1998) *Women Street Traders in Urban South Africa: A Synthesis of Selected Research Findings*, CSDS Research Report, Number 15, 36, University of Natal, Durban.

Majale, M. (2003) 'Towards a sustainable shelter strategy for the urban poor in Kenya and India'. Paper presented at the International Workshop on Integrated Urban Housing Development, 17–18 March, Rugby, UK.

Majale, M. and Albu, M. (2001) *Livelihoods among the Roofing Construction Subsector in Nakuru, Kenya: Tools for Understanding Sustainable Livelihoods Involving Micro and Small-scale Enterprise* (http://www.livelihoods.org/ lessons/docs/roofingKENYA.pdf).

Manuel, T.A. (2001) *Address to the National Assembly on the Introduction of the Adjustments Appropriation Bill and the 2001 Medium Term Budget Policy Statement*, 30 October (www.finance.gov.za).

Manuel, T.A. (2002) *Budget Speech 2002* (www.finance.gov.za).

Martínez de Jiménez, L. (2002) *La Política de Vivienda en la Argentina: del Estado*, Bienestar al Estado Post-Ajuste, unpublished manuscript.

Materu, J. et al. (2000) *Decentralised Cooperation and Joint Action: Building Partnerships between Local Government and Civil Society in Africa*, ECDPM, Maastricht.

Meikle, S., Ramasut, T. and Walker, J. (2001) *Sustainable Urban Livelihoods: Concepts and Implications for Policy*, Working Paper No. 112, Development Planning Unit, University College London, London.

Menegat, R. (2002) Participatory democracy and sustainable development: integrated urban environmental management in Porto Alegre, Brazil, *Environment and Urbanization*, 14(2): 181–206.

Milliken, J. and Krause, K. (2002) State failure, state collapse and state reconstruction, *Development and Change*, 33(5): 753–772.

Ministerio de Economía (2000) *Evaluación del Fondo Nacional de Vivienda (FON-AVI)*, Dirección de Gastos Sociales Consolidados, Buenos Aires.

Mitlin, D. (2001) 'Civil society and urban poverty – examining complexity, *Environment and Urbanisation*, 13(2), 151–173.

Mogale, T., Mabin, A., Durand-Lasserve, A. (2003) 'Residential tenure security in South Africa. Shifting relationships between customary, informal and formal systems'. Paper prepared for the Franco-South African Programme of Co-operation in Scientific Research.

Moser, C. (2003) Advantages and disadvantages of combining qualitative methods: the experience of a four city comparative study, in: Moser, C. *Urban Longitudinal Research Methodology: Objectives, Contents and Summary of Raised at the Joint DPU-ODI-World Bank-DFID Workshop*, Working Paper No. 124, The Development Planning Unit, University College London, London, pp. 83–92.

Moser, C.O.N. (1995) Urban social policy and poverty reduction, *Environment and Urbanisation*, 7(1): 159–171.

Moser, C.O.N. (1996) *Confronting Crisis: A Comparative Study of Household Responses to Poverty and Vulnerability in Four Poor Urban Communities*, World Bank, Washington, D.C.

Moser, C.O.N. and McIlwaine, C. (1999) Participatory urban appraisal and its implications for research on violence, *Environment and Urbanization*, 11(2): 203–226.

Moser, C.O.N and Winton, A. (2002) *Violence in the Central America Region: Towards an Integrated Framework for Violence Reduction*, ODI Working Paper 171, Overseas Development Institute, London.

Murphy, D. (1972) A glimpse of people's celebration: impressions of ZOTO, *Church Labor Letter No. 128*. Paper read at the second convention of ZOTO (www.daga.org/press/urm/urm1/chap305.htm).

Murphy, D., Gerlock, E., Chion-Javier, E., Dizon, A.M. and Quijano, S. (2001) *A Social Movement of the Urban Poor: The Story of Sama-sama*, Urban Research Consortium, Quezon City.

Murphy, D. (undated) *Naga City; An Organized People, An Astute Mayor*. Case study, Urban Poor Associates, Quezon City.

Mwaura, J. (2000) *NACHU Housing Credit Scheme: Huruma Informal Settlement*, Working Paper 3 (http://itdg.org/docs/shelter/iuhd_wp3_nachu_housing_huruma.pdf).

Naidoo, R. (2003) 'The union movement and South Africa's transition, 1994–2003'. Unpublished paper presented at the Harold Wolpe Memorial Trust/Centre for Policy Studies seminar, 23 June, Johannesburg.

National Capital Region Community Organizers Forum (NCRCOF, Community Organizers Multiversity (CO-M,) Urban Poor Associates (UPA) and Partnership of Philippine Support Services Agencies (PHILSSA) (2001) *Community Organizing of the Urban Poor in Crisis Situations: A Guidebook For Community Organizers and Social Development Workers*, PHILSSA, Quezon City.

National Economic Development Authority (2003) *The Medium-Term Philippine Development Plan, 2001–2004: Pursuing the National Anti-Poverty Program*, Powerpoint presentation made by NEDA Social Development Director Erlinda M. Capones at the Workshop on Government – Civil Society Partnership For Poverty Alleviation in the Philippines, sponsored by the National Anti-Poverty Commission and the Konrad Adenauer Stiftung, 29 November 29, Antipolo City.

Ng'ayu, M. (2003) 'Integrated Urban Housing Project (IUHP), Nakuru, Kenya: Project Impact Assessment', unpublished report.

Nordstrom, C. (2000) Shadows and sovereigns, *Theory, Culture and Society*, 17(4): 35–54.

North, D.C. (1990) *Institutions, Institutional Change and Economic Performance*, Cambridge University Press, Cambridge.

North, D.C. (1991) Institutions, *Journal of Economic Perspectives*, 5(1): 119–127.

North, D.C. (1995) The Adam Smith Address; Economic theory in a dynamic economic world, *Business Economics*, 30(1): 7–13.

Office for National Statistics (1999) *Tracking People: A Guide to Longitudinal Social Sources*, ONS, London.

Orozco, M. (2002) *Remittances to Latin America and the Caribbean: Money, Markets and Costs*, Inter-American Development Bank, San José, Costa Rica.

Orozco, M. (2001) *Globalization and Migration: The Impact Family Remittances in Latin America*, San José, Costa Rica.

Payne, G. (ed.) (2002) *Land, Rights and Innovation. Improving Security of tenure for the Urban Poor*, ITDG Publishing, London.

Pennant, T. (1990) The growth of small-scale renting in low-income urban housing in Malawi. In: Amis, P. and Lloyd, P. (eds) *Housing Africa's Urban Poor*, Manchester University Press, Manchester, pp. 189–201.

Perlman, J.E. (1987) *Megacities and Innovative Technologies*, The Mega-Cities Project, Publication MCP–017, Berkley, CA.

Perlman, J.E. (2003) Longitudinal panel studies in squatter communities: lessons from a re-study of Rio's favelas: 1969–2003, in: Moser, C. (2003) *Urban Longitudinal Research Methodology: Objectives, Contents and Summary of Raised at the Joint DPU-ODI-World Bank-DFID Workshop*, Working Paper No. 124, The Development Planning Unit, University College London, London, pp. 58–67.

Pieterse, E. (undated) In Praise of Transgression: Notes on Institutional Synergy and Poverty (http://www.interfund.org.za/pdffiles/vol3_four/transgression.pdf).

Plummer, J. (2000) *Municipalities and Community Participation; A Sourcebook for Capacity Building*, Earthscan, London and Sterling, VA.

Potts, D. (1995) Shall we go home? Increasing urban poverty in African cities and migration processes, *The Geographic Journal*, 161(3): 245–264.

Potts, D. (2001) Urban growth and urban economies in Eastern and Southern Africa: an overview, in: Bryceson, D. and Potts, D. (eds) *African Urban Economies: Viability, Vitality or Vitiation of Major Cities in East and Southern Africa*.

Preston, S.H. (1979) Urban growth in developing countries: a demographic reappraisal, *Population and Development Review*, 5(2): 195–215.

Przeworski, A. (1987) *Capitalism and Social Democracy*, Cambridge University Press, Cambridge.

Pugh, C. (1995) The role of the World Bank in housing, in: Aldrich, B.C. and Sandhu, R.S. (eds) *Housing the Urban Poor: Policy and Practice in Developing Countries*, Zed Books, London, pp. 34–92.

Racelis Hollnsteiner, M. 1976 People power: community participation in the planning of human settlements, *Philippine Studies*, 24; also in *Assignment Children* (UNICEF), 40 (October–December 1997).

Racelis, M. (2001) 'Community Empowerment, People's Organizations, and the Urban Poor: Struggling for Shelter, Infrastructure, Services, and Dignity in the Philippines' in Chifos, C. and Yabes, R. (eds) *Southeast Asian Urban Environments: Structured and Spontaneous*, Program for Southeast Asian Studies, Tempe, Arizona State University, pp. 3–27.

Racelis, M. (2000) *New Visions and Strong Actions: Civil Society in the Philippines, Funding Virtue; Civil Society Aid and Democracy Promotion*, Ottaway, M. and Carothers, T. (eds) Carnegie Endowment for International Peace, Washington, D.C., pp. 159–187.

Raczynski, D. (ed.) (1995) *Strategies for Combatting Poverty in Latin America*, Inter-American Development Bank, Washington DC.

Republic of Kenya (ROK) (1986) *Sessional Paper No. 1 of 1986 on Economic Management for Renewed Growth*, Government Printer, Nairobi.

Republic of Kenya (ROK) (1992) *Sessional Paper No. 2 of 1992 on Small Enterprises and Jua Kali Development,* Ministry of Planning and National Development, Nairobi.

Republic of Kenya (ROK) (2002) *National Development Plan 2002–2008,* Government Printer, Nairobi.

Republic of Kenya (ROK) (2003a) *Economic Recovery Strategy for Wealth and Employment Creation 2003–2007,* Ministry of Economic Planning and National Development, Nairobi.

Republic of Kenya (ROK) (2003b) *Report by the Task Force on Micro and Small Scale Enterprises,* Ministry of Labour and Human Resource Development, Nairobi.

Republic of South Africa, Ministry for Agriculture and Land Affairs (2003) Communal Land Rights Bill, with Department of Land Affairs proposed Amendments, 27 November.

Rigdon, S. (2003) Identifying causes of long-term poverty within families: experimental use of an anthropological data base, in: Moser, C. (2003) *Urban Longitudinal Research Methodology: Objectives, Contents and Summary of Raised at the Joint DPU-ODI-World Bank-DFID Workshop,* Working Paper No. 124, The Development Planning Unit, University College London, London, pp. 48–57.

Roberts, B. (1996) The social context of citizenship in Latin America, *International Journal of Urban and Regional Research* 20(1): 38–65.

Robredo, J.M. (1999) *The Role of Government to Implement National Poverty Alleviation Programs in the Philippines. Manila Social Forum: The New Social Agenda for East and Southeast Asia,* Asian Development Bank, Metro Manila.

Rodríguez, V. (1997) *Decentralization in Mexico: From Reforma Municipal to Solidaridad,* Westview Press, Boulder, CO.

Rodrik, D. (1999) *The New Global Economy and Developing Countries: Making Openness Work,* Overseas Development Council, Washington, D.C .

Rose, D. (2000) Household panel studies: an overview, in: Rose, D. (ed.) *Researching Social and Economic Change: The Uses of Household Panel Studies,* Routledge, London.

Royston L. (2002) Security of tenure in South Africa: overview of policy and practice, in: Durand-Lasserve, A. and Royston, L. (eds) *Holding their Ground: Secure Land Tenure for the Urban in Developing Countries,* Earthscan Publications, London, pp. 165–181.

Rubio, M. (1997) Perverse social capital:some evidence from Colombia, *Journal of Economic Issues,* 31(3): 805–816.

Sahley, C. and Pratt, B. (2003) *NGO Responses to Urban Poverty: Service Providers or Partners in Planning?,* INTRAC, Oxford.

Sandle, D. (1999) *Capturing the Complexity of Conflict,* Pinter Books, London and New York.

Sandoval, S.A.M. (2001) 'The demobilization of the Brazilian Labour Movement and the emergence of alternative forms of working-class contention in the 1990s', unpublished paper.

Sanyal, B. (1991) Organising the self-employed: the politics of the urban informal sector, *International Labour Review,* 130: 35–56.

Sassen, S. (1994) *Cities in a World Economy,* Pine Forge Press, Thousand Oaks, London, New Delhi.

Sassen, S. (2002) Locating cities on global circuits, *Environment and Urbanization,* 14(1): 13–30.

Satterthwaite, D. (2001) Reducing urban poverty: constraints and the effectiveness of aid agencies and development banks and some suggestions for change, *Environment and Urbanization,* 13(1): 137–157.

Satterthwaite, D. (2002) *Coping with Rapid Urban Growth,* The Royal Institution of Chartered Surveyors, available from http://www.rics.org/downloads/research_reports/urban_growth.pdf

Satterthwaite, D. (undated) *Reducing Urban Poverty: Some Lessons From Experience*, DFID/IIED (pdf).

Schilderman, T. (2002) *Strengthening the Knowledge and Information Systems of the Urban Poor*, Policy Paper (http://www.itdg.org/html/shelter/docs/kis_urban_poor_policy_paper.doc).

Scott, C. (2003) Some reflections on the use of household panel data for the micro-economic analysis of poverty, in: Moser, C. (2003) *Urban Longitudinal Research Methodology: Objectives, Contents and Summary of Raised at the Joint DPU-ODI-World Bank-DFID Workshop*, Working Paper No. 124, The Development Planning Unit, University College London, London, pp. 9–16.

Shah, G. (1997) *Public Health and Urban Development: The Plague in Surat*. Sage Publications, New Delhi.

Shankland, A. (2001) *Matching Macro and Micro: Building Bridges Between Policy and Livelihoods*, www.id21.org.

Sihlongonyane, M.F. (2001) The rhetoric of the community in project management: the case of Mohlakeng township, *Development in Practice*, 11(1): 34–44.

Skinner, C. (2000) Getting institutions right? Local government and street traders in four South African cities, *Urban Forum*, 11(1): 48–71.

Skocpol, T. and Katznelson, I. (1996) *Social Policy in the US: Future Possibilities in Historical Perspective*, Princeton University Press, Princeton, NJ.

Solimano, A. (2003) 'Workers remittances to the Andean region: mechanisms, costs and development impact'. Paper for the Multilateral Investment Fund-IDB's Conference on Remittances and Development, Quito.

Stiglitz, J. (2002) Argentina, shortchanged: why the nation that followed the rules fell to pieces, *The Washington Post*, 12 May.

Sutcliffe, M. (2000) *Democracy and Demarcation*. Summary of seminar held at the Centre for Policy Studies, with the support of the Friedrich Ebert Stiftung, Centre for Policy Studies, Johannesburg.

Sutherland, E. and Cressey, D. (1978) *Criminology*, Lippincott, Philadelphia, PA.

The Pew Hispanic Centre, Fondo Multilateral de Inversiones, Banco Interamericano de Desarrollo (2003a) *Receptores de Remesas en Centroamérica*, Quito.

The Pew Hispanic Centre, Fondo Multilateral de Inversiones, Banco Inter-Americano de Desarrollo (2003b) *Receptores de Remesas en Ecuador. Una Investigación del Mercado. Receptores de Remesas en Mexico: Una encuesta de opinión pública*, Quito.

The Pew Hispanic Centre, Fondo Multilateral de Inversiones, Banco Inter-Americano de Desarrollo (2003c) *Remittance Senders and Receivers: Tracking the Transnational Channels*, Washington, D.C.

Thulare, P. (2004) *Trading Democracy: Johannesburg Informal Traders and Citizenship*, Policy. Issues and Actors, Centre for Policy Studies, Johannesburg.

Tipple, A.G. and Willis, K.G. (1991) Tenure choice in a west African city, *Third World Planning Review*, 13 (1): 27–45.

Tomlinson, M. (1996) *From Rejection to Resignation: Beneficiaries' Views on the Government's Housing Subsidy Scheme*, Research Report, Centre for Policy Studies, Johannesburg.

Tomlinson, M. (1997) *Mortgage Bondage?: Financial Institutions and Low-cost Housing Delivery*, Research Report, Centre for Policy Studies, Johannesburg.

Toner, A. and Howlett, D. (2001) *Goodbye to Projects? The Institutional Impacts of a Livelihood Approach on Development Interventions*, Working Paper Series, Paper No 1, Annotated Bibliography on Livelihood Approaches and Development Interventions.

Toulmin, C. and Quan, J. (eds.) (2000) *Evolving Land Rights, Policies and Tenure in Africa*, IIED, Natural Resources Institute, DFID.

Trejo, G. and Jones, C. (1998) 'Poverty, inequality and the politics of welfare reform,' in S. Kaufman Purcell and L. Rubio (eds.), Mexico Under Zedillo, Lynne Rienner, Boulder.

Turner, J. (1968) Housing priorities, settlement patterns and urban development in modernising countries, *Journal of the American Institute of Planners*, 34(5): 354–363.

UNCHS (1989) *Strategies for Low-Income Shelter and Services Development: The Rental Housing Option*, United Nations Centre for Human Settlements (Habitat), Nairobi.

UNCHS (1990) 'Rental housing: proceedings of an expert group meeting to review rental systems and rental stability'. Paper presented at the Jointly organised by the United Nations Centre for Human Settlements (Habitat) and the Institute for Housing Studies, Rotterdam, 9–13 October, Nairobi.

UNCHS (1993) *Support Measures to Promote Rental Housing for Low-Income Groups*, United Nations Centre for Human Settlements (Habitat), Nairobi.

UNCHS (1999) *UNCHS Global Campaigns: Governance and Secure Tenure*, accessed on 17 November, 2000 at http://www.unchs.org, UNCHS

UNCHS (Habitat) (1996) *An Urbanizing World: Global Report on Human Settlements*, Oxford University Press, Oxford and New York.

UNCHS (Habitat) (1997) *The Istanbul Declaration and The Habitat Agenda*, UNCHS (Habitat), Nairobi.

UN–Habitat (2002a) *The Role of Cities in National and International Development*, HSP/WUF/1/ORG/Paper 1.

UN–Habitat (2002b) *The Role of Local Authorities and Other Habitat Agenda Partners: Dialogue on Effective Decentralization, including Principles And Legal Frameworks in Support of The Implementation of the Habitat Agenda*, HSP/WUF/1/DLG.I/Paper 1.

UN–Habitat (2002c) *International Role of Non-Governmental Organizations in the Implementation of the Habitat Agenda*, HSP/WUF/DLG.I/Paper 3.

UN–Habitat (2003a) *Rental Housing: An Essential Option for the Urban Poor in Developing Countries*, United Nations Human Settlements Programme (UN-Habitat), Nairobi.

UN–Habitat (2003b) *The Challenge of Slums. Global Report on Human Settlements 2003*, UN-Habitat and Earthscan Publications.

UN–Habitat (2003c) *Handbook on Best Practices. Security of Tenure and Access to Land. Implementation of the Habitat Agenda.*

United Nations (1982) *Estimates and Projections of Urban, Rural and City Populations, 1950–2025; The 1980 Assessment*, Department of International Economic and Social Affairs, ST/ESA/SER.R/45, New York.

United Nations (2002) *World Urbanization Prospects; The 2001 Revision*, Population Division, Department of Economic and Social Affairs, United Nations, ST/ESA/SER.A/216, New York.

van der Gaag, J. and Lipton, M. (eds) (1993) *Including the Poor*, Proceedings of a Symposium Organized by the World Bank and the International Food Policy Research Institute, World Bank, Washington, D.C.

Vanderschueren, F. (1996) From violence to justice and security in cities, *Environment and Urbanisation*, 8(1): 93–112.

Vanderschueren, F., Wegelin, E. and Wekwete, K. (1996) *Policy Programme Options for Urban Poverty Reduction: A Framework for Action at the Municipal Level*, The World Bank, Washington, D.C.

Wahab, E.A. (1984) T*he Tenant Market of Baldia Township: Towards a More General Understanding of Tenancy in Squatter Settlements*, Working Paper 3, Institute of Cultural Anthropology/Sociology of Development, Free University, Amsterdam.

Ward, P. (1990) The politics of housing production in Mexico, in :van Vliet, W. (ed.) *The International Handbook of Housing Policies and Practices*, Greenwood Press, Boulder, CO.

Watson, V. and McCarthy, M. (1998) Rental housing policy and the role of the household rental sector: evidence from South Africa, *Habitat International*, 22 (1): 49–56.

White, C. et al. (2000) 'The social determinants of energy use: synthesis report', unpublished report submitted to the Department of Mineral and Energy Affairs.

Widner, J. (1991) Interest group structure and organisation in Kenya's informal sector: cultural despair or a politics of multiple allegiances?, *Comparative Political Studies*, 24(1): 31–55.

World Bank (1974) *Sites and Services*, World Bank, Washington, D.C.

World Bank (1975) *Housing*, Sector Policy Paper, World Bank, Washington, D.C.

World Bank (1983) *Learning by Doing: World Bank Lending for Urban Development: 1972–82*, World Bank, Washington, D.C.

World Bank (1993) *Housing: Enabling Markets to Work*, Policy Paper, World Bank, Washington, D.C.

World Bank (1995) *Better Urban Services: Finding the Right Incentives*, Development in Practice Series, World Bank, Washington, D.C.

World Bank (1996*) Poverty Reduction and the World Bank: Progress and Challenges in the 1990s*, World Bank, Washington, D.C

World Bank (1997) *Poverty Reduction and the World Bank: Progress in Fiscal 1996 and 1997*, World Bank, Washington, D.C.

World Bank (1999a) *A Strategic View of Urban and Local Government Issues: Implications for the Bank*, October 1999 Draft, The World Bank Transportation, Water and Urban Development Department, Urban Development Division (http://www.worldbank.org/html/fpd/urban/strategy/full.htm)

World Bank (1999b) *Project Appraisal Document for the FOVI Restructuring Project*, Report No. 18854-ME, World Bank, Washington, D.C.

World Bank (2000a) *Poor People in a Rich Country: A Poverty Report for Argentina*, Report No. 19992-AR, World Bank, Washington, D.C.

World Bank (2000b) *World Development Report 2000–2001: Attacking Poverty*, Oxford University Press, Oxford.

World Bank (2001a) *Argentina at a Glance*, World Bank, Washington, D.C.

World Bank (2001b) *Building Institutions for Markets*, World Development Report 2002, Oxford University Press, Oxford and New York.

World Bank (2002) *Mexico Low Income Housing: Issues and Options*, Mexico Country Management Unit, Report No. 22534-ME, World Bank, Washington, D.C.

World Bank (2003) *Breaking the Conflict Trap: Civil War and Development Policy*, Oxford University Press, Oxford.

Wratten, E. (1995) Conceptualising urban poverty, *Environment and Urbanisation*, 7 (1): 11–36.

Yahya, S. et al. (2001) *Double Standards, Single Purpose: Reforming Housing Regulations to Reduce Poverty*, London: ITDG Publishing.

Yahya, S.S. (2003) 'Management approaches for enhancing land tenure security'. Paper presented at the USK/CASLE/UN-Habitat Regional seminar on Security of Land Tenure, 12 June, Nairobi, Kenya.

Yujnovsky, O. (1984) *Claves Políticas del Problema Habitacional Argentino: 1955–1981*, Grupo Editorial Latinoamericano, Buenos Aires.

Zanetta, C. (2004) *The Influence of the World Bank on National Housing and Urban Policies: A Comparison of Mexico and Argentina during the 1990s*, Ashgate, London.

Index